Literacy in Context (LinC)

Literacy in Context (LinC)

CHOOSING INSTRUCTIONAL STRATEGIES TO TEACH READING IN CONTENT AREAS FOR STUDENTS GRADES 5-12

Mimi Miller
California State University, Chico

Nancy Veatch
Evergreen Union School District

Boston   Columbus   Indianapolis   New York   San Francisco   Upper Saddle River
Amsterdam   Cape Town   Dubai   London   Madrid   Milan   Munich   Paris   Montreal   Toronto
Delhi   Mexico City   São Paulo   Sydney   Hong Kong   Seoul   Singapore   Taipei   Tokyo

Vice President, Editor in Chief: Aurora Martínez Ramos
Editorial Assistant: Meagan French
Executive Marketing Manager: Krista Clark
Senior Project Manager: Janet Domingo
Project Manager: Susan Hannahs
Cover Designer: Karen Salzbach
Photo Researcher: Annie Pickert
Full-Service Project Management: Joseph Malcolm, PreMediaGlobal
Composition: PreMediaGlobal
Text Printer/Bindery: Edwards Brothers
Cover Printer: Lehigh/Phoenix Color
Text Font: Times 10/12

Credits and acknowledgments borrowed from other sources and reproduced, with permission, in this textbook appear on the appropriate page within the text.

Many of the designations by manufacturers and seller to distinguish their products are claimed as trademarks. Where those designations appear in this book, and the publisher was aware of a trademark claim, the designations have been printed in initial caps or all caps.

Some pages from this text may be reproduced for classroom use only.

Library of Congress Cataloging-in-Publication Data

Miller, Mimi.
    Literacy in context (LinC) : choosing instructional strategies to teach reading in content areas for students grades 5-12 / Mimi Miller, Nancy Veatch.
        p. cm.
    Includes bibliographical references and index.
    ISBN-13: 978-0-13-503484-2
    ISBN-10: 0-13-503484-1
1. Content area reading.   2. Reading (Secondary)   3. Reading (Elementary)   I. Veatch, Nancy.   II. Title.
    LB1050.455.M56 2011
    428.4071—dc22

                                                                                                2010033033

10 9 8 7 6 5 4 3 2 1 14 13 12 11 10

ISBN 10:   0-13-503484-1
ISBN 13: 978-0-13-503484-2

TABLE OF CONTENTS

PREFACE

Recent data show that adolescent learners struggle with reading content area text. There are many effective strategies that can be used to support this learning, but how do teachers choose and use them? The aim of *Literacy in Context* (LinC) is to provide middle and high school teachers with an instructional model to embed literacy instruction into content area teaching. This book details literacy strategies that can be used with content area instruction to promote the development of vocabulary, fluency, comprehension, and motivation. Unique to this book is the focus on process—it provides guidance about how to choose the most effective literacy instructional strategies for different contexts and classes of students. The book models how teachers use the LinC Cycle (assess, reflect, plan, and teach/reteach) to make decisions about which instructional assessments and strategies to choose for their adolescent students.

It is our expectation that this book will provide teachers with two types of resources—first, instructional strategies and, second, a model to help teachers select strategies that will readily impact student literacy and content learning. We invite you, as a reader, to join us as we begin to reverse the effects of the adolescent literacy crisis.

TEXT ORGANIZATION

Chapter 1: Addressing the Adolescent Literacy Crisis describes the current state of adolescent literacy and the challenges presented by content area text. It gives an overview of the LinC Cycle, a model for embedding literacy in content teaching.

Chapters Two through Five focus on describing effective, research-based strategies to support reading and learning in fifth through twelfth-grade academic subject areas. Each chapter highlights a specific literacy component (*Chapter 2: Strategies to Build Vocabulary, Chapter 3: Strategies to Foster Fluency, Chapter 4: Strategies to Increase Comprehension*, and *Chapter 5: Strategies to Initiate and Sustain Motivation*) and provides research-tested instructional strategies for improving content area reading. Each chapter begins by defining the literacy component (e.g., vocabulary), identifying goals for effective instruction, and explaining how the goal relates to content area instruction. The remainder of the chapter describes instructional strategies, complete with procedural directions and examples across content area classrooms. Student work from fifth to twelfth-grade classrooms, captured in handwriting or electronically, exemplifies these strategies.

Chapters Six through Nine illustrate how to effectively choose and use these strategies. The chapters follow a teacher as she engages in the LinC Cycle—Assess, Reflect, Plan, and Teach/Reteach. *Chapter 6: Assess—Learning About Students* explains how the teacher uses assessments to evaluate students' proficiency levels in English language proficiency, vocabulary, fluency, comprehension, and motivation. *Chapter 7: Reflect—Finding Patterns and Drawing Conclusions* demonstrates the process of reflection, in which the teacher carefully considers knowledge about students and the curriculum before planning and teaching. *Chapter 8: Plan—Making Informed Decisions* describes how the teacher uses these reflections to help her decide which instructional strategies from Chapters Two through Five will best meet the needs of her students. These strategies become part of a LinC Teaching Plan, focused on fostering content knowledge, reading proficiencies, and motivation. *Chapter 9: Teach and Reteach—Using the LinC Cycle* chronicles the implementation of a LinC Teaching Plan with a class of students and addresses how teachers—individually and collaboratively—assess student learning and design future instruction.

PEDAGOGICAL FEATURES

This book provides several pedagogical features to support reading. Boxed text, entitled *Pause and Reflect,* asks the reader to stop and consider how the book connects with a personal teaching experience. In addition, marginal icons signal additional support for readers. The *Resources* icon directs the reader to supplementary text and Web-based teaching resources to expand learning in particular areas. The *Learning Log* icon invites readers to turn to a Learning Log Appendix and practice using LinC instructional strategies and assessments. The *Teacher Tools* icon refers the reader to a Teacher Tools Appendix where black-line masters are available for use in the classroom.

ACKNOWLEDGEMENTS

We would like to thank the teachers who inspired us to begin the process of writing this book. Our colleagues asked for guidance in how to assess, reflect, plan, teach, and reteach using strategies that promote literacy. It is our hope that this book will help all teachers as they continually strive to give their best.

We thank our students—middle school, high school, and college— who enabled us to envision a world in which every individual uses reading as a tool for continual learning. The future of our country depends upon the literacy instruction provided to them today.

Our appreciation goes out to Linda Bishop whose belief in our project guided us in our initial steps to create a book that would be teacher-friendly and inspiring. Aurora Martinez and Meagan French supported us in taking the next steps to bring the book to production. The production and copy editing team, especially Janet Domingo, was an invaluable help and resource as we moved through the copy editing process. In addition, we thank our reviewers for their insightful comments. These reviewers include: Amy MacKenzie, Manhattanville College; Merleen D. Ivey, Mississippi College; Susan Frank, Caroline County Public Schools; Erika Daniels, California State University, San Marcos; Jonella A. Mongo, Oakland University; Mary J. Drucker, Utica College; Vickie S. Brown, Arlington Baptist College; Dawn Downes, University of Delaware; Rosemary Fessinger, University of New Mexico; Leslie Hopping, The Columbus Academy; Deborah Ellermeyer, Clarion University of Pennsylvania.

Finally, we thank our families. We appreciate our parents (our first teachers), Jane and Paul Beretz and Christine and Herb Wimmer, who taught us to value learning. Our husbands, Andy Miller and Steve Veatch, unselfishly and lovingly encouraged us to follow our dream of writing this book. In addition, we thank our children, Benton and Cora Miller and Katie and Cody Veatch, for their patience throughout the writing process. We hope that our children, like us, will be open to continual growth and will grasp opportunities to make the world a better place.

Mimi Miller and Nancy Veatch

ABOUT THE AUTHORS

Dr. Mimi Miller is an Associate Professor of Education at California State University, Chico, where she teaches and supervises pre-service teachers. She earned her PhD in Educational Psychology from Stanford University and her BA in Psychology from the University of Notre Dame. Before coming to CSU, Chico, Dr. Miller taught middle school in the California public schools, served as a K-12 teacher educator for Project Read/Text Analysis Project at Stanford, and was senior editor for Interact Simulations. Dr. Miller's professional interests include content literacy instruction, curriculum integration, rural education, and authentic assessment. She lives in Durham, California, with her husband and two children.

Nancy Veatch is a National Board Certified sixth-grade teacher at Evergreen Middle School in Cottonwood, California. She earned her BS in Human Development and MA in Education from the University of California at Davis. Prior to teaching, she worked as the Project Evaluator for the National Science Foundation's Nuclear Age Education Institute and for the California Foreign Language Project. Mrs. Veatch has 19 years of teaching experience in the Northern California public schools. She has also taught content literacy classes as a part-time instructor at California State University, Chico. Her professional interests include early childhood development, adolescent literacy, and content area instruction. She lives with her husband and two children in Cottonwood, California.

Addressing the Adolescent Literacy Crisis

The bell rang, and the 30 high school juniors took their seats at the chemistry lab tables. Mr. Davis knew that he had to grab their attention right away. "Are you an acid or a base? That's the question of the day." Students looked at him. Some raised their eyebrows as they waited to hear what was next. "And to answer that, you'll be testing your saliva." Some of the students said "ewwww," but they kept their eyes on Mr. Davis. They had recently learned about the structure of different substances, and today they would be learning the difference between an acid and a base.

"Before you begin the experiment, we'll be going over the procedure on page 52 of your textbook."

They took out their textbooks, which were too difficult for most of them. Mr. Davis knew this, so he had carefully structured activities that would support student literacy as they learned content. First, he showed the students the text, and he pointed out the headings that divided the text into an introduction and a two-part procedure.

He began reading. As he read the first part of the introduction aloud, he modeled a technique that his students had used before— Reciprocal Teaching. With Reciprocal Teaching, students engage in a series of reading strategies. They make predictions about the upcoming text. Then, after reading a section of the text, they ask for clarification about unknown words, ask questions about the content, and summarize the text. To model Reciprocal Teaching, Mr. Davis read a paragraph of the textbook aloud to the class, and then he paused to summarize and clarify terms in the text ("litmus," "phosphorus"). He asked students a question to see if they understood and challenged them to think about how they might test for acidity.

Mr. Davis then directed the students to break into lab groups and use Reciprocal Teaching to read the procedure together. He and his students both enjoyed this method. They could talk to each other, and the talk was focused on understanding what to do for the experiment. As he walked around and checked in with the groups, he knew that they would be ready to carry out the procedure and effectively conduct the experiment.

In this scenario, Mr. Davis is committed to both teaching essential content and helping his students gain access to the text. He, like many of his colleagues, has repeatedly heard the saying: "Every teacher is a teacher of reading." He loves science, but he noticed that year after year students arrived in his class without the literacy skills that are necessary to understand what they read. And in science, that meant they made some serious, even dangerous, mistakes in their lab experiments.

Mr. Davis did, in fact, recognize a crisis—one that includes *all* adolescents, from advanced students to struggling readers. Both standardized test scores and reports from teachers in the classroom attest to the fact that many adolescents struggle to read, especially when facing

expository, content area text. What can teachers do? Studies suggest a common solution that is in reach of all teachers—to embed literacy into content area instruction (Biancarosa & Snow, 2004; Kamil, 2003). This chapter explains the challenge and describes a practical solution to address the crisis—Literacy in Context (LinC).

PAUSE and REFLECT 1.1

Consider your experiences with advanced, proficient, and struggling readers in grades 5 through 12. From these experiences, what conclusions can you draw about the state of adolescent literacy?

UNDERSTANDING THE CHALLENGE

The call to action began when adolescents' performance on standardized tests revealed that many middle and high school students were not proficient readers. Prompted by this information, researchers and educators identified some of the unique demands of content reading and shared possible solutions.

Troubling Statistics

In 1998, *The Nation's Report Card* revealed that just 33 percent of eighth-grade students and 40 percent of twelfth-grade students performed at or above the proficient level in literacy (Donahue, Voelkl, Campbell, & Mazzeo, 1999). A year later, the International Reading Association released a position statement acknowledging that adolescent literacy deserved some attention (Moore, Bean, Bridyshaw, & Tycik, 1999). Since the late 1990s, adolescent literacy has gotten some attention, so much that it has earned the title of "Hot Topic" from the International Reading Association every year from 2007–2010 (Cassidy & Cassidy, 2010). Much of the attention to the topic is a result of troubling statistics.

- Sixty-nine percent of all eighth graders are below the proficient level in their ability to comprehend text written at their grade level (Lee, Grigg, & Donahue, 2007).
- For high school students, scores on the *Nation's Report Card* were the lowest they had been since 1992 (Grigg, Donahue, & Dion, 2007).
- In typical high poverty schools, half of the incoming ninth graders read at sixth or seventh grade level (Balfanz, McPartland, & Shaw, 2002).
- Eight million students in grades 4 through 12 are struggling readers (Grigg, Daane, Jin, & Campbell, 2003).

A surprising number of students enter high school without the skills and strategies that are necessary to face the rigors of reading in their content area classes. Once in high school, they continue to struggle in all high school courses, missing the opportunity to engage in learning and thinking. Many struggling readers drop out of school. In fact, readers who score in the bottom quartile of standardized tests are 20 times more likely to drop out of high school than proficient readers (Carnevale, 2001). And those who do go to college often need remediation. Over half of all college students need to take remedial courses to learn the skills they did not learn in high schools (Wirt, et al., 2001). These students are not prepared for the demands of content reading.

The Demands of Content Reading

To understand the challenge, it is critical to be aware of the content reading demands placed upon adolescent learners. **Reading** is a complex process in which the reader constructs meaning from the text. When reading content-rich materials, students face a challenging task. As students read the text, they must learn new concepts and consider the meaning of complex ideas. In middle and high school, the concepts in each domain increase in complexity. As a result, content area literacy becomes more specialized as students become more engaged with different disciplines.

Broadly defined, **literacy** is the ability to identify, understand, interpret, create, communicate, compute, and use printed and written materials associated with varying contexts (National Institute for Literacy [NIFL], 2009). In learning from a text, students gradually move from basic literacy, to intermediate literacy, to disciplinary literacy (Shanahan & Shanahan, 2008). **Basic literacy** includes skills such as decoding that give a reader access to print and help them break the code of text. **Intermediate literacy** involves learning to comprehend texts of different types and learning literacy strategies that cross domains. **Disciplinary literacy** is a specialized literacy that occurs in a discipline. When students are thinking like a historian, scientist, or mathematician, they are engaging in disciplinary literacy.

Effective instruction in content reading gradually moves students from basic literacy to disciplinary literacy. This instruction occurs within each domain. National content standards in various disciplines define what students need to know and be able to do in order to be literate within that domain. For example, the National Science Standards state that for an individual to be scientifically literate, he or she must be able to ask questions about everyday experiences, describe natural phenomena, read with understanding, and engage in conversations about the validity of the reading (National Academy of Sciences, 1995). According to this definition, literacy is an integral part of science education.

How can teachers move students toward disciplinary literacy, specifically reading literacy? When considering effective instruction for content reading, four particular elements of reading emerge: comprehension, vocabulary, fluency, and motivation (National Association of State Boards of Education, 2006). Each of these areas poses challenges for adolescent readers when they approach content text.

COMPREHENSION   Many adolescents can read words but struggle to fully comprehend what they read (NIFL, 2009). For the purpose of this book, **reading comprehension** is defined as the process of using one's own prior knowledge and the writer's cues from the text to infer the author's intended meaning (Irwin, 1991).

Content area text requires strategic reading that is sustained and intentional. Proficient readers know when and how to use reading strategies, and they have the flexibility to adapt them to different reading contexts (Afflerbach, Pearson, & Paris, 2008). For example, reading in the social sciences requires that students comprehend, analyze and compare texts. Reading in chemistry requires that students understand important interactions and processes. In math, reading is used to evaluate and interpret mathematical ideas. In each subject area, students must learn to go beyond what is said on the page to process and build a broad meaning of the text.

VOCABULARY   The difficulty of the words, or the **vocabulary**, in content text poses challenges for readers. The text is filled with terms that represent new concepts. In addition, there are familiar words that are used in different ways and academic language that is found in school subjects but not in everyday communication.

Research in reading has consistently shown the strong, positive relationship between reading comprehension and vocabulary knowledge (Baumann, Kame'enui, & Ash, 2003). Adolescents' comprehension can be challenged or strengthened by the difficulty of language in content area text. Proficient reading requires a complete and flexible knowledge of vocabulary words (Nagy & Scott, 2000). Words in content texts might be familiar, but their meanings change when they appear in a different context. To succeed with content area text, adolescents need to build their vocabularies as they build conceptual understanding.

FLUENCY   **Fluency** involves reading a text accurately, at an appropriate rate, with appropriate expression. The sentence structure, word choice, and use of punctuation in content texts challenge even the most experienced reader.

While fluency is often a part of elementary reading instruction, it is often missing from middle and high school instruction (Rasinski, Padak, McKeon, Wilfong, Friedauer, Heim & 2005). However, research shows that fluency continues to develop as students are exposed to new and varied texts (National Institute of Child Health and Human Development [NICHD], 2004). As students delve more deeply into subject areas, they need to be given opportunities that foster their fluency, strengthening their proficiency with reading text aloud. In addition, research shows a strong correlation between fluency and comprehension, suggesting that fluent readers have more cognitive space that would free them to focus on building meaning from text (LaBerge & Samuels, 1974). Adolescent readers who struggle with fluency also struggle with comprehension (Rasinski et al., 2005). Fluency instruction should continue as students learn to read content.

MOTIVATION   **Motivation** is a process by which a goal-directed activity is both instigated and sustained (Schunk, Pintrich, & Meece, 2008). In general, as students progress through the grades, their motivation and engagement in school experiences decline (Keene, 2007). Content reading poses particular motivational challenges. Reading an algebra, chemistry, or world history text is likely the most difficult reading that a student has ever experienced. Adolescent readers, and readers in general, are likely to sustain attention if they value the reading task and believe they will be successful (Guthrie & Wigfield, 1997). Thus, one of the most important jobs of a teacher is to help students find value in their academic reading.

It is not surprising that motivation is also strongly connected to reading comprehension (Alvermann, 2002). Proficient content readers are able to sustain reading and apply strategies necessary to build vocabulary, fluency, and comprehension. As students continue to engage in content reading, they become more skilled and strategic. They see themselves as better readers, and they want to read. If a student, for whatever reason, is not motivated to read, he or she will not have the sustained attention that is needed to engage in content reading and gain important practice with understanding text. Initiating and sustaining students' motivation is a critical goal for every content teacher; without it, literacy development will not occur.

Each of these demands of content reading—comprehension, vocabulary, fluency, and motivation—needs to be addressed when focusing on adolescent literacy development.

PAUSE and REFLECT 1.2

What do you think are the greatest demands of reading content area text?

Possible Solutions

A number of research briefs, written by researchers, educators, and policy makers, make recommendations to address the crisis in adolescent literacy. Figure 1.1 lists eight reports, a representative sample of the many that include possible plans of action for states, districts, and teachers, to assist in program design and selection of research-based strategies.

One of these reports, *Reading Next* (Biancarosa & Snow, 2004), presented results of research that studied school programs designed to foster adolescent literacy. After identifying and examining exemplary programs, they noticed 15 elements that these programs shared. These 15 elements, shown in Figure 1.2, include characteristics of classroom instruction and characteristics of the school context—both of which are important in supporting literacy development. Each of these elements provides guidance for educators and administrators who are committed to supporting literacy growth in adolescents. *Reading Next* suggests that teachers embed effective reading instruction in the course content (Biancarosa & Snow, 2004). However, to enact these important practices, teachers need a supportive context that includes such elements as the opportunity to meet with colleagues to plan instruction.

Title	Author/Year	Purpose	Available At
1. Academic Literacy Instruction for Adolescents: A Guidance Document from the Center on Instruction	Torgesen et. al, 2007	To offer researched-based recommendations, advice from experts, and descriptions of successful programs to help improve content literacy.	The Center on Instruction www.centeroninstruction.org
2. Effective Instruction for Adolescent Struggling Readers: A Practice Brief	Boardman et. al, 2008	To provide best practices for struggling adolescent readers.	The Center on Instruction www.centeroninstruction.org
3. Double the Work: Challenges and Solutions to Acquiring Language and Academic Literacy for Adolescent English Language Learners	Short & Fitzsimmons, 2007	To identify the challenges faced by adolescent English learners, and to outline recommendations to address those challenges through teaching practices, professional development, research, and policy changes.	Alliance for Excellent Education www.all4ed.org
4. Interventions for Adolescent Struggling Readers: A Meta-Analysis with Implications for Practice	Scammacca et. al, 2007	To describe reading interventions that lead to positive results for struggling adolescent readers.	The Center on Instruction www.centeroninstruction.org
5. Literacy Instruction in the Content Areas: Getting to the Core of Middle and High School Improvement	Heller & Greenleaf, 2007	To outline recommendations focused on developing advanced literacy skills and provide guidance for the strategies necessary in each academic discipline.	Alliance for Excellent Education www.all4ed.org
6. Reading at Risk: The State Response to the Crisis in Adolescent Literacy	National Association of State Boards of Education, 2006	To outline the steps needed for states to implement a literacy plan for adolescents.	National Association of State Boards of Education www.nasbe.org
7. Reading Next: A Vision for Action and Research in Middle and High School Literacy	Biancarosa & Snow 2004	To guide projects focused on adolescent literacy—identifying what works, when it works, and for whom it works	Alliance for Excellent Education www.all4ed.org
8. Writing to Read: Evidence for How Writing Can Improve Reading	Graham & Hebert, 2010	To offer specific instructional practices for helping adolescents develop writing proficiencies which in turn help them to improve their reading abilities.	Alliance for Excellent Education www.all4ed.org

FIGURE 1.1 Documents Guiding Adolescent Literacy Instruction

  1. Direct, explicit comprehension instruction
  2. Effective instructional principles embedded in content
  3. Motivation and self-directed learning
  4. Text-based collaborative learning
  5. Strategic tutoring
  6. Diverse texts
  7. Intensive writing
  8. Technology integration
  9. Ongoing formative assessment of students
  10. Extended time for literacy
  11. Professional development
  12. Ongoing summative assessment of students and programs
  13. Teacher teams
  14. Leadership
  15. Comprehensive and coordinated literacy programs

FIGURE 1.2   The Fifteen Elements of Effective Adolescent Literacy Programs   *(Biancarosa & Snow, 2004, p. 12)*

TEACHING LITERACY IN CONTEXT: THE LinC CYCLE

This text uses the Literacy in Context (LinC) Cycle to illustrate how literacy can be taught in the context of content instruction. The model supports *Reading Next* (Biancarosa & Snow, 2004) in that it includes both instructional strategies for the teacher and tools to support the use of best practices. The LinC Cycle is not a "new program." It takes the thinking of expert teachers of content and literacy and makes it explicit. So often teachers are handed a book of 50 or 100 strategies for teaching content reading, but rarely do teachers have an opportunity to see the process of how and why teachers choose and use these strategies.

Teachers who use the LinC Cycle engage in four connected steps: Assess, Reflect, Plan, and Teach. Figure 1.3 shows the LinC Cycle. Teachers begin the process with assessing student literacy needs and reflecting on students' strengths and areas for growth. Based upon this information and the knowledge of strategies to address these needs, teachers create a LinC Teaching Plan that incorporates best practices for literacy instruction. After teaching, formative assessment helps the teacher decide next steps for instruction.

Assess

To **assess** is to gather evidence of student learning. With the LinC Cycle, the purpose of assessment is to inform instruction. The LinC Cycle promotes balanced literacy—an approach to literacy instruction that focuses on student needs (Reutzel & Cooter, 1996). Teachers identify the students' learning needs before making decisions about what to teach.

As the previous section explains, many factors contribute to reading performance and student learning, including language proficiency, vocabulary, fluency, comprehension, and motivation. However, because of the demands on teachers' time, it is nearly impossible to use the available data in a productive way. The LinC Cycle attempts to make the process more manageable. It includes assessments that can be conducted by teachers who are not certified reading specialists, but who are committed to the literacy growth of their students.

The commitment to using data fits with two educational models: Professional Learning Communities and Response to Intervention. Many schools are in the process of developing **Professional Learning Communities** (DuFour, 2004). In a Professional Learning Community (PLC), teachers take collective responsibility for the learning of all students at their school. To meet that end, they collaboratively examine evidence of student learning, such as test scores and

Resource

For a complete description of the Professional Learning Community model, see *Learning by Doing* by DuFour and colleagues (DuFour, DuFour, Eaker & Many, 2006).

student classroom work. Teachers work together to refine their teaching practices, which leads to increased opportunities for student learning.

Similarly, the **Response to Intervention** model (Fuchs & Fuchs, 2001) focuses on using data to make instructional decisions. Response to Intervention (RTI) became well-known when the 2004 revised Individuals with Disabilities Education Act encouraged earlier intervention for struggling students. With the RTI model, students participate in instructional interventions around needed skills and strategies, and, struggling readers frequently engage in a variety of reading assessments. The data generated from these assessments allow instruction to be tailored to students' needs.

When using the LinC Cycle, teachers and other school personnel work together to collect and compile data on student literacy. This data becomes the springboard for teaching aimed at developing students' literacy skills and strategies in the context of content area instruction. Too often, because of multiple demands on teachers' time, useful data sits untouched in a computer database or a three-ring binder. Chapters six through nine of this book give teachers guidance on how to effectively use this valuable information, along with their professional knowledge, to foster student learning.

Reflect

Each day, teachers make decisions based on their professional knowledge and the information in the environment (Colton & Sparks-Langer, 1993). To **reflect**, teachers give careful attention to their experiences and the instructional choices they make. Reflective teachers observe, analyze, hypothesize, and test those hypotheses. According to John Dewey, this reflective thought is the only thinking that is truly educative (Dewey, 1933). Reflection about teaching leads to growth for teachers and students.

The LinC Cycle provides opportunities for teachers to reflect on their professional knowledge and their students' needs. Teachers use evidence to draw conclusions about students' needs

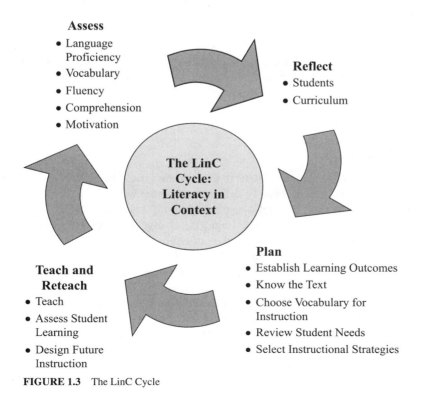

FIGURE 1.3   The LinC Cycle

and make decisions about future instruction. Ideally, the reflective process is collaborative; it includes individuals who have an investment in the success of the learner.

The focus on reflection aligns well with the philosophies of schools that are committed to the success of *all* students. In schools that are or aspire to be Professional Learning Communities, reflection is an essential step between gathering evidence of student learning and teaching the next lesson (DuFour, 2004). When engaged in the LinC Cycle, teachers are reflective decision makers who use many sources of data to improve student learning.

Plan

In the LinC Cycle, planning takes on a pivotal role in connecting knowledge about students with teaching practice. When **planning** for instruction, teachers systematically make decisions about what students should learn and the methods to use for instruction and assessment. The relationship between the teacher and the instructional materials is a dynamic one. Rather than delivering curriculum, teachers work with resources to construct plans that guide instruction (Remillard, 2005). Teachers use their expertise in the content area to understand the standards and evaluate the material provided in the textbook. Once they draw conclusions about class needs, the standards, and the text, teachers begin to select instructional strategies that impart disciplinary literacy of content knowledge and provide for literacy skill development. Using their knowledge of individual students and the class as a whole, teachers develop a LinC Teaching Plan for a lesson that teaches reading while focusing on important subject matter. The plan includes instructional strategies to support the development of vocabulary, fluency, comprehension, and motivation. The LinC Teaching Plan is not an intervention for a select group of students. Rather, it is a plan that accounts for the needs of the individual and the needs of the group.

One unique element of the LinC Cycle is the role of instructional strategies. The use of instructional strategies to support literacy is intentional and based upon student needs. Teachers often have an instructional tool bag filled with instructional strategies. Many teachers, especially new ones, have difficulty deciding when to use a particular strategy. The planning stage of the LinC Cycle gives teachers guidance in choosing strategies to support student vocabulary, fluency, comprehension, and motivation.

Ideally, planning with the LinC Cycle is done collaboratively among teachers at the same school site. For example, in one middle school, teams of teachers meet regularly to discuss student literacy data and plan instruction. These meetings include teachers who all teach the same grade level, even though their subject areas differ. Collaborative planning, when possible, provides opportunities for teachers to share promising teaching practices and to keep each other informed of student progress.

Teach and Reteach

After planning, teachers move on to the next stage of the LinC Cycle, teaching and reteaching. The act of teaching is complex and can be defined in different ways. In the LinC Cycle, **teaching** is a process in which the teacher, a reflective decision maker (Colton & Sparks-Langer, 1993), implements instruction aimed at positively impacting change in students. Teachers use the LinC Teaching Plan to ensure that the instructional strategies they use are carefully chosen. After teaching, they evaluate student learning and make decisions about future instruction. When **reteaching**, a teacher implements instruction in a different way to lead to positive learning outcomes.

When using the LinC Cycle, teachers use **instructional strategies** to guide students in their development of **reading strategies**. Instructional strategies are teaching methods chosen to reach a particular learning outcome. Reading strategies are deliberate actions that readers make in an effort to construct meaning from text (Afflerbach et al., 2008).

The LinC Cycle supports two important principles of reading instruction. First, students most effectively learn to use reading strategies when these strategies are taught explicitly rather than implicitly. **Explicit strategy instruction** gives students the tools to succeed with demanding texts (Pressley, 2006). If a strategy is taught explicitly, the teacher shows students how and when to use that strategy as a tool to help their comprehension.

Second, when teaching students a new strategy, effective teachers **scaffold** student learning. In scaffolded instruction, teachers first demonstrate the strategy, and then they gradually release responsibility for using the strategy to the student. The term scaffolding (Wood, Bruner, & Ross, 1976) describes learning situations that are "socially mediated," with one person carefully supporting another with new learning (Vygotsky, 1978). Scaffolded instruction includes:

1. *Modeled Practice.* During modeled practice, a teacher demonstrates a procedure. For example, a teacher thinks aloud while modeling how to use a reading strategy. This process allows students to observe the strategy used by a proficient reader.
2. *Guided Practice.* During guided practice, a student repeats the modeled procedure with teacher support. The teacher assists students as they practice the strategy, gradually giving them control over the use of the strategy.
3. *Independent Practice.* During independent practice, a student repeats the procedure without direct teacher intervention. Teachers work toward having students use the strategy individually, but they are still present for guidance and support (Pearson & Gallagher, 1983).

Independent use of strategies requires a heavy mental load, especially when using a new reading strategy to learn difficult content. By gradually releasing responsibility, the teacher ensures that students have mastered the strategy before they use it independently.

PAUSE and REFLECT 1.3

Recall a time when you used scaffolding during a lesson sequence. Consider whether you used modeled practice, guided practice, and/or independent practice. How did the learner respond to your teaching?

Once the lesson sequence is complete, the teacher assesses student progress and plans future instruction. A hallmark of the LinC Cycle is its continuity. During and after instruction, teachers assess students' progress and use that information to design future instruction. Observational, informal, and formative data is valuable to help make these decisions. The LinC Cycle begins, once again, and the teacher engages in assessment, reflection, planning, and teaching. Data provided from ongoing, informal reading assessments shapes instruction to meet the needs of all students.

The teaching cycle described here greatly simplifies the process of targeted, embedded literacy instruction. In addition, it leads to positive learning outcomes. Over a two-year period, a team of sixth grade teachers used the LinC Cycle to improve student performance with expository text. In the two years prior to the study, students had moved into and through sixth grade with very little growth in their proficiency with content reading material. During the two-year pilot, teachers began using assessment data to plan targeted reading instruction for their students. In both years, mean scores for students rose from 62 to 70 percent proficient in 2007/08 and from 56 to 63 percent proficient in 2008/09. More studies are underway to measure both the qualitative and quantitative effects of the LinC Cycle on student learning.

A study of a similar teaching/learning cycle in another context also had positive effects on learning. Teachers learned to use the cycle to reflect on student outcomes and make instructional decisions. The focus was on reading and writing with 120 students, kindergarten through seventh grade. Results showed that student learning was accelerated; over 12 weeks, the average gain on multiple measures of reading performance was half of an academic year (Jinkins, 2001). Matching resources and approaches to students' needs leads to intentional decisions and a greater impact on student learning.

Chapter Summary

The statistics on adolescent literacy are troubling. Many adolescents are not prepared to face the progressively demanding literacy tasks of high school, college, and beyond. By using the LinC Cycle, teachers can embed literacy in context, helping students reach disciplinary literacy by developing their vocabulary, fluency, comprehension, and motivation. Teachers who use the LinC Cycle engage in a continuous cycle of assessment, reflection, planning, teaching, and reteaching to help foster literacy for all.

Resources

Biancarosa, G., & Snow, C. (2004). *Reading next: A vision for action and research in middle and high school. A report to Carnegie Corporation of New York.* Washington, DC: Alliance for Excellent Education.

Boardman, A. G., Roberts, G., Vaughn, S., Wexler, J., Murray, C.S., & Kosanovich, M. (2008) *Effective instruction for adolescent struggling readers: A practice brief.* Portsnouth, NH: RMC Research Corporation, Center on Instruction.

DuFour, R., DuFour, R., Eaker, R., & Many, T. (2006). *Learning by doing: A handbook for professional learning communities at work.* Bloomington, IN: Solution Tree.

Graham, S., & Hebert, D. (2010). *Writing to Read: Evidence for How Writing Can Improve Reading—A report from the Carnegie Corporation of New York.* Washington, DC: Alliance for Excellent Education.

Heller, R., & Greenleaf, C. L. (2007). *Literacy instruction in the content areas: Getting to the core of middle and high school improvement.* Washington, DC: Alliance for Excellent Education.

National Association of State Boards of Education. (2006). *Reading at risk: The state response to the crisis in adolescent literacy.* Alexandria, VA: NASBE.

Scammacca, N., Roberts, G., Vaughn, S., Edmonds, M., Wexler, J., Reutebuch, C. K., et al. (2007). *Interventions for adolescent struggling readers: A meta-analysis with implications for practice.* Portsmouth, NH: RMC Research Corporation, Center on Instruction.

Short, D., & Fitzsimmons, S. (2007). *Double the work: Challenges and solutions to acquiring language and academic literacy for adolescent English language learners. A report from the Carnegie Corporation of New York.* Washington, DC: Alliance for Excellent Education.

Torgesen, J. K., Houston, D. D., Rissman, L. M., Decker, S. M., Roberts, G., Vaughn, S., et al. (2007). *Academic literacy instruction for adolescents: A guidance document from the Center on Instruction.* Portsmouth, NH: RMC Research Corporation, Center on Instruction.

References

Afflerbach, P., Pearson, P. D., & Paris, S. G. (2008). Clarifying differences between reading skills and reading strategies. *The Reading Teacher, 61*(5), 364–373.

Alvermann, D. E. (2002). Effective literacy instruction for adolescents. *Journal of Literacy Research, 34*(2), 198–208.

Balfanz, R., McPartland, J. M., & Shaw, A. (2002). *Re-conceptualizing extra help for high school students in a high standards era.* Baltimore, MD: Center for Social Organization of Schools, Johns Hopkins University.

Baumann, J. F., Kame'enui, E. J., & Ash, G. E. (2003). Research on vocabulary instruction: Voltaire redux. In J. Flood, D. Lapp, J. R. Squire & J. M. Jensen (Eds.), *Handbook of research on teaching the English language arts* (2nd ed., pp. 752–785). Mahway, NJ: Erlbaum.

Carnevale, A. P. (2001). *Help wanted...college required.* Washington, DC: Educational Testing Service, Office for Public Leadership.

Cassidy, J., & Cassidy, D. (2010). What's hot for 2010. *Reading Today, 27,* 1, 8, 9.

Colton, A. B., & Sparks-Langer, G. M. (1993). A conceptual framework to guide the development of teacher reflection and decision making. *Journal of Teacher Education, 44*(1), 45–54.

Dewey, J. (1933). *How we think: A restatement of the relation of reflective thinking to the educative process.* (Rev. ed.). Boston, MA: D.C. Heath & Co.

Donahue, P., Voelkl, J. R., Campbell, J., & Mazzeo, J. (1999). *NAEP 1998 Reading Report Card for the Nation and the States.* Washington, DC: U.S. Department of Education. Office of Educational Research and Improvement. National Center for Education Statistics.

DuFour, R. (2004). What is a professional learning community? *Educational Leadership, 61*(8), 6–11.

Fuchs, D., & Fuchs, L. S. (2001). Responsiveness to intervention: A blueprint for practitioners, policymakers, and parents. *Teaching Exceptional Children, 38*(1), 57–61.

Grigg, W., Daane, M. C., Jin, Y., & Campbell, J. R. (2003). *The Nation's Report Card: Reading 2002.* Washington, DC: National

Center for Educational Statistics, Institute of Education Sciences, U.S. Department of Education.

Grigg, W., Donahue, P., & Dion, G. (2007). *The Nation's Report Card: 12th Grade Reading and Mathematics 2005.* Washington, DC: U.S. Department of Education, National Center for Education Statistics.

Guthrie, J. T., & Wigfield, A. (1997). Reading engagement: A rationale for theory and teaching. In J. T. Guthrie & A. Wigfield (Eds.), *Reading engagement: Motivating readers through integrated instruction* (pp. 1–12). Newark, DE: International Reading Association.

Irwin, J. W. (1991). *Teaching reading comprehension processes* (2nd ed.). Boston, MA: Allyn & Bacon.

Jinkins, D. (2001). Impact of the implementation of the teaching learning cycle on teacher decision-making and emergent readers. *Reading Psychology, 22,* 267–288.

Kamil, M. L. (2003). *Adolescents and literacy: reading for the 21st Century.* Washington, DC: Alliance for Excellent Education.

Keene, E. O. (2007). The essence of understanding. In K. Beers, R. E. Probst, & L. Rief (Eds.), *Adolescent literacy: Turning promise into practice* (pp. 27–38). Portsmouth, NH: Heinemann.

LaBerge, D., & Samuels, S. J. (1974). Toward a theory of automatic information processing in reading. *Cognitive Psychology, 6,* 293–323.

Lee, J., Grigg, W., & Donahue, P. (2007). *The Nation's Report Card: Reading 2007.* Washington, DC: National Center for Education Statistics, Institute of Education Sciences, U.S. Department of Education.

Moore, D. W., Bean, T. W., Bridyshaw, D., & Tycik, J. A. (1999). Adolescent literacy: A position statement for the Commission on Adolescent Literacy of the International Reading Association. Newark, DE: International Reading Association.

Nagy, W. E., & Scott, J. A. (2000). Vocabulary processes. In M. Kamil, P. Mosenthal, P. D. Pearson & R. Barr (Eds.), *Handbook of reading research* (Vol. 3) (pp. 269-284). Upper Saddle River, NJ: Erlbaum.

National Academy of Sciences (1995). National Science Education Standards. Washington, DC: National Academies Press.

National Institute of Child Health and Human Development (NICHD). (2004). *Teaching children to read: An evidence-based assessment of the scientific research literature on reading and its implications for reading instruction.* Bethesda, MD: NICHD.

National Institute for Literacy (NIFL). (2009). About the National Institute for Literacy. Retrieved January 10, 2010, from http://www.nifl.gov/about/aboutus.html.

Pearson, P. D., & Gallagher, D. R. (1983). Instruction of reading comprehension. *Contemporary Educational Psychology, 8*(3), 317–344.

Pressley, M. (2006). *Reading instruction that works: The case for balanced teaching* (3rd ed.). New York: Guilford.

Rasinski, T., Padak, N., McKeon, C. A., Wilfong, L. G., Friedauer, J. A., & Heim, P. (2005). Is reading fluency a key for successful high school reading? *Journal of Adolescent & Adult Literacy, 48*(1), 22–27.

Remillard, T. J. (2005). Examining key concepts in research on teachers' use of mathematics curricula. *Review of Educational Research, 75*(2), 211–246.

Reutzel, D. R., & Cooter, R. B. (1996). *Teaching reading: Putting the pieces together* (3rd ed.). Upper Saddle River, NJ: Merrill.

Schunk, D. H., Pintrich, P. R., & Meece, J. L. (2008). *Motivation in education: Theory, research and applications* (3rd ed.). Upper Saddle River, NJ: Pearson, Merrill, Prentice Hall.

Shanahan, T., & Shanahan, C. (2008). Teaching content area literacy to adolescents: Rethinking content area literacy. *Harvard Educational Review, 78*(1), 41–59.

Vygotsky, L. (1978). *Mind in society.* Cambridge, MA: Harvard University Press.

Wirt, J., Choy, S., Gerald, D., Provasnik, S., Rooney, P., Watanable, S., et al. (2001). *The Condition of Education.* Washington, DC: National Center for Educational Statistics, U.S. Department of Education Institute of Education Sciences.

Wood, D. J., Bruner, J. S., & Ross, G. (1976). The role of tutoring in problem-solving. *Journal of Child Psychology and Psychiatry, 17*(2), 89–100.

CHAPTER **2**

Strategies to Build Vocabulary

 *Learning Log*

Use the Vocabulary Rating Guide found in the Learning Log Appendix (LL1) to learn this chapter's vocabulary concepts in a meaningful context. The Vocabulary Rating Guide is an effective instructional strategy that will be discussed later in the chapter.

The classroom was buzzing as students discussed what they had read in the introductory section of their math chapter on congruent triangles. One ninth-grade geometry student in particular caught the teacher's attention.

"Hey, Ms. J … What does this word mean—e-qui-ang-ul-ar?" Tanner shouted across the classroom.

Emmi intervened. "Break it down. It has 'equal' and 'angle' in it. That means all of the angles are equal."

"You sure know your stuff, Em. I didn't know I could look for smaller words to figure it out."

"Duh. That's what Ms. Jackson keeps telling us to do. What do you normally do?" replied Emmi.

Tanner admitted, "Most of the time I just skip it if I don't know how to say it or what it means."

"Well, how's that gonna help you in math or when you're reading something else?" said Emmi.

"I guess it's not …" grumbled Tanner.

In middle and high school classrooms across the country, students often skip key, content area terms. Unfortunately, students who do not actively seek to learn new words are at a disadvantage for success in content area classes. Research by Graves (2008) estimates that once students enter school, they learn an average of 3,000 to 4,000 new words per year. At this rate, they will have learned 25,000 words by the eighth grade and 50,000 new words by graduation from high school. However, students who do not seek to learn new words or who are given few opportunities to develop word knowledge at school and at home, are likely to have smaller vocabularies than their classmates. This concept is referred to as the **Matthew Effect**, where "The rich (rich with vocabulary) get richer, and the poor (limited vocabulary) get poorer" (Stanovich, 1986). Under these conditions, a vocabulary-deprived tenth grader can be performing an average of two grade levels behind his or her peers. Subsequently, this limited vocabulary can affect reading comprehension, content knowledge, and future success.

For decades, research has shown a strong, positive relationship between vocabulary knowledge and reading comprehension (Anderson & Freebody, 1981; Baumann, Kame'enui, & Ash, 2003). This is especially true in content area reading where a student's knowledge about a content concept can hinge upon the understanding of a single vocabulary word. Students who fail to increase their vocabulary knowledge have limited reading comprehension proficiency and therefore struggle to understand the content.

To complicate matters, as a student progresses through school, the amount of academic vocabulary increases. **Academic vocabulary** includes words that are specific to learning in the content areas; these terms describe content-specific knowledge and complex processes, and they create cohesion in discourse (Zwiers, 2003). They can be grouped into two categories: content-specific academic vocabulary and content-general academic vocabulary. **Content-specific academic vocabulary** is associated with a particular discipline, such as the word "abolitionist" as presented in history. **Content-general academic vocabulary** includes words that occur across domains, such as the words "evidence" and "describe." These content-general words can sometimes change meaning depending upon the context.

Many features of content area textbooks have been put in place to help support vocabulary development (Cardinale, 1991). Authors often use techniques such as analogies to explain the new concepts and aid students' understanding of vocabulary. In addition, many new content area textbooks have academic vocabulary bolded so that students will focus on these words. (All the academic vocabulary in this text is bolded. Definitions are embedded within the text. You can also find the definitions in the Glossary.)

Despite these improvements with content area texts, learning content area vocabulary continues to pose a unique set of challenges. Not only must students devote time to learning new **labels**, (words given to represent objects or ideas), but they must also understand the **concept** (abstract thoughts), that the new labels represent. For example, in a life science class, students must learn the labels "prophase" and "anaphase." In addition, they must also comprehend the concept of "meiosis" involving these stages. To complicate matters even more, as students learn new labels and concepts in the different content areas, they must often learn new meanings for familiar terms (Blachowicz & Fisher, 2000).

What can teachers do to support students in building their vocabulary knowledge? A review of the research shows that there are many interventions that have been successful, especially with students who struggle with reading (Blachowicz & Fisher, 2000). The most effective vocabulary instruction has these three goals in mind:

- Build full concept knowledge
- Teach words in a meaningful context
- Encourage independent use of strategies

This chapter describes instructional strategies teachers can use to meet these three goals. They are outlined in Figure 2.1.

Teachers can reflect upon their students' needs from assessment data and teach using instructional plans that include the thoughtful use of these strategies paired with the careful selection of significant vocabulary terms. (Chapter 8 will describe how teachers can choose which strategies and words should be taught.) Such instruction will lead to literacy-based content learning that enriches students' vocabulary knowledge. When new vocabulary knowledge develops, students will be able to create a deeper understanding of the text and the content it represents.

Literacy Component	Goals of Instruction	Strategies for Instruction
Vocabulary	Build Full Concept Knowledge	• Concept of Definition Map • Semantic Feature Analysis • Pre-Teaching Vocabulary
	Teach Words in a Meaningful Context	• Vocabulary Rating Guide • List-Group-Label • Vocabulary Visits
	Encourage Independent Use of Strategies	• Word Analysis • Contextual Redefinition • Dictionary Use • Personal Dictionary

FIGURE 2.1   Vocabulary Strategy Summary Chart

BUILD FULL CONCEPT KNOWLEDGE

One way to expand vocabulary and to help students comprehend content text is to build full concept knowledge of words that are *significant* in the content area or text passage being studied. Often, in middle and high school, vocabulary terms represent labels and concepts that are new to students. To develop conceptual understanding, students need to first recognize and have basic knowledge of the word. Ideally, students must move beyond this stage to having complete and flexible knowledge with an understanding of the word's multiple meanings and an ability to use it appropriately in different contexts (Nagy & Scott, 2000).

Educators have identified a continuum of four levels of word knowledge students progress through as they seek to build conceptual understanding of words (Allen, 1999). They are:

Level 1: No Association: I don't recognize this word, and I have never heard it before.

Level 2: Recognition: I recognize the word, but I don't know what it means.

Level 3: Partial Concept Knowledge: I have a basic understanding of the word.

Level 4: Full Concept Knowledge: I understand the word and can use it flexibly in most contexts.

To better understand these stages, review the following examples. Tyler read the word "vector" in his calculus lesson, and he has not ever heard or seen this word before (Level 1: No Association). Kristina read the word "carbohydrate" in her health textbook and can recognize the word from things she has heard, but she cannot explain its meaning (Level 2: Recognition). During economics class, Brandon read the words "unemployment rate" and has a basic understanding of the term, but he cannot tell you how it is calculated or used in different contexts (Level 3: Partial Concept Knowledge). Kamarin read the word "chivalry" in her world history textbook passage entitled "Feudal Societies," and she had a full understanding of the word because she had been exposed to it in other classes (Level 4: Full Concept Knowledge). She even used it as the topic for a piece of writing she completed in literature class. All four of these students are at different stages of word knowledge with each of these terms.

PAUSE and REFLECT 2.1

One of the strategies that teachers can use to build full concept knowledge involves *semantic mapping*. Which stage along the continuum best represents your understanding of this term? 1) No Association, 2) Recognition, 3) Partial Concept Knowledge, or 4) Full Concept Knowledge

---

In order to attain full concept knowledge, students must experience repeated multiple exposures to each label or concept (National Institute of Child Health and Human Development [NICHD], 2000). Building full conceptual knowledge of new or familiar, targeted vocabulary in each of the content areas is critical to proficiency. Examples for history, science, math, language arts, and electives will help explain this significance.

History

Students in a world history course must understand the label for "empire" as it relates to the geographical realms of the Byzantines, Romans, and British. In addition, they must have a conceptual understanding of how the definition of the term can change depending upon which political structure the empire has in place. American government students need to understand the concept "revolution" as it connects to the American and Industrial Revolutions. They must also develop a fluid knowledge of the term "revolution" as it is applied in other domains.

Science

In order to be successful in comprehending a chapter on plant science, students in a biology course must understand the labels and concepts involved with photosynthesis (e.g., "chloroplast," "carbon dioxide," "glucose"). In chemistry, many students begin the class with an understanding of the term "conservation" as it relates to biology. Now they must add to their definition that "conservation" of matter involves the arrangement of atoms.

Mathematics

In Algebra I, students learn the term "inequality." As they move into Algebra II, they expand their understanding of this definition to include negative integers and variables. Furthermore, calculus students must understand the concept of a "derivative" so they can calculate the covariant and the partial derivative.

Language Arts

In English, understanding the terms associated with sentence structure (e.g., "verb phrases," "prepositional phrases," "appositives") allows students to understand lessons about how to improve their writing using these features. Furthermore, American literature teachers must be sure their students fully understand the concept of "persona," the role or personality of a writer, before they turn them loose to independently analyze this feature in a classic novel.

Electives

In a visual art course, fully understanding the vocabulary associated with art elements (e.g., "hue," "emphasis," "unity") is a critical basis for all art that is produced or critiqued. And in an economics course, students must build full concept knowledge of the "law of demand" if they are to become informed consumers who understand the American market.

PAUSE and REFLECT 2.2

In each discipline, there are some central concepts that are essential to building a full understanding. What are some important vocabulary labels and/or concepts in your subject area?

As explained, building full concept knowledge is essential in all content areas. There are three effective instructional strategies teachers can use to help students build full concept knowledge. These are: Concept of Definition Map, Semantic Feature Analysis, and Pre-Teaching Vocabulary.

Concept of Definition Map

Studies suggest that an effective way to build conceptual understanding is to combine words with visual images. This type of strategy, called **semantic mapping**, uses lines and geometric shapes to show the relationship between concepts and sub-concepts. One type of semantic map, a Concept of Definition (CD) Map, helps build a broad, multidimensional meaning of a word (Schwartz & Rafael, 1985). It includes three different components:

- *Category:* What is it?
- *Properties:* What's it like?
- *Illustrations:* What are some examples?

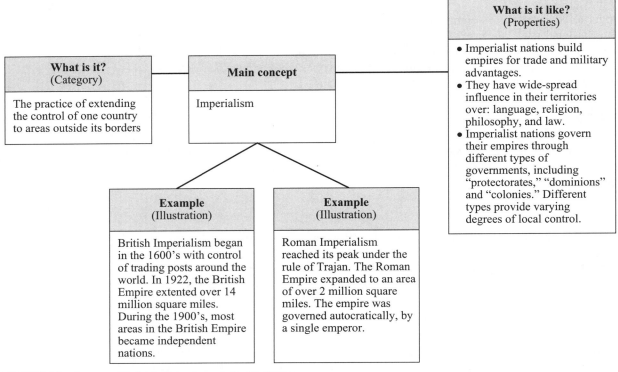

FIGURE 2.2 Concept of Definition Map Example for World History

All information is recorded on the CD Map. Figure 2.2 is an example from a world history class learning about the concept of "imperialism."

PROCEDURE

1. Choose a term that is central to the curriculum. Place that term in the "Main Concept" box.
2. Define the concept for the students. If the word is defined in the text, guide students to that definition. Have students record the definition in the "What is it?" box.
3. Explain to students the difference between this concept and other similar concepts by discussing and recording its properties in the "What's it like?" box. (This can include synonyms.)
4. With the class, generate examples. Add words, descriptions, and/or images in the "Example" boxes.
5. Students complete their individual CD Maps as the teacher discusses the content and completes a class CD Map on the board, overhead, or Interwrite board. CD Maps can then be used by students as they continue to encounter this concept throughout the section or to review at the end of the chapter.

VARIATIONS   There are several variations to the CD Map. With the Frayer Method, students add examples and non-examples to the definition. After recording some non-examples, the teacher then asks students to explain the difference between examples and non-examples (Frayer, Frederick, & Klausmeier, 1969). In Figure 2.3, the students needed to understand the term "isosceles" triangle in their geometry class before they could begin to understand the basic theorems for isosceles triangles.

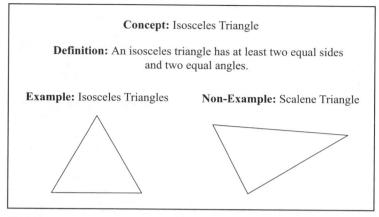

FIGURE 2.3   Frayer Method Example for Geometry

In the Visual Association Chart, students add images, beyond the definition, to help them visualize the word's meaning. They record this under the "What does it look like?" column. In the example (Figure 2.4), a middle school student worked to expand her vocabulary knowledge as she read a passage in her literature textbook about the study of archeology.

Another variation involves recording targeted words on a Vocabulary Note Card. Students write the term in the middle of the note card. Then they add the definition, properties, examples, and non-examples into four quadrants on the card. Students can use their Vocabulary Note Cards to help them when reading, taking notes, or completing work in that particular content area. They can also use them as a study aid for quizzes and tests. Figure 2.5 shows an example of a seventh-grade student's Vocabulary Note Card from his study of weather.

Teacher Tool

A blank Concept of Definition Map (TT1), Visual Association Chart (TT2), and Vocabulary Note Card (TT3) can be found in the Teacher Tools Appendix.

Vocabulary Word	What is it?	What does it look like?
fossil	fossil is a part of imprint of something that was once alive	
artifacts	artifacts, objects created by and used by humans.	
Primary Source	an account created by someone who witnessed the event.	
Secondary Source	gathered info told to someone	

FIGURE 2.4   Visual Association Chart Example for Literature

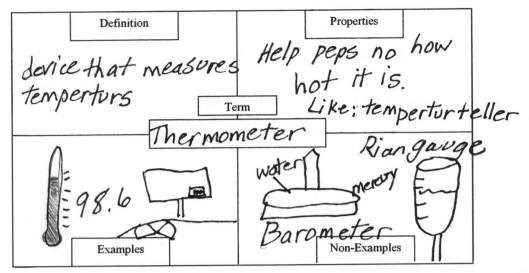

FIGURE 2.5   Vocabulary Note Card Example for Earth Science

Semantic Feature Analysis

Semantic Feature Analysis is another way to build conceptual knowledge, but in this case, students are prompted to focus on the relationships between terms. This type of analysis is useful in helping students understand the **semantic features**, or differences that can be noted among the meanings of words, concepts, events, and processes. The process acknowledges the relationship between the words and requires that students participate actively with word meaning (Blachowicz & Fisher, 2000).

PROCEDURE

1. Identify concepts and/or terms to be learned and the features of these concepts that can be used to compare them (see Figure 2.6).
2. Create a chart that lists the concepts down the left-hand side and the features across the top.
3. Guide students through a discussion of each concept. As each feature is considered, decide whether the concept exemplifies that feature (+) or does not exemplify that feature (−).
4. Use the chart to explore the concepts further, generate questions, and conduct research.

   In the example shown in Figure 2.6, the tenth-grade chemistry students used a chart that identified the four stages of matter: solid, liquid, gas, and plasma. As they learned about each stage, they entered a "+" or "−" on the chart. The comparison between these four stages led to a discussion of examples that they had seen in their lives. Some students had heard of plasma televisions, and they wondered whether this technology made use of the fourth stage of

Concept	Changes Form	Changes Volume	Can Form a Free Surface	Can Conduct Electricity
Solid	−	−	−	+
Liquid	+	−	+	+
Gas	+	−	−	−
Plasma	+	−	−	+

FIGURE 2.6   Semantic Feature Analysis Chart Example for Chemistry

matter. This led to discussion and research on plasma's use in projecting images. In addition, they were able to draw on previous demonstrations and laboratory experiments in which they had discussed water's ability to form a free surface inside a container.

VARIATIONS   Semantic Feature Analysis can be used before, during, and after instruction. Before beginning the reading of a passage, the teacher might introduce the terms and find out what students already know. The initial "+" and "−" marks can be written in one color. Then, during or after reading a section of text, students can come back to the chart and revisit their evaluation of the features. After reconsidering, some might be changed from "+" to "−", and vice-versa. These new, revised marks can be made in a different color. This approach allows students to engage in continual thinking about the concepts and to record their learning.

Pre-Teaching Vocabulary

Another way to ensure that students gain full concept knowledge is to make them aware of important concepts before they begin reading the text. When teachers pre-teach vocabulary (Feldman & Kinsella, 2003), they introduce unfamiliar terms to students before they begin to read the text, and students have a heightened awareness of the vocabulary that they will encounter while reading. In addition, pre-teaching selected vocabulary allows students to see that some words have academic definitions that are different from their everyday meanings. This focus on multiple meanings is especially important for English learners or students who need extra support with academic language.

Research suggests that pre-teaching vocabulary can significantly improve comprehension of passages that contain the target words (Carney, Anderson, Blackburn, & Blessing, 1984). Additionally, it can lead to an increase in the use of these terms in writing (Amaral, Garrison, & Klentschy, 2002).

PROCEDURE

1. Choose terms that are essential to understanding the text. Then, for each term:
   a. Pronounce the new word and have students repeat.
   b. Provide an explanation of the word or a synonym.
   c. Rephrase the explanation, asking students to complete the statement by substituting the new word aloud.
   d. Show a visual image of the word, if possible. This can be effectively done using a PowerPoint® presentation.
   e. Check for beginning understanding of the word by asking questions to assess students. This can be done whole group as students respond with thumbs up (partial concept knowledge/recognition) or thumbs down (no association yet).
   f. Ask students to generate their own examples. Students can generate these examples with a partner, and then report back to the group.
2. After the teacher introduces the new terms, students complete a Pre-Teaching Vocabulary Chart as shown in Figure 2.7. This chart can then be used as a reference when students are engaged during the reading and post-writing activities associated with the text passage.

Teacher Tool

A Pre-Teaching Vocabulary Chart (TT4) can be found in the Teacher Tools Appendix.

VARIATIONS   There are many ways that vocabulary can be pre-taught to students. The key is to choose a variation that makes students aware of the terms that are essential to their understanding of the reading or the lesson *before* it begins. For example, the Concept of Definition Map may be used to pre-teach vocabulary before reading a passage. When used as a pre-reading lesson, the teacher guides students as they investigate words and their meanings before beginning to read the text. Vocabulary Note Cards can also be used to pre-teach vocabulary so that students will develop knowledge of the word prior to being exposed to it.

Conclusion

Building full concept knowledge of vocabulary is critical to content area proficiency and literacy development. When teachers use these strategies—Concept of Definition Maps, Semantic Feature Analysis, and Pre-Teaching Vocabulary—they will help adolescent learners

Term	Synonym	Definition/Example	Image
Normal distribution	Bell curve	Describes any variable that tends to cluster around a mean	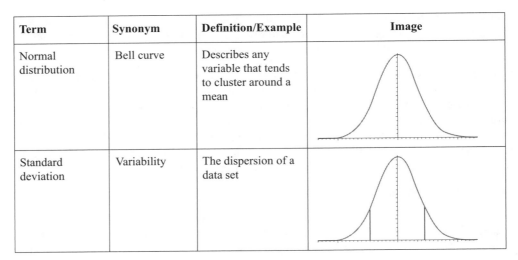
Standard deviation	Variability	The dispersion of a data set	

FIGURE 2.7   Pre-Teaching Vocabulary Chart Example for Calculus

move toward developing full concept knowledge of terms and help them to further build their literacy.

TEACH WORDS IN A MEANINGFUL CONTEXT

When teachers think back to how they learned new vocabulary as middle or high school students, they may recall memorizing a list of terms and their definitions out of **context** of content learning. In other words, the terms were unrelated to the text passage being read and to the classroom instructional content. Some classrooms, unfortunately, still frequently use this method of instruction. Students are asked to study lists of words that are disconnected.

For example, a teacher gave her ninth-grade literature class five days to learn the words "annihilate," "transitory," and "rhapsody" along with a list of 22 other random words. These terms were not related to the novel *Lord of the Flies* (Golding, 1973) that they were reading in class or to the content in their literature textbook. Research suggests that learning vocabulary is not successful when taught this way. Students must have the opportunity to learn and use vocabulary in meaningful, authentic situations. A review of the research on vocabulary studies indicates that the only time that comprehension is not impacted by vocabulary instruction is when it is superficial or disconnected (Beck & McKeon, 1991).

For vocabulary learning to continue to build and help comprehension, students must make deep connections between words and their meanings and use the words in multiple contexts over a long period of time (Pressley, 2000). Take the example of Carter. In fifth and sixth grade, he learned and practiced new terms in the context of meaningful instruction. When he moved to junior high in seventh and eighth grade, he learned new words by completing paper-and-pencil activities with weekly word lists. On the state standardized subtest measuring vocabulary, his scores dropped from a 100 percent in fifth and sixth grades, to 62 percent in seventh grade and 50 percent in eighth grade. As measured by these tests, learning random words out of context was not beneficial to his vocabulary development.

The strategies described in this section focus on how to infuse vocabulary instruction into a lesson or sequence of lessons. Central to this notion of teaching words in a meaningful context is the concept of scaffolding, as described in Chapter 1. When teachers scaffold instruction, they make the vocabulary comprehensible in the context of learning new concepts. Scaffolding helps students expand their vocabulary knowledge and understand content better.

Before Reading. Teaching vocabulary *before* reading can significantly improve comprehension of passages (Carney, et al., 1984). Various instructional strategies can be used to focus students on these terms. When used before reading, the Concept of Definition Map and its variants help students to start building conceptual knowledge of a word before reading the text. The Semantic Feature Analysis Chart can also provide such support. Other strategies such as the Text Box/Bag Activity or the Survey Strategy & Guide, which will be described in Chapter 4, are also effective to highlight vocabulary before reading.

During Reading. New vocabulary can also be built *during* reading. Students who are exposed to new words during reading will more likely develop an understanding of that word (Nagy, Herman, & Anderson, 1985). Teachers often use artifacts or photos to illustrate terms as they appear in the text. For example, while reading a passage about Mt. Everest, a sixth-grade language arts teacher brought **realia**, or actual objects—a carabineer, climbing rope, harness, quick-draws and a helmet—to illustrate unfamiliar terms. Another powerful during-reading vocabulary activity is the Interactive Think Aloud strategy that will be explained in Chapter 4, as it builds both vocabulary and reading comprehension.

After Reading. Vocabulary development continues *after* the reading of the text. Research indicates that exposing students to a word in different contexts increases student understanding and use of the target word (McKeown, 1985). One way to support vocabulary after reading is to post terms on a Word Wall. With this, a visual display of words is posted for students to use as a resource to support them in their reading and writing associated with the content instruction. As Wagstaff noted (1999), Word Walls do not simply act as a bulletin board decoration; they are useful works in progress built over time as words are harvested from meaningful contexts. They should be memorable, useful, practical, hands-on, space efficient, and suited to meet the needs of the students and content being studied.

Resource

To learn more about using Word Walls, refer to *Word Wall— A Support for Literacy in Secondary School Classrooms* at http://www.curriculum.org/tcf/teachers/projects/wordwalls.shtml.

Vocabulary can also be supported after the lesson when it is incorporated into a writing assignment. Figure 2.8 shows a sixth-grader's summary paragraph written after a lesson about the ancient Roman baths. The underlined words are terms the teacher identified at the beginning of the lesson and supported throughout. Following this writing assignment, the teacher asked students to read their paragraph aloud to their classmates, correctly pronouncing the new vocabulary terms. This written and oral practice is necessary for vocabulary to become useful (Baumann, et al., 2002).

A critical feature of scaffolding vocabulary instruction comes as teachers select which vocabulary should be targeted before, during, and/or after reading. Chapter 8 will explain how

---

"A Debate about the Roman Baths"

You have just finished reading "A Debate about the Roman Baths." The literacy goal for reading this article was to focus on drawing conclusions. The social science goal was to understand more about ancient Rome. Which of the two debaters—Marcus or Petronius—do you think makes the strongest argument? Give details to support your opinion.

In the expository passage, "A Debate about the Roman Baths," two very strong <u>opinionated</u> men state what their feelings are about the Roman baths. Marcus, a serious <u>Stoic</u>, believes that the Roman bathhouse is a dirty, <u>bothersome</u> place of no beauty. He also thinks that without <u>hard-working</u>, serious people, Rome will basically fall apart. Marcus clearly doesn't enjoy the baths at all. My honest opinion is that Marcus has the strongest argument and that he is most correct about the Roman bathhouse. In conclusion, my opinion matches that of Marcus. I also believe that the baths are a dirty place for lazy <u>citizens</u>.

FIGURE 2.8   Summary Paragraph Example of Teaching Vocabulary Words in a Meaningful Context for Social Science

Vocabulary Knowledge Rating
The Great Wall

High Knowledge
4 = I could teach it to the group.
3 = I am pretty sure what it means.

Low Knowledge
2 = I recognize it but need a review.
1 = I have no clue what it means.

Word	Before Instruction				After Instruction				Definition and Synonym
	4	3	2	1	4	3	2	1	
blueprint	✶				✶				a reproduction of tech. drawing or plans. - plan -
terrain		✶			✶				The surface of an area - land -
durable	✶					✶			Able to continue for a prolonged period of time. -unbreakable-
stonemassons		✶			✶				Person that works with stone. -worker-
steppe		✶				✶			level land without trees -land / plains -
ingenious	✶				✶				ingenuity; clever - skillfull -
insurmountable		✶			✶				incapable of being overcome. -incapable - ? invincible -
grueling	✶					✶			very tired - exausted -tacing -
vying		✶							Challenging - getting -
extravagance	✶				✶				overly lavish in expenditure; wasteful -overlavish - exceeding -
imposed	✶				✶				to enact or apply as compulsory; to obtrude or force oneself to De's
nomadic		✶				✶			being a member of a group of people who wander from place to place ; -wanderer
domain	✶				✶				a territory under one government; a field of activity or interest. -empire, country-

FIGURE 2.9   Vocabulary Rating Guide Example for Literature

8. As a class, students share what they have learned about each word. (If the class has been divided into pairs, the teacher leads the class in completing the definition and synonym portion of the Vocabulary Rating Guide together.)

9. (During reading) Students use the Vocabulary Rating Guide during the reading of the text passage to review word meaning.

10. (After reading) After the text reading has been completed, students revisit the Vocabulary Rating Guide and complete the "After Reading" rating section to see if they have made vocabulary growth over time. The teacher says each word. Students rate their new understanding, assigning a 1, 2, 3, or 4. If a student has rated his or her understanding as either 3 or 4, the teacher can challenge him or her to put that word in a sentence.

11. Debrief about how students' understanding of the key terms improved during the lesson. The teacher can also request that students show a hand signal—thumbs up (increase), thumbs down (decrease), or a flat hand (no change) to show whether their rating changed over time.

Teacher Tool

A Vocabulary Rating Guide (TT5) can be found in the Teacher Tools Appendix for use with your students.

VARIATIONS   In one similar word rating method, Stoplight Vocabulary, students use colors rather than numbers to rank their knowledge level of each term. Students record their vocabulary words on a handout and shade in a small stoplight printed next to each word with red (low level of knowledge), yellow (some level of knowledge), or green (high level of knowledge) (Lubliner & Smetana, 2005). Another option is for teachers to hang vocabulary terms on small posters around the walls of the classroom. Students then move from poster to poster and sign their names in green, yellow, or red, depending upon their knowledge of the word. Both of these variations include pre-teaching words, referring to them during, and revisiting them after reading to re-rank understanding.

List-Group-Label

A second instructional strategy that exemplifies teaching words in a meaningful context is the List-Group-Label (LGL) strategy. LGL encourages students to use inductive reasoning to categorize related vocabulary words (Taba, 1967). As students sort words into categories, they connect familiar words with new words, expanding their conceptual understanding of vocabulary. Then, during and after reading, they revisit their categories to expand and make changes.

PROCEDURE

1. (Before reading) The teacher writes a word or topic on the board.
2. List. Students suggest words they associate with the topic. If they have difficulty providing words, the teacher can give clues. If students still struggle, the teacher can provide words.
3. Group. Students work to organize these words into groups with common features. As they discuss, students share ideas regarding why these words fit together.
4. Label. Students generate and write a label for each category of words listed.
5. (During reading) Students then read the text, looking for the terms they categorized.
6. (After reading) Students revisit their concept groups, eliminating words that no longer fit and regrouping based on information from the text.

When using the LGL strategy, it is especially important to revisit the vocabulary groupings after reading. In one study where students categorized science words, researchers found that students did not consistently group the words into science-related categories (Meyerson, Ford, Jones, & Ward, 1991); they often used a non-science meaning of the term to group the word. By revisiting during and after reading, the teacher can ensure that students are learning the word meaning that is connected to the area of study.

VARIATIONS   The LGL strategy assumes that some students in the class will have prior knowledge about the focus topic. If, however, this is not the case, the teacher can choose the list of terms to use. Then, students continue with the process of grouping and labeling, as described in steps 3 through 6. Figure 2.10 shows an example built under these circumstances when an art class prepared to read a passage entitled "Features of Art." The teacher provided the list, and the students grouped and labeled each set of sorted terms as they progressed through the reading.

Vocabulary Visits

Another way to build context for new word learning is to build connections between abstract concepts and tangible objects, or realia. A Vocabulary Visit highlights vocabulary words that surround a field trip, or field experience. It has been shown to lead to increased vocabulary knowledge in elementary students (Blachowicz & Obrochta, 2005). When extended to middle and high school students, it can also be used to prepare students for an experience, such as conducting a lab experiment or listening to a guest speaker.

PROCEDURE

1. (Before reading) Collect related texts and photos that represent the experience.
2. Prepare a large blank poster that can be transported. Ask students to look at the text and photos and to list on the poster the vocabulary terms that they associate with that experience.
3. Go to the site for the experience and bring the poster, text selections, and pictures along as a reference. While there, have students add additional words to the poster. These words may be from the resources the teacher has brought or from auditory or visual experiences gleaned during the experience.

Categorize and Classify Art Vocabulary

Group the following terms together in the correct category and classify them.

Abstract	Focal point	Negative Space	Secondary
Analogous	Foreground	Neutral	Shade
Background	Form	Opaque	Sketch
Complementary	Gesture	Perspective	Still life
Contour	Horizon line	Portrait	Tertiary
Cool	Hue	Primary	Tint
Curvilinear	Landscape	Proportion	Warm
Figurative	Line		

FIGURE 2.10   List-Group-Label Example for Visual Art

4. Lead the students in grouping related words and giving these groups labels, either at the experience site or upon return to the classroom.
5. (During reading) Read sections of the text and have students note (with a signal) when they hear one of the words. If necessary, add more words to the poster that students suggest will belong, and group these new words accordingly.
6. (After reading) Use these words to conduct other word study activities and extension activities.

In the example Figure 2.11, a ninth-grade biology class visited a salmon fish hatchery to learn about principles of ecology. Before the trip, the class developed a list of terms from their text chapter on ecology and from photos and information from the fish hatchery's Web site. During the trip, the class added terms to the list from the informational presentation boards, handouts, and from the hatchery tour guide's presentation. Then, upon return to the classroom, the class arranged the terms into groups and gave them labels. Figure 2.11 is a copy of the poster that was created. The teacher used these grouped vocabulary terms to engage in in-depth discussion about the declining salmon population in the northwestern United States. Students were able to use these terms in a meaningful context throughout this discussion.

VARIATIONS   The Vocabulary Visit does not require that students leave campus for a field trip. The "visit" can be to another location on campus or an experience can come to campus. For example, English teachers may find the Vocabulary Visit strategy helpful if they take their students to the library to conduct research and use tools available there. A social science class studying the Civil War may use the Vocabulary Visit strategy in conjunction with a presentation by Civil War reenactors who come to school to speak about life in the southern encampments. There are unlimited variations with this strategy.

Salmon Hatchery

Vocabulary Generated Before the Field Experience:

Migration
Fish Ladder
Spawn
Coho
Eggs
Stream
Ocean
Toxins
Predators

After the Field Experience:

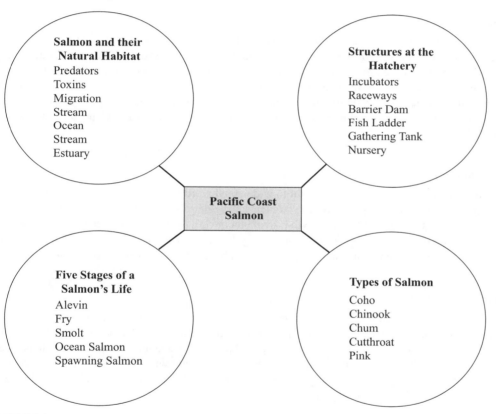

FIGURE 2.11   Vocabulary Visit Example Poster for Biology

Conclusion

Teaching words in a meaningful context helps students develop full knowledge of selected vocabulary terms and deepen their content knowledge along the way. By using Vocabulary Rating Guides, List-Group-Label, and Vocabulary Visits, teachers can achieve this goal.

ENCOURAGE INDEPENDENT USE OF STRATEGIES

In middle and high school classrooms, it is necessary for teachers to help students develop full conceptual knowledge of selected new vocabulary words by creating a powerful, supportive context. However, for students to build an extended vocabulary, word learning must continue outside of the daily content lessons. Therefore, one of the goals of vocabulary instruction is to provide students with a set of word learning strategies that they can use when reading independently (Harmon, Wood, & Hedrick, 2008). Teachers across all content areas must model for students how to determine the meaning of new words and, over time, encourage the independent use of these strategies.

History

Students in world and American history classes will find that independent word learning is essential to their success in this content area. Academic vocabulary terms fill the pages of these textbooks, and teachers must guide students to use the features of the text (boldface terms and glossaries) to decipher meaning as they are asked to read independently. When clues are not available, students can be prompted to record unfamiliar words and review them with support in class.

Science

Likewise, biology, life science, physical science, chemistry, agricultural science, and physics textbooks are filled with academic vocabulary terms that are essential to learning. Students must be given opportunities to learn strategies to comprehend text filled with such words. Beyond learning about features of the text to help in comprehension of content, science teachers can also help students use word parts to uncover meaning. For example, students studying paleontology need to learn what the word part "zoic" means as it relates to the terms "Ceno*zoic*" "Meso*zoic*" and "Paleo*zoic*" eras.

Mathematics

Mathematics students need to be taught to understand word structure to help them read their text independently. For example, geometry students struggle to understand prefixes like "equi" and "con" in their texts, and word work will provide them with the knowledge necessary to determine the meaning of these words. Furthermore, using the glossary of the math text will help students find meanings and equations that will prove invaluable in their comprehension of the content.

Language Arts

In English, it is essential to build an understanding of these types of strategies, for many content standards require instruction in word analysis and dictionary skills. Then, as students complete independent reading assignments and are exposed to varied vocabulary words, they can use these strategies to build their vocabularies. Many English teachers will find it helpful for students to create their own personal dictionary related to their recreational, online, and/or fictional reading to encourage students to build their vocabulary.

Electives

Whether students are reading their keyboarding manual, a textbook in health sciences, or a manual in wood shop, teachers must model how to use context clues to determine word meaning. Over time, students will eventually be able to implement these strategies on their own as they progress through their independent reading assignments.

PAUSE and REFLECT 2.4
Can you describe why it is important to encourage the independent use of vocabulary strategies in your content area?

As explained, encouraging independent use of strategies will vary somewhat for the different content areas. However, the goal is the same—to help students learn strategies that promote independent word learning. The following section describes Word Analysis, Contextual Redefinition, Dictionary Use, and Personal Dictionaries as strategies that students can learn and use.

Word Analysis

Many of the words used in content area instruction are multisyllabic—a fact that can sometimes daunt adolescent readers. Tanner, the student you met in the introduction to this chapter, is not aware that the word *equiangular* can be dissected into word parts to find meaning. He needs to understand that within syllables are the clues to word meaning. The meanings of over 60 percent of multisyllabic words can be determined by knowing the meaning of word parts. Understanding the meaning of common affixes (prefixes and suffixes) and roots, or base words, can give students an edge in deciphering the meaning of an unfamiliar term.

Using word structure to determine meaning, also called **morphological analysis**, is important because it enables students to see the patterns of words and word families. When students are taught about the generative nature of words, they can unlock the meaning of the words in a strategic way (Padak, Newton, Rasinski, & Newton, 2008). Even by second grade, students can be taught to use word parts as a vocabulary strategy (Biemiller, 2005).

Research suggests that an effective way to teach affixes is through word sorts. While this method has existed for decades, publications by Donald Bear and colleagues have made the phrase "word sort" a familiar one among teachers (Bear, Invernizzi, Templeton, & Johnston, 2000).

In **word sorts**, terms are sorted into categories based upon word structure. With repeated exposure to word parts, students will more readily recognize these affixes when they encounter new words in their text; they will be able to independently use this as a strategy. Figure 2.12 shows a Prefix Word Sort Example used in an eleventh-grade health class. Students completed a word sort with the words. Then, as they engaged in the reading passages for the week, they were able to independently use their knowledge of these prefixes to independently determine meanings of words, and they were more successful at comprehending the content of the health topics.

PROCEDURE

1. Prepare for the sort.
   a. Choose prefixes that students need to learn, and identify several words that contain these affixes. Word lists can be found in *Words Their Way* (Bear, et al., 2000).
   b. Copy student lists, distribute, and have students cut the words apart.

dis-	bio-	anti-
disable	biochemical	antiallergenic
discarnate	biochemist	antibiotic
diseased	biodegradable	antibodies
disembowel	biodiversity	antidepressant
disfigurement	bioengineer	antidote
disinfect	biogas	antifungal
disjoint	biogeochemical	antigen
displace	biophysicist	antiperspirant
disproportionate	biosensors	antiviral

FIGURE 2.12 Prefix Word Sort Example for Health

2. Introduce the sort.
   a. Have students sort the words into groups.
   b. Once words are sorted, focus students on each group of words. Have a discussion about the prefix and the word meanings. What does the prefix do to the word? If there are questions about word meanings, use a dictionary to talk about the words.
3. Repeat the sort. For additional practice, have students shuffle their words and resort into the same categories.
4. Cut-up sort. Have students cut the prefixes off of the words. Ask them to combine prefixes and base words to make new words. Have students write down these words and guess the definitions. (They will ask you whether certain words are "real," so keep dictionaries available). During the process of guessing, point out to students any word parts that they have already studied. They can use these familiar parts to guess the meaning of unfamiliar words.
5. Word Hunt. Have students look for these words in their text and write them down in word study notebooks.

Resource

Wordexplorations.com features lists of word parts and their definition and origin (from Latin and Greek sources).

VARIATIONS   The above example focuses on prefixes, but suffixes and base words can be taught in the same way. Additionally, word sorts can be used to teach spelling patterns, phonics, and word recognition (Joseph & Orlins, 2005). There are various Web sites available that can help teachers prepare lists and define words during these sorts.

Contextual Redefinition

When reading, students will often come upon words they cannot define or sometimes even pronounce. For example, a world history student who was reading about Chinese foot binding came upon this sentence: "If the bindings were too tight, it could cut off *circulation*, which could, in turn, lead to *gangrene* and blood poisoning." The words "circulation" and "gangrene" were difficult for her to say and comprehend. When students struggle with words during direct instruction within the classroom, teachers can encourage them to use **context clues** to make sense of the unfamiliar term. The use of context can be a powerful way to build one's vocabulary; the reader must put together the clues and information from the text to determine the meaning of the unknown word.

Several types of context clues can be used when reading content area text. Four common ones are:

- *Synonym:* Surrounding sentences give similar terms for the target term.
- *Antonym:* Surrounding sentences describe the opposite of the target term.
- *Explanation:* Surrounding sentences give an explanation or definition of the target term.
- *Example:* Surrounding sentences give examples of the target term.

However, context alone might misguide students to word meanings (Blachowicz & Fisher, 2000). Findings suggest that using context clues can be effective when students receive feedback and guidance. Such guidance and feedback are especially important when using context clues with content area text; words may have more than one meaning—but only one of the meanings makes sense. Therefore it is critical that teachers guide students carefully toward independent use of this strategy.

One specific strategy for teaching students to use context clues is Contextual Redefinition (Tierney & Readence, 2000). This strategy combines word level clues (such as using knowledge of word affixes) with context clues in the sentence. Students can record their learning on a Contextual Redefinition Chart, as seen in Figure 2.13. Students can also use this chart to expand their vocabulary during independent reading that they complete outside of school.

Sentence: "The Nuclear Arms Non-Proliferation Treaty was created to limit the spread of nuclear weapons."

Term	Word-level Clues	Context Clues	Predicted Meaning	Actual Meaning
proliferation	Pro = Before or forward	Antonym: Nuclear arms non-proliferation, limits spread of nuclear weapons	Spread	To cause to grow or increase rapidly

FIGURE 2.13   Contextual Redefinition Chart Example for World History

PROCEDURE

1. While reading, teachers guide students to monitor their vocabulary knowledge and comprehension. Students share when they come across words that they do not understand.
2. Students record the term on their Contextual Redefinition Chart under the column marked "Term."
3. The teacher directs students to examine the word for word-level clues. For example, in Figure 2.13, the affix "pro" will let the reader know that the term's meaning includes a notion of "before" or "forward." Students record this word-level clue on the chart under "Word-level Clues."
4. Identify any context clues given. Surrounding text may give synonyms, antonyms, explanations, or examples of the target term. Record the context clue on the chart under "Context Clues."
5. Predict meaning. Based on the word-level and context clues, predict the term's meaning and record it under "Predicted Meaning."
6. Use a dictionary or other authoritative source to verify the word's meaning and record the meaning derived from all sources under "Actual Meaning."

Teacher Tool

A Contextual Redefinition Chart (TT6) can be found in the Teacher Tools Appendix to copy for your students.

VARIATIONS   Some teachers use a modified cloze procedure to provide students with opportunities to practice using context clues. (Chapter 5 explains directions on how to use content area text to create a cloze activity for this purpose.) The teacher removes several words from a paragraph, and students attempt to fill in the blanks. As students choose words, they discuss what factors were considered. What were the context clues? What was the explanation in the surrounding sentence? What was the part of speech of the target term? This variation will help students become more explicitly aware of the context.

Dictionary Use

The age-old adage seems to be "If you don't know what a word means, look it up." However, research suggests that dictionaries, when used alone, might be the least effective way of learning a new word. Choosing to use a dictionary or glossary first requires that the reader is motivated to stop reading and look up the word. Then, to be able to find a word, students must be able to spell it, locate it, and decipher the multiple definitions. Teachers often teach students alphabetization and use of guide words to begin the process of independently using a glossary or dictionary at a young age. This is a critical first step and a basic skill that students should master in their language arts classes.

However, repetitive direct instruction in how to look up words and determine the most appropriate definition is necessary beyond this point. When students find the word, that is when the most challenging part begins—deciphering the definitions. Whether a student uses a paper dictionary or an online dictionary, he or she is bound to encounter multiple meanings.

Resource

The *Collins COBUILD New Student's Dictionary* (Harper-Collins, 2005) and the *Longman Study Dictionary of American English* (2006) provide many excellent examples of student-friendly definitions.

Therefore, dictionaries should be thought of as a powerful tool when used with context and word elaboration activities (Rhoder & Huerster, 2002). Students can be taught to analyze the word's context and then choose the appropriate definition from the dictionary. This strategy should be used in conjunction with the strategies previously mentioned as students refer to dictionary definitions to help them develop full concept knowledge or analyze words in pre-teaching activities. With repeated practice, students will become more proficient at deciphering appropriate definitions when they are working on their own. With this procedure, the teacher initially models effective use of a dictionary, gradually moving students from guided into independent practice.

PROCEDURE

1. Locate the unknown word in a dictionary. (In many cases, students will have to use their knowledge of the root word in order to locate it. For example, "indentation" would be found under "indent.")
2. Read the various definitions, and substitute each definition given for the word in the sentence.
3. Have students ask themselves: "Does it make sense?" for each potential definition.
4. Record the definition that makes the most sense on whatever worksheet the student is using (e.g., Vocabulary Rating Guide, Contextual Redefinition Chart).

Resource

An animated, interactive math dictionary with definitions of over 600 common math terms in simple language can be found at http://www.amathsdictionaryforkids.com/. *The Scholastic Science Dictionary* (2000) is a fantastic reference tool for science- and nature-oriented kids in elementary and middle school featuring more than 2,400 terms.

VARIATIONS   If students have access to an online dictionary, they will find some help in choosing the correct definition. On *Dictionary.com*, each entry includes a feature called "use (target word) in a sentence." A click on that link generates online examples of how the target word is used. In addition, a link will allow students to hear the pronunciation of that word. Students who are conducting word study in a specific content area may wish to refer to a content-specific dictionary as a resource.

Personal Dictionary

A Personal Dictionary is a record of words that an individual doesn't know, but wants to understand. As students read their assignments in class or at home, they record words, their definitions, and the context in which the words were discovered. These Personal Dictionaries can travel from home to school with students and are the focus of word study activities in class. When students are asked to track their word learning, they are thought to be increasing their word consciousness, or their awareness of the features of words and language (Manzo & Manzo, 2008).

PROCEDURE

1. Model for students how to monitor vocabulary understanding while reading.
2. Demonstrate what to do when students come to an unknown word. Stop reading and record the word and the page and paragraph numbers in a Personal Dictionary, as is shown in Figure 2.14.
3. Each day, encourage students to add to their dictionaries.
4. During class, have opportunities for students to build their understanding of these words. This support could include direct instruction, an activity with a partner, or a whole class sharing of the words and their meanings. Regardless of which activity is chosen to complete, it is important that the students have access to the vocabulary word in context as they work to determine its meaning.
5. Encourage students to take their Personal Dictionaries home and add any new terms they come across in their assignments. (Students who are using a Personal Dictionary for literature classes can be recording words from their independent reading.)

Date	Source	Page	Term	Definition
March 5	Life Science Text	234	nephron	A part of the kidney that carries out the kidney's function—to carry waste from the body. It filters the blood to remove waste.
"	"	234	Lipase enzyme	An enzyme that is necessary to absorb and digest nutrients and fats. It is a catalyst in the hydrolysis of fat to glycerol and fatty acids.
"	"	235	glucogenesis	The generation of glucose from carbon substrates that are not carbohydrates
March 6	Mayo Clinic.com		Lupus	A disease that causes inflammation of the kidneys
"	"		Kidney stones	Mineral and acid salt deposits in the kidney

FIGURE 2.14   Personal Dictionary Example for Life Science

In Figure 2.14, groups of students in this Life Science class are becoming experts on one of the body's major organs. As one student learns about kidneys, he records words in his Personal Dictionary. Some words originate in his text; others from research conducted online.

VARIATIONS   One English teacher describes a slightly different approach to the Personal Dictionary (Nelson, 2008). When students identify words worth learning, they record these words on a designated area of the whiteboard. These words then become the focal words of the class. Students begin by uncovering their meaning, specifically as they are used in the course. They then engage in activities with the words, insert these words into their lexicons, and develop quizzes for their peers. These words can also be posted on a Word Wall in the classroom.

Personal Dictionaries can also be used across content areas. If students create a "Personal Dictionary" section in their binders, they can record words in every class. This record of terms can then serve as a reference for test review and future reading, writing, listening, and speaking activities.

Teacher Tool

A Personal Dictionary (TT7) can be found in the Teacher Tools Appendix for your students to use.

Conclusion

In conclusion, independent strategy use will help students develop skills for the classroom and beyond. However, none of these strategies can initially be used independently; students must be given teacher guidance. Students need instruction on how to use the strategy, modeling of the strategy, a gradual release of responsibility, and continual support (Pearson & Gallagher, 1983). With appropriate guidance, students who use these strategies will deepen content knowledge and continue to develop their vocabulary.

Learning Log

Revisit the Vocabulary Rating Guide found in the Learning Log Appendix (LL1) to build a deeper knowledge of the vocabulary concepts presented in this chapter and to practice implementing the last steps of this effective vocabulary strategy.

Chapter Summary

This chapter has highlighted three important goals of vocabulary instruction: build full concept knowledge, teach words in a meaningful context, and encourage independent use of strategies. Teachers embed vocabulary instruction into the content areas so that students build conceptual understanding in their content reading. When students understand vocabulary labels and the complexity of the concept that label represents, their comprehension increases.

With explicit vocabulary instruction in place, students will no longer be skipping words if they don't know how to say them or what they mean. Instructional strategies, such as those described in this chapter, provide the tools for meeting these goals. It is critical that teachers use the process of assessment and reflection to choose which instructional practices would be appropriate to meet the needs of their students.

The beginning of the chapter describes Tanner, a ninth-grade geometry student who skipped a word that was central to conceptual understanding. How can a teacher respond? By integrating knowledge of building vocabulary strategies with an understanding of the learner, teachers can make an informed decision about the type of instruction that would be appropriate and necessary. Thoughtfully applying instructional strategies following the LinC cycle of assessment, reflection, planning, and instruction will help content literacy grow. Tanner will begin to understand more vocabulary along the way, increasing both his fluency and comprehension.

PAUSE and REFLECT 2.5

List the three goals of vocabulary instruction. Can you think of ways that you could improve your content instruction by integrating some of the strategies described in this chapter?

Resources

Bear, D., Invernizzi, M., Templeton, S., & Johnston, F. (2000). *Words Their Way* (2nd ed.). Upper Saddle River, NJ: Pearson/Merrill/Prentice Hall.

Berger, M. & Bonner, H. (2000) *The Scholastic Science Dictionary*. New York, NY: Scholastic.

Cleveland-Marwick, K. , Fox, C., Handorf, S. & Stern, K. (Eds.). (2006). *Longman Study Dictionary of American English*. White Plains, NY: Pearson Longman.

Collins COBUILD New Student's Dictionary (3rd Ed.). (2005). New York, NY: Harper-Collins.

Golding, W. (1973). *Lord of the Flies*. London, UK: Faber and Faber.

Hellweg, P., LeBaron, J. & LeBaron, S. (Eds.). (2003). *The American Heritage® Student Thesaurus* Boston, MA: Houghton Mifflin Harcourt.

References

Allen, J. (1999). *Words, Words, Words: Teaching Vocabulary in Grades 4–12*. New York: Stenhouse.

Amaral, O. M., Garrison, L., & Klentschy, M. (2002). Helping English learners increase achievement through inquiry-based science instruction. *Bilingual Research Journal, 26*(2), 213–239.

Anderson, R. C., & Freebody, P. (1981). Vocabulary knowledge. In J. T. Guthrie (Ed.), *Comprehension and teaching: Research reviews* (pp. 77–117). Newark, DE: International Reading Association.

Baumann, J. F., Edwards, E. C., Font, G., Tereshinski, C. A., Kame'enui, E. J., & Olejnik, S. (2002). Teaching morphemic and contextual analysis to fifth-grade students. *Reading Research Quarterly, 37*, 150–176.

Baumann, J. F., Kame'enui, E. J., & Ash, G. E. (2003). Research on vocabulary instruction: Voltaire redux. In J. Flood, D. Lapp, J. R. Squire, & J. M. Jensen (Eds.), *Handbook of research on teaching the English language arts* (2nd ed., pp. 752–785). Mahwah, NJ: Erlbaum.

Beck, I. L., & McKeon, C. A. (1991). Conditions of vocabulary acquisition. In R. Barr, M. L. Kamil, P. B. Mosenthal, & P. D. Pearson (Eds.), *Handbook of reading research* (Vol. II, pp. 789–814). New York: Longman.

Biemiller, A. (2005). Size and sequence in vocabulary development: Implications for choosing words for primary grade vocabulary. In E. H. Hiebert & M. L. Kamil (Eds.), *Teaching and learning vocabulary: Bridging research to practice* (pp. 223–242). Mahwah, NJ: Erlbaum.

Blachowicz, C. L., & Fisher, P. J. (2000). Vocabulary instruction. In M. L. Kamil, P. B. Mosenthal, P. D. Pearson & R.Barr (Eds.), *Handbook of reading research* (Vol. 3, pp. 503–523). Mahwah, NJ: Erlbaum.

Blachowicz, C. L., & Obrochta, C. (2005). Vocabulary visits: Virtual field trips for content vocabulary development. *The Reading Teacher, 59*(3), 262–268.

Cardinale, L. (1991). Paper presented at the Annual Convention of the Association for Educational Communications and Technology.

Carney, J. J., Anderson, D., Blackburn, C., & Blessing, D. (1984). Preteaching vocabulary and the comprehension of social studies materials by elementary school children. *Special Education, 48*(3), 195–197.

Feldman, K., & Kinsella, K. (2003). Narrowing the language gap: Strategies for vocabulary development. Retrieved from http://www.fcoe.net/ela/pdf/Vocabulary/Narrowing%20Vocab%20Gap%20KK%20KF%201.pdf.

Frayer, D., Frederick, W. C., & Klausmeier, H. J. (1969). *A schema for testing the level of cognitive mastery*. Madison, WI: Wisconsin Center for Education Research.

Graves, M. F. (2008). *Teaching individual words: One size does not fit all*. Paper presented at the International Reading Association.

Harmon, J. M., Wood, K. D., & Hedrick, W. B. (2008). Vocabulary instruction in middle and secondary content classrooms: Understandings and direction from research. In A. E. Farstrup & S. J. Samuels (Eds.). *What research has to say about vocabulary instruction* (pp. 150–181). Newark, DE: International Reading Association.

Joseph, L. M., & Orlins, A. (2005). Multiple uses of a word study technique. *Reading Improvement, 42*(2), 73–79.

Lubliner, S., & Smetana, L. (2005). Effects of comprehensive vocabulary instruction on Title 1 students' metacognitive word-learning skills and reading comprehension. *Journal of Literacy Research, 37*(2), 163–2000.

Manzo, U. C., & Manzo, A. V. (2008). Teaching vocabulary-learning strategies: Word consciousness, word connection and word prediction. In A. E. Farstrup & S. J. Samuels (Eds.), *What research has to say about vocabulary instruction* (pp. 80–105). Newark, DE: International Reading Association.

McKeown, M. G. (1985). The acquisition of word meaning from context by children of high and low ability. *Reading Research Quarterly, 20*,482–496.

Meyerson, M. J., Ford, M. S., Jones, W. P., & Ward, M. A. (1991). Science vocabulary of third and fifth grade students. *Science Education, 75*, 419–428.

Nagy, W. E., Herman, P. A., & Anderson, R. C. (1985). Learning words from context. *Reading Research Quarterly, 20*(1), 233–253.

Nagy, W. E., & Scott, J. A. (2000). Vocabulary processes. In M. Kamil, P. Mosenthal, P. D. Pearson & R. Barr (Eds.). *Handbook of Reading Research* (Vol. 3). Upper Saddle River, New Jersey: Erlbaum.

National Institute of Child Health and Human Development (NICHD). (2000). *Report of the National Reading Panel: Teaching children to read: An evidence-based assessment of the scientific research literature on reading and its implications for reading instruction.*

Nelson, D. L. (2008). A context-based strategy for teaching vocabulary. *English Journal, 97*(4), 33–37.

Padak, N., Newton, E., Rasinski, T., & Newton, R. M. (2008). Getting to the root of word study: Teaching Latin and Greek word roots in elementary and middle grades. In A. E. Farstrup & S. J. Samuels (Eds.), *What research has to say about vocabulary instruction.* Newark, DE: International Reading Association.

Pearson, P. D., & Gallagher, D. R. (1983). Instruction of reading comprehension. *Contemporary Educational Psychology, 8*(3), 317–344.

Pressley, M. (2000). What should comprehension instruction be the instruction of? In M. L. Kamil, P. B. Mosenthal, P. D. Pearson, & R. Barr (Eds.), *Handbook of reading research* (Vol. III, pp. 545–561). New York: Longman.

Rhoder, C., & Huerster, P. (2002). Use dictionaries for word learning with caution. *The Journal of Adolescent and Adult Literacy, 45*(8), 730–735.

Schwartz, R. M., & Rafael, T. E. (1985). Concept of definition: A key to improving students' vocabulary. *The Reading Teacher, 39*, 198–205.

Stanovich, M. E. (1986). Matthew effects in reading: Some consequences of individual differences in the acquisition of reading. *Reading Research Quarterly*,21, 360–406.

Taba, H. (1967). *Teacher's handbook for elementary social studies.*Reading, MA: Addison-Wesley.

Tierney, R. J., & Readence, J. E. (2000). *Reading strategies and practices: A compendium* (5th ed.). Boston, MA: Allyn & Bacon.

Wagstaff, J. (1999). Word walls that work. *Instructor, 110* (5), p. 32–33.

Zwiers, J. (2003). The third language of academic English. *Educational Leadership, 62*(4), 60–63.

CHAPTER 3

Strategies to Foster Fluency

The tenth-grade biology room was alive with discussion. Groups of students were engaged in repeated reading of their text and taking notes about cellular structure.

As the teacher circulated around the room, he stopped to listen to Ariel and Sarah. Ariel, a developing reader, was not stopping at the end of sentences, and it was difficult for Sarah to understand her. Sarah, a fluent student with high comprehension, told Ariel that she needed to slow down and pay attention to periods and commas or they were going to have to read independently. Sarah then modeled aloud one paragraph and encouraged Ariel to echo read the paragraph after her, reminding her to pay attention to periods and commas.

Ariel reread each sentence with appropriate accuracy, rate, and prosody. She told her teacher, "I was reading and not stopping at the end of sentences, and Sarah was getting tired of listening to me read . . . plus I don't think she understood what I was saying, so I am practicing taking breaths. I think it sounds better. Don't you?"

Her teacher agreed she was easier to understand and that she would most likely be able to better comprehend what she had read with improved fluency.

Fluency is something that students begin to actively develop in preschool/kindergarten programs when they first learn their letters and corresponding sounds. It describes one's ability to read accurately, at an appropriate rate, using expression. Recall, as described in Chapter 1, that fluency is an essential component of literacy development because fluent readers have more cognitive space available to focus on building meaning from text (LaBerge & Samuels, 1974). Therefore, if students can read a textbook fluently, they will be more able to focus on the content. Fluency includes three major components: rate, accuracy, and prosody.

RATE   **Rate** is often referred to as automaticity (LaBerge & Samuels, 1974). As a reader's eyes pass across the words, their brain is signaled to decode the words they are reading. Fluency rate, which is recorded in words read per minute, tells whether or not a student can decode words automatically. A student's rate can be impacted by the vocabulary in the text and the complexity of the content.

ACCURACY   **Accuracy** involves reading or decoding the text without making errors. This involves omissions, leaving words out, additions, adding words to the text read, and miscues, reading the word incorrectly. An error in reading can affect the reading and subsequent comprehension of that text.

PROSODY   **Prosody** refers to the intonation and vocal stress in speech. The characteristics of prosody include intonation, expression, and phrasing.

Intonation is the rising or falling of pitch of the voice and has to do with putting stress on certain words in a sentence to give the sentence meaning. Try reading the following five sentences, stressing the boldfaced word:

1. ***The*** blue hat is not yours. (Implying the one and only)
2. The ***blue*** hat is not yours. (Implying the color is significant)
3. The blue ***hat*** is not yours. (Implying it is a hat, as opposed to some other object)
4. The blue hat ***is not*** yours. (Implying that it, under no circumstances, belongs to you)
5. The blue hat is not ***yours***. (Implying it does not belong to you, as opposed to someone else)

These examples show that intonation carries meaning; proper intonation implies that the student comprehends the text as he or she is reading. Monotonous reading or improper stress can signal a lack of understanding by the reader.

Expression involves using a correct tone of voice based upon grammatical symbols within the text. For example, quotation marks, question marks, and exclamation points all signal to the reader that a change in voice should occur when reading. The expression used by the reader will have an effect on the reading of the text and also on the understanding of that text.

The **phrasing** used by the reader will also have an effect upon the reader's fluency and subsequent comprehension of the text. Commas and periods are used throughout the text to denote pauses and breaks in thought. These symbols signal the reader to pause (comma) or take a breath (period).

Using or omitting these marks can lead to misunderstandings. For example, read the differences between these two statements found on caution signs.

Slow, children crossing

Slow children crossing

In the first, drivers are being asked to slow down because children are crossing the street. In the second, the lack of a comma makes it sound as though slow children are crossing the street.

Phrasing can lead to understanding or misunderstanding.

Some educators argue that fluency development is one of the precursors of comprehension. However, research shows that fluency is a component that continually develops as vocabulary and comprehension expand over time. Even the most proficient reader's fluency can vary depending upon the text type and the reader's familiarity with vocabulary (National Institute of Child Health and Human Development [NICHD], 2004). Therefore, all adolescents (from struggling readers to those who are advanced) must be specifically given opportunities to use strategies that help them develop their fluency.

Many struggling adolescent readers are not able to read grade level text fluently because they lack phonetic decoding skills or are unfamiliar with the vocabulary. Educational researchers find that when these readers exert a great deal of effort toward these tasks, they have less attention and energy available for comprehension. Consequently, as students become more fluent, they can focus more effort toward comprehension (LaBerge & Samuels, 1974; NICHD, 2004). Figure 3.1. shows this continuum.

Wyatt is an eighth-grade student who struggles to decode grade level text. He devotes most of his effort to decoding and pronouncing new vocabulary words. Conversely, Savanna, also an eighth-grader, devotes little of her energy toward decoding the eighth-grade level text and is therefore able to spend more of her energy on comprehension. It therefore is extremely important for content area teachers to give struggling adolescent readers ample instruction and time to develop fluency skills so they can direct their attention to the challenges of comprehending content area text.

To develop this type of fluency, students need instruction that is rich with opportunities to move beyond automatic decoding of words. The Deep Processing Fluency Model (Topping, 2006) is a continuum of four levels of fluency development that students progress through

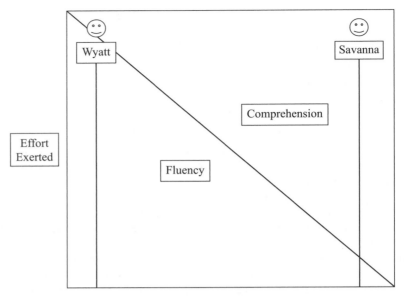

FIGURE 3.1   Fluency/Comprehension Continuum

as they move toward being able to read like Savanna, with absolute fluency (appropriate rate, accuracy, and prosody to achieve optimal comprehension). Level 1 includes factors that predispose fluency. Without these "entry requirements" in place, little can be achieved.

- Level 1: Predisposing factors: the use of appropriately leveled text, time given and used effectively, concurrent vocabulary activities, scaffolded comprehension activities, and strategies to motivate.

Subsequent levels include:

- Level 2: **Surface fluency**: the use of phonological decoding, sight-word recognition, prediction from context, and prediction from grammatical structure with text to produce automaticity (accuracy and rate).
- Level 3: **Strategic fluency**: the balancing between speed control, meaning extraction, and level of confidence with text to comprehend and read with expression (rate control and prosody).
- Level 4: **Deep fluency**: the explicit awareness of one's own text processing, intrinsic motivation to practice, and autonomy (absolute fluency).

As students move along this fluency development continuum, they expand their literacy skills and move toward more comprehensive content competency. This continuum continues to cycle back as students become engaged with more complex text.

Unfortunately, in middle schools and high schools, some common reading practices do not promote deep fluency. For example, research shows that Round Robin reading, in which students read aloud in turn, is ineffective as a method to build fluency (Rasinski & Hoffman, 2003). In fact, it can be detrimental to both reading and motivation. Rather than allowing students to *practice* fluency, this method *tests* their fluency and subjects them to potentially embarrassing mispronunciations.

The focus of this chapter is to explain research-based strategies that teachers can use to help struggling and proficient adolescent learners build their fluency: rate, accuracy, and prosody, in connection with content area learning. Fluency can best be fostered using strategies that combine all three of these sub-skills (rate, accuracy, and prosody) together and move students toward developing "deep fluency."

Literacy Component	Goals of Instruction	Strategies for Instruction
Fluency	Model Fluency	• Teacher Read Aloud • Generated Read Aloud
	Guide Fluency	• Guided Fluency Instruction • Adapted Retrospective Miscue Analysis
	Provide Practice for Fluency	• Repeated Reading • Wide, Independent Reading

FIGURE 3.2   Fluency Strategy Summary Chart

The most effective strategies to use for fluency development can be grouped into three key instructional categories that represent the goals of fluency instruction. They are:

1. Model fluency
2. Guide fluency
3. Provide practice for fluency

These strategies are outlined in Figure 3.2.

These goals parallel the **Gradual Release of Responsibility Model** (Pearson & Gallagher, 1983); teachers model strategies for students and give opportunities for guided practice before students independently apply the strategy. By using the knowledge gained about students through the process of assessment and reflection, described in Chapters 5 and 6, in combination with the strategies that are presented in this chapter, teachers will be better able to meet the needs of their students in content area instruction and to foster their fluency.

MODEL FLUENCY

It shouldn't be a surprise to learn that students must hear fluent reading being modeled if they are to understand how they should sound when they read fluently. Much research has been conducted to determine the effectiveness of reading aloud to students. Findings indicate that students who are read to on a daily basis have larger vocabularies, stronger comprehension, a positive attitude toward reading, and a clearer understanding of what fluent reading sounds like (Rasinski, 2003). Modeling fluency often happens in elementary school, rather than middle and high school classrooms (Jacobs, Morrison, & Swinyard, 2000). However, even after elementary school, students benefit when teachers model fluency. As grade levels and text difficulty rise, fluency continues to develop. Therefore, modeling must become a frequent strategy used in all classrooms serving toddlers to adolescents. No matter what the content area, modeled fluency can be integrated and will help students move closer toward deep fluency.

History

Tenth-grade social science students learning about Dr. Martin Luther King can listen to his eloquent speech downloaded to the teacher's MP3 player via podcast, while students follow along with the text. Students who are nonnative English speakers or who are taking blended English can listen to an audio recording of their geography textbook section prior to completing an activity with the text passage. Students in Advanced Placement (AP) World History, using a college-level textbook, can download and listen to the chapter with the same intention.

Science

As with social science, students can use audio recordings of their various science textbooks to hear fluent reading being modeled. This is critical so they can hear a fluent model and have accessibility to the content text with support.

Mathematics

In mathematics, teachers can pair students together to read word problems. This provides support for students who are proficient with computation, but may struggle solely because they cannot fluently read the word problems. Mathematics teachers may also model reading by sharing about famous mathematicians, like Rene Descartes and his "rule of signs" used with single-variable polynomials in algebra.

Language Arts

Students in AP English Literature benefit from hearing Shakespeare's downloaded sonnets, rich with prosody and rhythm, read to them on the classroom iPod. In addition, teachers can read excerpts of award-winning or new novels to model reading and encourage students to connect with a high-quality book to read.

Electives

Students in a life skills class can use scan/read software systems to help them read the state driver's handbook in preparation for their driver's license test. Home economics students can benefit from the teacher reading reviews aloud about products and restaurants from magazines and newspapers.

PAUSE and REFLECT 3.1

It is beneficial for students to listen to fluent reading in all content areas. Can you describe two examples of how you could model reading aloud in your teaching?

Teacher Read Aloud and Generated Read Aloud are examples of instructional strategies that effectively model fluency.

Teacher Read Aloud

Teacher Read Aloud is a reading done by the teacher; usually the teacher reads to the entire class. Researchers recommend that a Teacher Read Aloud be conducted often, using a wide variety of genres. Cunningham and Allington (2006) suggest that teachers read four types of material aloud every day:

- Informational/Real World Texts, eg., newspapers, magazines, expository text
- Traditional Grade Level Favorites, eg., novels, series books, award winners
- Poetry
- Easy Books, eg., picture books that are old favorites

Resource

A great resource for choosing a read aloud can be found at http://www.trelease-on-reading.com/ or in *The Read-Aloud Handbook* by Jim Trelease (Trelease, 2006). Another read aloud resource is the Read Aloud America Book List found at http://www.readaloudamerica.org/booklist.htm.

This daily reading from four categories may be excessive for middle and high school classrooms, where there is a limited amount of time and important content to cover. However, Teacher Read Aloud can be used as often as seems appropriate.

Teacher Read Aloud can be integrated into any subject area to introduce or support a lesson, chapter, or theme. It can include varying genres (i.e., narrative, expository, newspapers) and high-interest passages (i.e., persuasion speeches about controversial topics, letters to the editor, commentaries). The length of Teacher Read Aloud sessions can also vary. Teachers may choose to read a short passage (150 words) or a novel that they read over the course of several weeks. Teachers can choose to read aloud from a text that is, or is not, visually available for the students to see. Class book sets and the use of the overhead or multimedia projector provide students with a visual copy of what is being read aloud. There is much flexibility with this strategy. The bottom line is, read aloud!

PROCEDURE

1. Choose a text to read aloud that is above the students' independent reading level. Be sure that students can adequately comprehend when they listen to it, even if students cannot read that text independently. The level of text will vary from class to class (i.e., a tenth-grade remedial reading class should be exposed to a different type of read aloud when compared to a twelfth-grade Advanced Placement Government class). There are limited times when a picture book that is written below students' reading level can be used to get a certain point across or to be read just for the fun of enjoying its text. For example, the picture book *We Share Everything* (Munsch & Martchenko, 2000) can be used to spark a discussion with a middle school social science class about how sharing homework answers is not a great idea.

2. Pre-read the text to be read aloud and practice prosody, also considering voice intonation, gesturing, and dialogue. For example, during the read aloud of the sentences, "Why *me*? Why would *I* want to do such a thing," the teacher may wish to gesture bringing his or her hand to the chest when reading the words *me* and *I*. In addition, character voices help students clearly understand who is doing the talking.

3. Activate and build background knowledge about the text topic. (More about this will be discussed in Chapter 4.)

4. Read aloud with accuracy, appropriate rate, and prosody. Pause and model word analysis strategies used when words and names are not easily decoded. (See Guided Fluency Development Instruction still to come in this chapter for more information.)

5. When the reading is complete, ask questions to encourage reflection about fluent reading.
   a. Did you notice anything about my accuracy?
   b. Did you notice anything about my rate?
   c. Did you notice anything about my prosody?

6. Make the text available to students after the read aloud has concluded.

VARIATIONS   One variation on the Teacher Read Aloud is to invite a guest speaker, parent volunteer, school staff member, or fluent student to read aloud. Guests model fluency for the students while they share important information about the content area being studied. For example, a group of eighth-grade students who recently participated in the Mars Student Imaging Project (MSIP) had the opportunity through Skype™ to listen to a scientist from Arizona State University read aloud a section of their exemplary team report about the findings they had made. Another option is to invite parent volunteers and school staff to conduct a visitor's read aloud. A tenth-grade home economics/cooking class invited a cafeteria staff member to read aloud the new nutritional guidelines proposed by the state for the school lunch menu. Finally, a teacher might ask a student to read aloud if that student could effectively model deep fluency for the class. Varying the reader prompts a discussion about how different people show different strengths with their fluency.

Generated Read Aloud

As mentioned above, the goal of conducting a read aloud is to model fluent reading for all adolescent learners, whether struggling or advanced. If a "live" read aloud is not possible, students can listen to a Generated Read Aloud. These include: audio CDs that are part of the content curriculum program, audio recordings of text from a Web site or online store on MP3 players, iPods™, and Kindle™ 2, and scan/read software systems that read text aloud to students.

   Audio CDs.   Many textbooks currently provide Audio CD read alouds to foster fluency and comprehension. For example, in an eighth-grade social science classroom, students who labor to keep up with content area reading take home an audio CD. They listen to the read aloud of the chapter the night before they are required to read it in class. They are then more prepared to reread the text the next day. Then, the evening after in-class reading, they can use the audio CD to complete their notes. As a result of the National Instructional Materials Accessibility Standard (NIMAS), CDs are becoming a standard part of the curriculum package. Under this requirement, publishers must produce digital versions of textbooks that can easily be converted to Braille, audio, e-text, and large print.

Resource

Classic poetry can be heard via podcast at http://classicpoetryaloud.podomatic.com/. Audio narrations of Aesop's Fables can be found at http://www.aesopfables.com/.

Audio Recordings.   Another read aloud option is available via technology. Many Web sites have audio text or podcasts to download to MP3 players and iPods. Preliminary anecdotal evidence analyzing the use of audio recordings suggests that most teenagers prefer to listen to a recording on an iPod, as opposed to a traditional CD or tape player (Dell & Newton, 2008). Amazon has a product, the Kindle 2, that allows users to download a textbook and have that text read to them. There is some concern that the reading may be too computer-generated and may infringe on an author's audio copyright law. Nonetheless, our advanced technology in audio recordings continues to move us into the twenty-first century with read alouds and away from the old days of using books-on-tape. For example, Recording for the Blind and Dyslexic (RFBD) now uses CDs rather than four-track tapes to make materials accessible to individuals with visual and learning disabilities. With continued improved technology in this area, audio recordings will likely become more and more popular for teachers to use as a read aloud and for students to access outside of school.

Scan/Read Software Systems.   Another type of Generated Read Aloud can come from scan/read software systems. There are several that exist on the market, and all combine the use of a computer, scanner, optical character recognition software, and speech output to read aloud printed text. The computer produces a visual display of the text, creating a synchronized auditory and visual presentation of the text (Hecker, et al., 2002). Colored highlighting helps readers keep their eyes on a line of text, while the speech output provides ongoing auditory feedback, modeling "strategic fluency" for students. Research by Hecker, et al.(2002) found that secondary students with attention disorders who used the Kurzweil 3000^{TM} to read assignments and take tests in English were able to attend better to their reading, reduce distractibility, read faster, and complete assignments in less time. A downfall of scan/read software systems is that it can be time consuming to scan pages of text. To make this task less daunting, it is important for teachers to become aware of Internet sites that provide e-texts that already exist in electronic format.

Whether using audio CDs, audio recordings, or scan/read software systems, a Generated Read Aloud should follow the relatively similar procedure as a Teacher Read Aloud.

PROCEDURE

1. Choose the text.
2. Listen to the selection to be sure it models fluency well. (This is different from a Teacher Read Aloud because the teacher should be evaluating the fluency of the text and not needing to pre-read and practice it.)
3. Activate and build background knowledge.
4. Play the read aloud.
5. Ask questions about fluency of the read aloud.
6. Make the read aloud passage accessible to students.

VARIATIONS   Generated Read Alouds can be varied by using them with the whole class, a small group, or an individual student in order to model fluency.

They can also be varied in that the teacher can use two Generated Read Alouds of text to help students draw comparisons and contrasts between the rate, accuracy, and prosody of the readings. This activity encourages readers to develop an auditory meta-cognitive awareness of fluency and promotes dialogue about it.

Conclusion

In conclusion, it is necessary for teachers to model fluency for students of all ages and abilities. Whether using a Teacher Read Aloud or one of the many Generated Read Alouds available, students must hear models of fluent reading.

PAUSE and REFLECT 3.2

Name one piece of text you could use to model fluency and one Generated Read Aloud that would provide your students with an opportunity to hear fluent reading being modeled in your content area.

GUIDE FLUENCY

In addition to modeling fluency, effective teachers of middle and high school students *guide* fluency. Hearing a good example is helpful, but if they are to integrate "deep fluency" into their everyday literacy, students must be given the opportunity to have guided practice in context. Students can engage in literacy activities under the direction of a fluent instructor who gradually releases responsibility to students—hearing fluency modeled, practicing fluency with a fluent reader, and independently practicing reading with fluency.

History

In history, students must read text embedded with many names of people, places, and events that are difficult to pronounce. Students can become more articulate, build their confidence in reading, and engage in conversation about history if they are guided in reading fluently. In addition, teachers who integrate guided fluency into their history lessons ensure that all students will have the content accessible to them. For example, a social science teacher who used guided fluency as the students learned about the geography of Ancient Greece found that students who were not yet fluent were able to comprehend the content with such support.

Science

Scientists are often asked "How does that work?" In order to give an explanation, students need to be fluent with scientific language. Therefore, guided fluency provides support for science students in much the same way it does for social science students.

Mathematics

Understanding the language of math is necessary in dialoguing about the steps involved in reaching a solution. Math students must therefore be provided opportunities to participate in guided fluency lessons, which will help them develop skills to more easily read their textbook directions and problem sets.

Language Arts

Guiding fluency is essential in language arts, especially with students who are not yet proficient in fluency. English language learners need guidance as they develop this skill that lays the groundwork for comprehension. Yet all students will benefit from their teacher using guided fluency with novels, short stories, plays, and poetry.

Electives

Teachers of electives can also use guided fluency in their instruction. In an agricultural mechanics class, a teacher can guide fluency on a daily basis as students read the manual directions for different welds. This will give these students guided opportunities with directional text—a skill many of these students will need later in life when they read manuals at work or assembly instructions for projects at home.

There are two strategies that teachers can use to guide fluency: Guided Fluency Development Instruction and Adapted Retrospective Miscue Analysis.

Guided Fluency Development Instruction (GFDI)

Guided Fluency Development Instruction (GFDI, named by the authors) takes components from successful elementary research-based fluency programs and combines them to meet the demands of older students and content area text. Shared Book Experiences, Oral Recitation Lessons, Fluency Development Lessons, and Fluency-Oriented Reading Instruction are all programs designed to help students bolster their fluency.

Shared Book Experiences (SBE), created by Holdaway (1982), leads to positive results for fluency development (Smith & Elley, 1997). The teacher introduces the book, reads aloud, and discusses concepts with students. After the initial reading, the teacher provides rereading opportunities for students with the teacher, with small groups, with a partner, and on their own.

Another instructional strategy, Oral Recitation Lessons (Hoffman, 1987) has led to positive results on fluency development (Reutzel & Holingsworth, 1993). In these lessons, the teacher uses a basal reading story to read aloud, discuss the story, provide for student reading and rereading, and check for accuracy and fluency during student performance of a text segment.

The Fluency Development Lesson uses a poem and has teachers read aloud, discuss the meaning with students, read chorally, allow for student reading practice, and orchestrate a performance of the poem (Rasinski, Padak, Linek, & Sturtevant, 1994). The Fluency Development Lesson has resulted in fluency gains, specifically with reading rate (Rasinski, et al., 1994).

Fluency Oriented Reading Instruction (Stahl & Heubach, 2005) requires the teacher to work with a basal reading passage to read aloud, develop vocabulary, facilitate comprehension, and provide time for rereading before moving on to another passage. The research on the effectiveness of this instructional strategy proved that there was an average gain of two years of reading growth for these second-grade students (Stahl & Heubach, 2005).

These instructional programs have had a positive effect on fluency for elementary students. Guided Fluency Development uses the combined version of these instructional programs and reports positive results for middle school students. The authors implemented and measured the effects of GFDI with 120 sixth-grade students over the course of a two-year period, and preliminary data analysis shows student gains in both fluency and comprehension. However, further research must be conducted to provide evidence of its success with other middle and high school students.

The goal of Guided Fluency Development Instruction is to guide fluency within the meaningful context of content text reading. With that goal in mind, teachers can integrate GFDI into daily text experiences.

The procedure below describes the steps to guide students' fluency development as it is embedded within a content lesson. It assumes that each student has a copy of the text to follow either in hard copy or on a screen. The description of the procedure focuses on the whole class, but the strategy can be effective for small groups or individuals. The procedure for GFDI addresses the "predisposing factors" for fluency described in the Deep Processing Fluency Model at the beginning of this chapter. It also maintains that students operate at varying levels of fluency development (surface, strategic, and deep). It provides modeled fluency for all students, guided practice for those who are developing strategies to read fluently, and independent practice to help all readers develop their skills.

PROCEDURE

1. Activate and build background knowledge of the text. (More can be learned about this in Chapter 4.)
2. Pre-teach vocabulary, as described in Chapter 2.
3. Fluently read aloud the text passage *to* the students, scaffolding vocabulary instruction.
   a. Model and demonstrate word analysis strategies when there are terms the students will have difficulty with.
      i. Names and places
         1. Read aloud the pronunciations of names and places. Most current textbooks provide a pronunciation in parentheses following the word to aid in decoding.
      ii. Vocabulary words
         1. Read aloud the vocabulary words, using the book pronunciation, if it is given, to help with decoding.
         2. If no pronunciation is given, model how to:
            a. Circle the prefix and/or suffix
            b. Underline the root
            c. Say the word parts independently
            d. Blend to say
   b. Model and demonstrate reflection of the word analysis by asking the following:
      i. Does that make sense?
      ii. Does that sound right?
      iii. Does that look right?
4. Provide time for a discussion to summarize the text's purpose and main ideas.
5. Fluently reread the text *with* the students using varying strategies:
   a. *Choral Reading:* read the text fluently and in unison with the students.
   b. *Echo Reading:* read aloud a small section of the text while students follow along; then have all the students echo the same passage in unison.
   c. *Cloze Reading:* read a section of the text aloud, purposefully omitting words and/or phrases. Students read the omitted parts aloud and in unison as the teacher pauses and waits to move on. Omissions should be significant to the meaning of the passage, which will enable students to practice their fluency (i.e., "The emperor of the Qin _____ (Dynasty), _____ (Shi Huangdi), began construction of _____ (the Great Wall of China) and was instrumental in beginning _____ (a massive road system).
6. If students are unfamiliar with skimming and scanning, model (or review) skim and scan strategies.
   a. Model how to **skim** by reading the first sentence of each paragraph to understand the main idea.
   b. Model how to **scan** your eyes over the text to locate specific information.
7. Have the students reread the text and complete the comprehension activities. (More information about comprehension strategies will be discussed in Chapter 4.) Rereading can occur either:
   a. with a group or partner (using Paired Reading, which will be discussed in Variations), or
   b. with a partner or *independently* (using Partner or Independent Practice, which will be discussed later in this chapter)
8. Monitor the reading and comprehension behaviors while circulating around the room; provide corrective feedback about fluency and the use of skim and scan strategies. Homan, Klesius & Hite (1993) found that teacher-provided corrective feedback has a significant impact on fluency and comprehension, especially in non-repeated reading.
9. Invite students to participate in a **Read Around**; students select their favorite section from the text (a paragraph or group of sentences) and take turns reading aloud to showcase their fluency to the teacher and the class.

VARIATIONS   There are several variations to GFDI. The instructional lesson sequence can vary, occurring over the course of one day or several days. For example, if students read a short text, they could complete all of the steps in one day. However, if the text passage is long, the teacher can use the sequence over several days.

Day 1: activate and build background knowledge, pre-teach vocabulary, read aloud fluently, and discuss the passage.

Day 2: the teacher rereads, models, and demonstrates skim and scan, and then provides time for student rereading (with a group, partner, or individually).

Day 3: students continue and finish with reading and comprehension activities.

Day 4: include time for a Read Around of a section of the text, a writing extension activity about the reading, or a quiz. With any of these methods, teachers can require that all students recite a text segment for the Read Around, as opposed to requesting volunteers. However, teachers need to be sure students can be successful in their attempts so that their confidence will grow.

Another adaptation of GFDI is to use Paired Reading during step 7, when the students are rereading the text and completing comprehension activities. In **Paired Reading**, groups or partners are placed together by the teacher according to literacy skill levels. Proficient readers are paired with developing readers (as in the vignette at the beginning of this chapter). As students reread the text section together, they provide corrective feedback and praise, when appropriate, to each other. The teacher acts as the facilitator and roams the room to monitor the process. Some educators think of Paired Reading as reading practice, but, because its goal is to provide reading with guidance, it best fits under the goal of guided reading. Paired Reading is beneficial to all students, especially English learners (Li & Nes, 2001).

To further adapt GFDI, teachers can use strategy lessons that provide specific opportunities to guide fluency. In **Say It Like the Character**, teachers use a piece of narrative text full of dialogue to teach how reading with different voices enhances meaning. Another alternative is to give students small amounts of text and varied emotion cards (e.g., excitement, sadness, elation) so that students can practice reading with emotion. When students attend to variations in tone, they begin to understand how a reader can orally manipulate the text.

Adapted Retrospective Miscue Analysis (ARMA)

Adapted Retrospective Miscue Analysis is another strategy that teachers can use to guide fluency development. Ken Goodman, the creator of Miscue Analysis, argued that miscues aren't negative; rather they help teachers understand the student's reading process (Goodman, 1969). "Retrospective" was later added by Chris Worsnop, a Canadian secondary school remedial reading teacher (Goodman, 2008). Under this new direction, students could use the analysis as a tool to reflect upon their reading. Retrospective Miscue Analysis (RMA) provides two things:

1. Insight for students into their transaction with text, providing them with opportunities to listen and talk about their miscues.
2. Information to teachers about a student's reading development, including their use of graphophonic, syntactic, semantic, and pragmatic cueing systems.

Research shows that RMA is successful in helping readers talk about their reading process strategies and meta-cognition. It is also helpful in allowing readers to become more fluent and increase their confidence in their abilities to learn about the reading process. With these things in place, reading proficiency is positively influenced (Goodman & Paulson, 2000).

Adapted Retrospective Miscue Analysis (ARMA) is similar to RMA, but it considers the unique contexts of content area classrooms. In its original form, RMA may be too overwhelming a task for content area teachers to effectively have time and resources to integrate into the classroom. But teachers can use Adapted Retrospective Miscue Analysis to analyze student reading at many different points during the content instruction, while the student is reading the text with a group, partner, or individually or when the student performs the reread of the text. Teachers may also select specific students to participate in ARMA that would benefit from such a guided reading opportunity. In some high schools, the English/language arts department can use the ARMA strategy and share results with content area teachers to help them develop an awareness of their students' miscues. Teachers can also use ARMA as a tool to analyze fluency growth. If a teacher uses ARMA twice during a lesson sequence, he or she can examine the results and analyze student growth.

PROCEDURE

1. Select content text that is at the student's instructional level.
2. Have the student read a section of the text aloud.
3. Record student miscues on a copy of the text and how long it took the student to read the passage. (For more information about how to record miscues, see Chapter 6.)
4. Meet with the student, and ask him or her questions about their miscues.
   a. Does what you read look right?
      i. If this is not the case, they are making graphophonic errors and fail to use the sound-symbol correspondences.
   b. Does what you read sound right and make sense?
      i. If this is not the case, students are making syntactic (structure and ordering of words) and semantic (meaning) errors.
   c. Does what you read seem to be used correctly?
      i. If this is not the case, students are making pragmatic (changing language for different purposes) errors.
5. Discuss any patterns found in the miscues. (This will shed light on the student's accuracy.)
6. Help the student determine their rate by counting how many words were accurately read in one minute.
7. Discuss the rate.
8. Discuss the prosody. (For more information about how to assess prosody, see Chapter 6.)
9. Have students record the information about their rate, accuracy, and prosody for the text passage so they can reflect on it during the next ARMA and notice their changes in fluency development.

VARIATIONS   There are several variations to ARMA. Teachers can have students orally record (via tape, CD, or computer) their reading at an independent station for analysis at a later time. Teachers can also request that students provide an oral retelling of the events or main points of the passage at the conclusion of the ARMA to shed light on how rate and accuracy is affecting comprehension.

Content area teachers may also find it helpful to use **Collaborative Retrospective Miscue Analysis** or Whole Class RMA Strategy Lessons (Goodman, 2008). In the collaborative approach, teachers must first model the role of the teacher in the recording and interpreting of the analysis results. In stages, the teacher works with groups of two to four students, transitioning from guided to independent practice. **Whole Class RMA Strategy Lessons** assist students with this process. In these lessons, the teacher uses the overhead or projector to display a copy of a student's miscue analysis and leads a discussion about how to recognize the different types of miscues. Samples from students who are in the class can be used with their permission. Engaging readers in such a discussion about their own reading has positive results.

Conclusion

Content teachers who choose to use Guided Fluency Development Instruction and/or Adapted Retrospective Miscue Analysis can be confident they are helping students become more fluent with content area reading and strengthening their literacy skills. When readers are engaged in guided practice and discussion about their own reading, positive results will ensue.

PAUSE and REFLECT 3.3

Consider your content area and your students. How might you apply Guided Fluency Development Instruction to a passage from your course text? How could you use Adapted Retrospective Miscue Analysis (ARMA) to support fluency development with your struggling readers?

PROVIDE PRACTICE FOR FLUENCY

With fluency, practice makes perfect. Students who practice fluency will become more fluent. Teachers must therefore provide opportunities for practice across all content areas.

History

History lends itself to opportunities for students to practice independent reading. There are a diversity of topics and a plethora of fiction and nonfiction books, passages, and articles available beyond the textbook—in libraries and online. In one tenth-grade World History class, students chose between several reading options about the Irish potato famine (narrative, expository, poems, etc.) to expand their knowledge about a topic beyond their textbook. Then, after they read different texts, they shared what different sources taught them about the topic.

Science

Independent reading can also be easily connected to science content. For example, in a twelfth-grade physics class where students are learning about kinetic energy, the teacher reads aloud the introduction, pre-teaches vocabulary, and then assigns parts of the chapter for students to independently practice reading.

Mathematics

After teaching a new mathematical concept, an algebra teacher assigns homework that includes independent reading of a textbook section. Reading through the sequence of steps of a mathematical computation helps students build upon the knowledge they gained during the math lesson that day in class.

Language Arts

Literature and English classes have historically offered opportunities for students to practice independent reading. From students enrolled in Freshman English to those in AP Literature, independent reading provides them with opportunities to foster their fluency and deepen their content competency.

Electives

Teachers of languages can encourage students to read independently about the culture and customs of the country as they relate to the content being studied. Technology teachers can provide students with opportunities to read about word processing, desktop publishing, and PowerPoint® presentations to build knowledge and fluency.

Providing practice for fluency is a goal that all teachers can easily accomplish. This can be accomplished by Repeated Reading and Wide, Independent Reading.

Repeated Reading

Research continues to document that repeated reading increases oral reading fluency (Vandenberg, Boon, & Fore, 2008). Repeated reading can happen in any content area after any of the strategies described in the previous sections—Teacher Read Aloud, Generated Read Aloud, or Guided Fluency Development Instruction.

With Repeated Reading, students either practice rereading with a partner or independently. **Partner Repeated Reading** is different from Paired Reading in that students are not necessarily giving each other corrective feedback during this activity. Each student practices reading with a student who may or may not match his or her skill level. Independent practice can either be silent or aloud. Both partner and independent reading provide an opportunity for students to reread the text passage either to practice, complete comprehension activities, or prepare for a Read Around.

PROCEDURE

1. Have students reread the text passage modeling word analysis and fluency strategies.
2. Circulate around the room to monitor the rereading.

VARIATIONS   Students are sometimes unmotivated to participate in the rereading of a text. **Reader's Theatre** is one variation that makes Repeated Reading more engaging. In Reader's Theatre, students repeatedly practice reading a passage to later perform it as part of a play or skit. This type of rereading is relevant and purposeful to students. They understand that they must reread in order to sound proficient during the performance. Reader's Theatre is one of the most common ways for teachers to give students rereading practice with text. Research has shown that classes using Reader's Theatre make significant gains in oral reading fluidity, expression, and vocabulary (Keehn, Harmon, & Shoho, 2008).

Another variation is **Revised Radio Reading** (Greene, 1979; Searfoss 1975) in which students are assigned a portion of text the day before it is to be read in class. They practice at home and prepare to read the text orally in the style of a radio announcer. The next day students read their part in the order it appeared in text. The addition of props, like a microphone, and time for audience questions, makes the activity even more engaging.

Resource

Two excellent sources for middle and high school Reader's Theatre scripts are: http://www.teachingheart. net/readerstheater.htm and http://scriptsforschools. com/. The book, *Reader's Theatre for Middle School Boys* (Black, 2008), is also very useful.

Wide, Independent Reading

In order for students to gain proficiency in the varying sets of content area standards, students must read material that exposes them to a wide variety of content. Since it has been shown that reading independently gives students an opportunity to develop their fluency skills (Archer, Gleason, & Vachon, 2003 Torgeson & Hudson, 2006), it is no surprise that Wide, Independent Reading is an essential practice that all teachers should use in conjunction with their content area instruction to build fluency and content knowledge.

Many school districts have adopted reading software programs to monitor this independent reading. Students are required to read for 20 to 30 minutes per night from books at their reading level available in the school or classroom library. When a student completes reading this book, he or she goes to the computer lab and takes a book quiz; the length of which depends upon the book's length and difficulty. The computer scores the quiz, and students earn points for reading the book. In theory, this sounds like a perfect way for teachers to get students to read independently, providing them fluency practice and monitoring their comprehension along the way. However, many current studies and responses by teachers reveal that these programs may indeed be effective for students when they are in the primary years, simply because it provides students with opportunities to practice reading. On the other hand, studies show that they are less effective, or not effective at all, for older readers (Thompson, Madhuri, & Taylor, 2008).

There are several possible reasons for this discouraging effect. First, in its bank of book quizzes, content area and nonfiction books make up only a small portion. Second, comprehension questions typically request recall of facts and information. Rarely do questions delve into the important, deeper levels of comprehension. In addition, there are limited numbers of books at each level. So, if a reader stays at the same level, she will often need to reread the same books until she scores enough on the quizzes to move to a higher level. And, third, increasing numbers of students are turned off to reading because they cannot read books they are interested in, and they feel forced to read books from the program just to get enough points (Prince & Barron, 1998). Their "love of reading" has been robbed.

Are there other alternatives to encourage Wide, Independent Reading of nonfiction, content area materials? One way is to create a classroom library that is filled with content area books. For example, in a social science classroom where the students are learning about ancient Egypt, it would be advisable to have the white board rail loaded with all types of narrative and expository books about the mummification process, pyramids, the afterlife, and Egyptian art. When resources are minimal and an extensive classroom library is unavailable, have students access the school or public library. Appropriate texts for Wide, Independent Reading include those that the student:

1. is motivated to read,
2. can connect to the content area they are studying,
3. has the ability to decode and read the vocabulary words independently,
4. can make use of the text structures, and
5. will be given an opportunity to practice their prosody while reading.

The Independent Reading Chart in Figure 3.3 can help students and teachers determine if a book or article is appropriate for a student to read independently. Training students to follow the procedure below will forever allow them to select books that are appropriate and continue to foster their reading development.

PROCEDURE

1. Students choose a book or article that aligns with the content and their interests—a book they are motivated to read.

Text Difficulty	Content	Word Difficulty	Prosody	Text Features	Support Available	Should I read this book?
Too Difficult	Unfamiliar with concepts and/or not connected to content	There are 4 to 5 or more words on the page I don't know.	I do not use expression, proper phrasing, or intonation.	I do not use the features of the text to help me understand.	There is no support for me when I attempt to read and comprehend this text.	NO
A Good Match	Familiar with some new concepts and connected to content	There are 2 to 3 words on the page I don't know.	I use fair expression, phrasing, and intonation.	I can use the features of the text to help me understand.	I can get help from my peers, teachers, or parents to read and comprehend.	YES
Too Simple	Very familiar with all concepts and connected to content	There is 0 or only 1 word on the whole page I don't know.	I have lots of expression, proper phrasing, and intonation.	I use all of the features of the text to aid in my understanding.	I can get help from others when reading this text, but won't need it.	NO

FIGURE 3.3 Independent Reading Chart

1. Randomly choose a page of text to read aloud that is filled with mostly text and limited amounts of pictures, graphs, and captions.
2. Begin reading the page, and put one finger up every time you come to a word that you don't know or struggle to read. Pay attention to your prosody—expression, phrasing, and intonation—when reading.
3. If you end up with all five fingers up before you get to the end of the page, this book is probably too difficult for you to read alone. You should consult the Independent Reading Chart to decide what to do.
4. If you get to the end of the page and you have one or two fingers up, this book's difficulty level is probably perfect for you. You should still consult the Independent Reading Chart to determine whether or not it would be a good choice for you to read.
5. If you get to the end of the page and you don't have any fingers up, this book is probably too easy for you to read. You should consult the Independent Reading Chart to decide what to do.
6. Use the Independent Reading Chart to note your prosody ranking for reading expression, phrasing, and intonation.

FIGURE 3.4   The Five Finger Test for Determining Word Difficulty and Prosody

2. Ask students to briefly read the back for a summary, or skim and scan the pictures and captions, to judge if they are familiar with the content and features of the text. Rank the level for the content and text features on the Independent Reading Chart.
3. Show students how to conduct the Five Finger Test (J. Veatch, 1979) to determine if the word difficulty and prosody will hinder their independent reading of this text. See Figure 3.4.
4. Ask students to rank the level for word difficulty and prosody on the Independent Reading Chart.
5. Finally, have them rank the level for support available on the chart.
6. If there are three or more rankings in the same category "Too Difficult," "A Good Match," or "Too Simple," that particular piece of text is just that—either too difficult, a good match, or too simple.
7. If it is a good match, the student can read the text for Wide, Independent Reading.

VARIATIONS   The **Newspapers in Education** (NIE) program is one variation of Wide, Independent Reading that gives students the opportunity to practice reading and learn more about the world around them. With this program, companies donate funds to newspapers, which in turn are able to provide classroom sets of newspapers for student lessons and independent reading. Studies show that using newspapers in the classrooms leads to increases in reading proficiency among students, particularly those who are at-risk for school failure (Palmer, 1989).

Conclusion

Both Repeated Reading and Wide, Independent Reading can and should happen across all content areas. Using Reader's Theatre and Radio Reading helps maintain students' interest in rereading; Wide, Independent Reading fosters students' reading rate, accuracy, and prosody. Exposure to many different text types, readability levels, and topics helps students connect with the content area to be studied and provides them with fluency practice.

PAUSE and REFLECT 3.4

How can you integrate opportunities for your students to practice fluency in your content area?

Chapter Summary

This chapter has explained how teachers foster fluency in their content area by modeling, guiding, and providing practice with it. Research shows that fluent readers have more free cognitive space to focus on building meaning from the text. Therefore, it is important that students continue to build skills to read increasingly complex text accurately, at an appropriate rate, and with appropriate expression. By embedding fluency into content area teaching, students will focus on their prosody so that they can be more intelligible when reading aloud or silently. To support fluency development, teachers use their knowledge of these strategies, plus their expert knowledge of students, gained through the process of assessment and reflection to plan accordingly.

Recall from the vignette at the beginning of this chapter that Ariel's teacher was using Paired Reading to foster her fluency. Ariel's teacher combined her understanding of fluency strategies and knowledge of her students' needs to decide the most appropriate instruction for Ariel and her classmates. Now Ariel and her peers are becoming more literate as they develop a deep understanding of biology.

PAUSE and REFLECT 3.5

List the three goals of fluency instruction. Can you think of ways that you can improve your content instruction by integrating some of the strategies described in this chapter?

Resources

Black, A. (2008). *Reader's Theatre for Middle School Boys*. Aurora, CO: Libraries Unlimited.

Munsch, R. N., & Martchenko, M. (2000). *We share everything*. New York, NY: Scholastic.

Trelease, J. (2006). The Read-Aloud Handbook (6th Ed.). New York, NY: Penguin.

References

Archer, A. M.,, Gleason, M. M., & Vachon, V. L. (2003). Decoding and fluency: Foundation skills for struggling older readers. *Learning Disability Quarterly, 26*(2), 89–101.

Black, A. (2008). *Reader's Theatre for Middle School Boys*. Santa Barbara, CA; Greenwood Publishing.

Coleman, P. (2000). *Girls: A History of Growing Up Female in America*. New York: Scholastic, Inc.

Cunningham, P. M., & Allington, R. L. (2006). *Classrooms that work: They can all read and write*. Boston: Allyn & Bacon.

Dell, A. G., & Newton, D. (2008). Assistive technology helps students compensate for reading difficulties. *Technology in Action, 3*(5), 1–8.

Goodman, K. (1969). Analysis of oral reading miscues: Applied psycholinguistics. In F. Gollasch (Ed.), *Language and literacy: The selected writings of Kenneth Goodman* (Vol. I, pp. 123–134). Boston: Routledge & Kegan Paul.

Goodman, Y. (2008). Retrospective Miscue Analysis. Retrieved June 26, 2009, from http://www.rcowen.com/WordDocs/RMA-OverviewChapter.doc.

Goodman, Y., & Paulson, E. J. (2000). *Teachers and students developing language about reading through retrospective miscue analysis*. Urbana, IL: National Council of Teachers of English.

Greene, F. (1979). Radio Reading. In C. Pennock (Ed.), *Reading Comprehension at Four Linguistic Levels*. Newark, DE: International Reading Association.

Hecker, L., Burns, L., Katz, L., Elkind, J., & Elkind, K. (2002). Benefits of assistive reading software for students with attention disorders. *Annals of Dyslexia, 52*(2), 243–273.

Hoffman, J. R. (1987). Rethinking the use of oral reading in basal instruction. *The Elementary School Journal, 87*, 367–373.

Holdaway, D. (1982). Shared book experience: Teaching reading using favorite books. *Theory into Practice, 21*(4), 293–300.

Homan, S.P., Klesius, J.P. and Hite, C. (1993). Effects of repeated readings and nonrepetitive strategies on students' fluency and comprehension. The Journal of Educational Research, *87*(2), 94–99.

Jacobs, J. S., Morrison, T. G., & Swinyard, W. R. (2000). Reading aloud to students: A national probability study of classroom reading practices of elementary school teachers. *Reading Psychology, 21*, 171–193.

Keehn, S., Harmon, J. M., & Shoho, A. (2008). A study of Readers Theater in eighth grade: Issues of fluency, comprehension and vocabulary. *Reading and Writing Quarterly, 24*(4), 335–362.

LaBerge, D., & Samuels, S. J. (1974). Toward a theory of automatic information processing in reading. *Cognitive Psychology, 6*, 293–323.

Li, D., & Nes, S. (2001). Using paired reading to help ESL students become fluent and accurate readers. *Reading Improvement, 38*(2), 50–61.

National Institute of Child Health and Human Development (NICHD). (2004). *Teaching children to read: An evidence-based assessment of the scientific research literature on reading and its implications for reading instruction.*

Palmer, B. C. (1989). *An investigation of the effects of newspaper-based instruction on reading vocabulary, reading comprehension and writing performance of at-risk middle and secondary school students.* The Knight Foundation.

Pearson, P. D., & Gallagher, D. R. (1983). Instruction of reading comprehension. *Contemporary Educational Psychology, 8*(3), 317–344.

Prince, R., & Barron, D. (1998). Technology and reading (Part II) computer-based reading programs and rewards: Some misleading intentions and possible side affects. *School Library Media Activities Monthly, 14*(8), 48–50.

Rasinski, T. (2003). *The fluent reader: Oral reading strategies for building word recognition, fluency and comprehension.* New York: Scholastic.

Rasinski, T., & Hoffman, J. R. (2003). Oral reading in the school literacy curriculum. *Reading Research Quarterly, 38*(4), 510–522.

Rasinski, T. V., Padak, N. D., Linek, W. L., & Sturtevant, E. (1994). Effects of fluency development on urban second-grade readers. *Journal of Educational Research, 87*, 158–165.

Reutzel, D. R., & Holingsworth, P. M. (1993). The effects of fluency training on second graders' reading comprehension. *Journal of Educational Research, 86*, 325–331.

Scieszka, J. (2005). *Guys Write for Guys Read.* New York: Scholastic, Inc.

Searfoss, L. (1975). Radio Reading. *The Reading Teacher, 29*, 295–296.

Smith, J., & Elley, W. (1997). *How children learn to read.* Katonah, NY: Richard C. Owen.

Stahl, S. A., & Heubach, K. M. (2005). Fluency-oriented reading instruction. *Journal of Literacy Research, 37*(1), 25–60.

Thompson, G., Madhuri, M., & Taylor, D. (2008). How the accelerated reader program can become counterproductive for high school students. *Journal of Adolescent & Adult Literacy, 51*(7), 550–560.

Topping, K. J. (2006). Building reading fluency: Cognitive, behavioral, and socioemotional factors and the role of peer-mediated learning. In S. J. Samuels & A. E. Farstrup (Eds.), *What research has to say about fluency instruction* (3rd ed.).

Torgeson, J. K., & Hudson, R. (2006). Reading fluency critical issues for struggling readers. In S. J. Samuels & A. E. Farstrup (Eds.), *Reading fluency: The forgotten dimension of reading success.* Newark, DE: International Reading Association.

Vandenberg, A. C., Boon, R. T., & Fore, C. (2008). The effects of repeated readings on the reading fluency and comprehension for high school students with specific learning disabilities. *Learning Disabilities: A Multidisciplinary Journal, 15*(1), 11–20.

Veatch, Jeannette. (1979). *Key words to reading: The language experience approach begins* (2nd ed.). Columbus, OH: Merrill. (Original work published 1973).

CHAPTER 4

Strategies to Increase Comprehension

The sixth-grade students were silently reading a short section of their literature textbook about the disappearance of Amelia Earhart. When they finished their reading, the teacher asked them to work with their table partners to discuss the reading and complete a Main Idea/Detail Graphic Organizer.

Austin and his partner, Kelsie, began right away to look in the text to record information about her disappearance, but within minutes they had to request the help of the teacher to delineate important from irrelevant details to record on the graphic organizer.

Anyone listening to Austin read would think that he is a strong reader. He is proficient with grade level vocabulary, and he is able to pronounce many complex words with ease. He is also relatively fluent; he meets the sixth-grade goal of 145 words per minute. When he reads grade level text aloud, his prosody is fair. However, Austin struggles with reading, not because he can't read, literally, but rather, because he cannot fully comprehend—construct meaning—from what he has read.

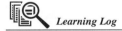
Learning Log

As you read Chapter 4, use the K-W-L in the Learning Log Appendix (LL2) to support your learning of the chapter's content and to experience an effective strategy to use with your students.

The two previous chapters have explained how to help build vocabulary and foster fluency of adolescent readers. But, what do teachers do when these elements are in place and students continue to struggle with comprehension?

As defined in Chapter 1, reading comprehension is the process of using one's own prior knowledge and the writer's cues from the text to infer the author's intended meaning. According to this definition, there are three sets of factors that influence comprehension: the reader, the text, and the context of reading (California Department of Education, 2000). Decades of research have shown how each of these sets of factors influences reading comprehension. For example, the reader brings prior knowledge to the text, which in turn helps her/him construct meaning. The text, such as the difficulty of vocabulary or the inclusion of visual aids, also can impact comprehension. And third, the context—the environment and motivation for reading—can impact this process. All three of these components work together for text comprehension.

There are hundreds of books and online sites that list instructional practices and strategies for helping students comprehend content area text. To help navigate that overwhelming body of work, researchers and educators have worked to synthesize some of the practices that have been proven, again and again, to lead to gains in reading comprehension. In 2000, a group of researchers and educators on the National Reading Panel synthesized the results of over 200 studies of reading comprehension (National Institute of Child Health and Human Development [NICHD], 2000). They identified goals of best practice for comprehension instruction, each of which is supported by research, and summarized them in a report by the Center of Instruction (Boardman, et al., 2008). They are:

1. Activate and build background knowledge,
2. Use graphic organizers,

Literacy Component	Goals of Instruction	Strategies for Instruction
Comprehension	Activate and Build Background Knowledge	• K-W-L Strategy Chart • Text Box/Bag Activity • Survey Strategy and Guide
	Use Graphic Organizers	• Main Idea/Detail Graphic Organizer • Outcome Graphic Organizer • Evidence Guide Graphic Organizer • Compare/Contrast Matrix • Inference Graphic Organizer
	Summarize	• Written Summaries • Oral Summaries • Visual Summaries • Cornell Notes
	Ask & Answer Questions	• SQ3R (Survey, Question, Read, Recite, Review) • QAR (Question-Answer Relationship)
	Monitor Comprehension	• Interactive Think Aloud • Comprehension Monitoring Strategy Guide
	Use Multiple Reading Strategies	• Reciprocal Teaching • PLAN (Predict, Locate, Add, Note)

FIGURE 4.1   Comprehension Strategy Summary Chart

3. Summarize,
4. Ask and answer questions,
5. Monitor comprehension, and
6. Use multiple reading strategies

Each of these goals represents a body of numerous instructional strategies designed to aid students in comprehending content area text. This chapter describes representative strategies from each as shown in Figure 4.1. The intent is for content area teachers to thoughtfully use these strategies, combined with what they glean from the processes of assessment and reflection, to meet the needs of their students.

ACTIVATE AND BUILD BACKGROUND KNOWLEDGE

Research suggests that students' prior knowledge about the content is one of the strongest predictors of their success with learning new content (Marzano, 2004). There are several theories used to explain this strong effect. **Schema theory** (Anderson & Pearson, 1984) is one that is commonly used in reading research to describe how readers use prior knowledge in reading. A schema can be described as an organized network of interrelated concepts. Learners possess schemata about the world, everyday events, areas of expertise, and even different types of text. They build upon this knowledge base when they are exposed to new concepts. For example, in a chemistry course, possession of a strong schema for the Periodic Table of Elements would allow a learner to understand where a newly named element would fit. That task would be nearly impossible for someone who was not knowledgeable about the periodic table.

For each reading task, a student's prior knowledge may vary in accuracy and amount, and this can affect comprehension. Students may often discount new information in the text because it does not match something they already know. In a two-year study of a struggling student, a teacher reported that prior knowledge sometimes hindered learning (Massey, 2007). The student believed he knew something about a topic that he learned on *The Discovery Channel*. Since this knowledge was inaccurate, it led him to discount new, more accurate knowledge from the text. If the student's prior knowledge is imprecise, it is important that new instruction help students to identify and disassemble misconceptions.

Students may also differ in the amount of knowledge they possess about the content at hand. It is often difficult to activate background knowledge in the content areas. Students may be quite knowledgeable about one topic and much less knowledgeable about another. In that case, knowledge needs to be built rather than activated.

Before reading, background knowledge can be built with two types of experiences, direct and indirect (Marzano, 2004). **Direct experiences** involve enriching experiences, such as visiting a natural history museum or handling historical artifacts. Ideally, with unlimited resources, direct experiences would be preferable. However, even in the classroom, with limited resources, teachers can create **indirect experiences**, such as the instructional approaches discussed in this chapter, to help students build background knowledge.

The strategies described in this section work both to *activate* and to *build* knowledge, so that a diversely experienced class of students can approach the new content on relatively equal footing. These instructional practices must be integrated in all content areas to promote comprehension.

History

Middle and high school history students need to *activate* their background knowledge in order to comprehend new concepts. History curricula frequently cycle repeatedly throughout a student's school career. For example, students may learn about United States history in Grades 5, 8, and again in Grade 11. Therefore, they have most likely studied about the Revolutionary War in previous years, but they may have minimal or inaccurate understanding of the specific details. Prior to study, students should have an opportunity to reflect upon what they already know. While several concepts may only require history teachers to *activate* background knowledge, most concepts presented are unfamiliar to students and therefore *building* knowledge is essential. For example, few students in world history classes have much background knowledge about the ancient Mayan civilization. Moreover, students in geography classes may not be familiar with information about European countries.

Science

Teachers of health can find much success with *activating* background knowledge about diet and substance abuse, since many students have personal experience with these topics. Students who enroll in Agricultural Science II classes will need to *activate* the background knowledge they have from the lessons learned during Agricultural Science I.

However, Agricultural Science I students, especially those who have not been engaged in 4-H programs as middle school students, should engage in strategies that help them *build* background knowledge of the concepts being presented. Building background knowledge may also be important for students who have had little previous exposure to chemistry or physics.

Mathematics

Instructors at all levels will find that background knowledge is critical to the development of their students' math skills along the continuum of growth; these strategies help to connect the new with the known, linking new concepts into students' schema. For example, prior to engaging in a lesson segment about word problems involving the multiplying and dividing of fractions, pre-algebra teachers can *activate* students' prior knowledge about the computational processes involved. These teachers *build* background knowledge by having students survey the chapter section to review the examples. In these examples, teachers show students how to determine the variables that constitute the product or quotient.

Language Arts

Language arts lessons provide many opportunities for teachers to *activate* students' background knowledge. For example, before assigning *Fahrenheit 451* (Bradbury, 1953) for an English class, a teacher can explore their students' understanding of the book's main idea—that television destroys one's interest in reading literature. In addition, these students would benefit from participating in activities that allow them to *build* background knowledge about Bradbury's intentions for writing the book.

Electives

For world language teachers, background strategies are a must, since many students find this area foreign to their lives in America. Experiences with artifacts, classroom guests, or videos can help *build* the background necessary to begin a unit of study. In visual and performing arts, a shared read aloud about a famous artist would *build* background knowledge prior to the lesson or unit. For example, the book *Linnea in Monet's Garden* (Bjork, 1987) takes readers into the settings of some of his famous paintings.

The following section describes the use of the K-W-L Strategy Chart as an example of how to *activate* background knowledge. The Text Box/Bag Activity and the Survey Strategy and Guide provide examples of how to indirectly *build* background knowledge.

K-W-L Strategy Chart

The K-W-L Strategy Chart (Ogle, 1986) is one of the most widely used instructional practices with expository text. The purpose of using the K-W-L is to help readers *activate* their prior knowledge about a topic. It also has the benefit of giving them a purpose for reading a particular piece of text, and it helps them monitor their comprehension along the way. The focal point of the strategy is a three-columned chart, labeled with the headings: *K-What We Know*, *W-What We Want to Learn*, and *L-What We Learned*. Students must have some understanding of the topic at hand in order to complete the chart; so, the K-W-L strategy is most effectively used to help *activate* and not build background knowledge.

In general, teachers using the K-W-L Chart ask students to first record what they already know about a topic. Next, the class generates questions they have about this topic. Finally, after instruction, the class lists what they have learned about the subject. The K-W-L Chart in Figure 4.2 shows information a student recorded about their agricultural science chapter entitled "Domestication, Biotechnology, and Genetics." He first recorded what he knew and wanted to learn. When he had finished reading the subsection entitled "Domestication," he recorded his notes in the *L* column.

When teachers repeatedly and explicitly teach this strategy to students through modeling, guiding, and independent practice, it can later become a strategy that readers may choose to use in order to better comprehend. As noted by Afflerback, Pearson, & Paris (2008), practicing strategies can lead students to later accomplish the same actions with less effort and awareness.

PROCEDURE

1. Choose appropriately leveled text that covers the concept needing to be taught.
2. Make a K-W-L Chart on a white board, chart paper, overhead, or Interwrite board that can be seen by all students.
3. Distribute paper and have students fold it into three columns, with appropriate headings. Students should each have her or his own K-W-L Chart on prepared paper or paper that has been folded burrito style (trifolded) with the appropriate headings. (If students do not have individual charts, they will be less likely to use the strategy independently and will be less engaged with the text.)

K-W-L STRATEGY CHART

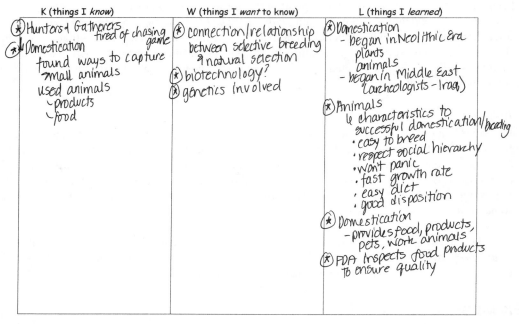

| K (things I *know*) | W (things I *want* to know) | L (things I *learned*) |

(*) Hunters & Gatherers — tired of chasing game
(*) Domestication
    found ways to capture
     small animals
    used animals
     ⌐ products
     ⌐ food

(*) connection/relationship between selective breeding & natural selection
(*) biotechnology?
(*) genetics involved

(*) Domestication
    - began in Neolithic Era
      plants
      animals
    - began in Middle East
      (archeologists - Iraq)
(*) Animals
    ⌐ characteristics to successful domestication/breeding
    • easy to breed
    • respect social hierarchy
    • won't panic
    • fast growth rate
    • easy diet
    • good disposition
(*) Domestication
    - provides food, products, pets, work animals
(*) FDA inspects food products to ensure quality

FIGURE 4.2   K-W-L Strategy Chart Example for Agricultural Science

4. Introduce the topic to the class and ask students to review the text. Model how to read captions under pictures and maps, boldfaced vocabulary terms, and headings and subheadings.

5. Ask students to record words, phrases, and terms they are familiar with about the area of study under the *K* column on their own individual K-W-L Chart. Students should record items on their charts; usually three to five is a reasonable goal.

6. After most students have recorded as many items as they can think of, encourage students to share their ideas with the class. Record their shared ideas under *K* on the classroom K-W-L Chart.

7. Next, have students record questions they have about the area of study on the *W* column of the chart. Again, encourage students to record at least three to five questions they have. Teachers may allow students to record short statements instead of questions.

8. After most students have written several questions or statements on their own K-W-L Chart, have individuals share their ideas with the class. Write them under the *W* on the classroom K-W-L Chart. There often are very similar questions or statements noted within this section. (The "W" activity can guide future instruction and increase motivation by giving students a purpose for reading.)

9. With the chart hanging on the wall, have students read the selection.

10. After the text has been read, students use the *L* column on their individual charts to record five to seven concepts that they learned while reading. (Teachers can have the students record concepts after reading the entire section or each subsection as was shown in Figure 4.2.)

11. Have the class share ideas from individual charts to complete the K-W-L Chart posted in the classroom.

12. Conduct a **Think Aloud**. The teacher shares orally what had been known prior to the reading (*K*), and then compares the questions or statements (*W*) with the concepts learned (*L*). It is important for the teacher to highlight or circle questions or statements (*W*) that were not answered in the reading of the text. This teaches students to monitor their own comprehension, identify knowledge that has been acquired, and plan for future inquiries.

13. Students who have an interest in pursuing an unanswered question can conduct research. This extension activity creates an opportunity for self-directed learning and further reading practice around the focal topic.

14. As appropriate, move from modeling the K-W-L Strategy Chart, to guiding student practice, to allowing students to complete it independently.

VARIATIONS   There are several variations of the K-W-L Chart.

The K-W-H-L Chart is one that can be used when students are reading from two or more pieces of text to learn new information. With the K-W-H-L Chart, another column (*H=How We Will Find Out*) is added in between the *W* and the *L*. This space is for recording sources used to find the answers to questions.

Another variation of the K-W-L Chart is the K-W-L-S Chart. Students record the previously described *Know, Want to Know, Learned* information, and then they finish the last column with S, listing what they *Still Want to Learn*.

The last variation commonly used is the B-K-W-L-S Chart. This uses the traditional K-W-L Chart at the core, but adds the *B* column before and the *S* column at the end. The *B* column is where students can record what they have learned from an activity that has been presented by the teacher in order to *build* background knowledge. In this chart, the *S* is used after reading the text for the student to record what they *Still Want to Learn*.

Text Box/Bag Activity

The purpose of the Text Box/Bag Activity is to help readers *build* background knowledge about a topic. According to Cambourne (2002), learners construct meaning by participating in authentic interactions that enable them to transform the knowledge they acquire. Fuhler, Farris, and Nelson (2006) expanded upon this idea acknowledging that the use of artifacts to build background knowledge allows students to bridge the gap between the words in the text and the objects or concepts they represent. With the Text Box/Bag Activity, students see and hold realia—real objects that are going to be featured in the text. These items can be stored in a central place in the room so that students have access to them.

The Text Box/Bag Activity is similar to Pre-Teaching Vocabulary described in Chapter 2. However, with this strategy, the teacher chooses realia based on the concept's importance in understanding the text. For example, an English teacher prepares to read Rappuccini's Daughter, by Nathaniel Hawthorne. In this short story, Rappuccini, an Italian scientist, grows plants that are poisonous to everyone but his daughter, Beatrice. Giovanni, a young visitor at the house, falls in love with her, but learns that she, too, is poisonous. To fill the text box, the teacher chooses items important to the theme—a purple flower, rubber gloves, a bottle labeled "antidote." By thinking about these items before they begin reading, students are poised to engage with the theme of the relationship between scientific inquiry and natural beauty.

PROCEDURE

1. Identify an appropriately leveled piece of text that covers the concept needing to be taught.

2. In preparation, identify 5 to 7 concepts within the text that are both important to the meaning of the text and can be represented by an object.

3. Gather objects representing these words or concepts, and place them into a box or bag.

4. When the lesson begins, give a brief introduction about the topic to the class—but don't give too much away. Pull an object out of the box, and with students, think aloud about the object and its possible connection to the text.

5. Continue to pull objects, thinking aloud about them. An example dialogue from a Text Box/Bag Activity can be found in Figure 4.3.

Teacher Tool

For your use, a blank K-W-L Strategy Chart (TT8) can be found in the Teacher Tools Appendix.

Teacher: Today we are going to read an article entitled "Modern India." I have several items in my bag that may help give you clues about our reading.

Look at the first item. What is it?

Student: A bag of rice.

Teacher: Yes, how do you think this may relate to the text?

Student: Maybe they like to eat rice, or maybe they grow it.

Teacher: Okay, how about the next item?

Student: It is pepper, and maybe they grow pepper in India. Actually, does pepper grow?

Teacher: Yes, pepper comes from a plant.

Look at this next item, and think about how it relates to the text.

Student: It is a bunch of cotton balls. Do they make cotton there?

Teacher: Cotton is also a plant, and so it grows. We will have to read about whether they grow it in modern India or not.

Can anyone identify this next item?

Student: I know what it is. It is a piece from a chess game. Maybe they like to play chess in modern India.

Teacher: How about this item?

Watch while I put it on.

Student: It's a really, really, really long piece of fabric.

Student: Oh...oh... I know... I have seen women at the store wearing one. What is it?

Teacher: This is called a sari and is the popular style of dress for women in modern India. It is made from a piece of 6- to 9-foot-long cloth that is draped around one's body.

The items that I have just shown you (rice, pepper, cotton, a chess piece, and a sari) are all featured in the text we will read today. As we read, I would like you to locate and highlight them in your text selection. We will discuss them again when we are done.

FIGURE 4.3 Text Box/Bag Activity Example Dialogue for World History

6. As students read the text, ask them to locate each of these concepts and/or words within the text and highlight or underline them.

7. At the conclusion of the reading, show each of the items, and review how they connected to the text.

VARIATIONS One variation of the Text Box/Bag Activity is to present a PowerPoint® slide show of 5 to 7 of the most unique concepts to be presented in the text. The purpose of using slides is to help all students, as a community, build a shared understanding of new and interesting concepts unique to the text.

Another variation is to have a bag or box that is unique for that particular piece of text. For example, when building background knowledge about a section of text on cellular structure, a biology teacher uses a spherical globe as the container, also representing the cell wall.

Survey Strategy and Guide

The purpose of the Survey Strategy is to help students *build* background knowledge about the actual text they will be reading. Surveying the key parts of the text is critical to helping students better understand what they are reading. In the primary years, teachers refer to this as "taking a picture walk" through the book before students begin to read. With older students, this strategy becomes more specific and deliberate, involving reviewing such features as the text type, main idea, headings, and subheadings, key vocabulary, significant diagrams, pictures, and maps of the section. Without this step, students do not know where they are headed, or what to expect in the reading. As studies show, previewing the text leads to increased reading performance by students (Spires, 1992).

Algebra II- Chapter 7

DEFINE THE VOCABULARY TERMS:

Exponential function *A function in the form f(x) = ab^x*

Base *The number in a power that is used as a factor*

Asymptote *A line that a graph approaches as the value of a variable becomes large or small*

Exponential growth *An exponential function of the form f(x) = ab^x in which b > 1*

Exponential decay *An exponetial function of the form f(x) = ab^x in which 0 < b < 1*

Inverse relation *The set of all ordered pairs inverted*

Logarithm *The exponent that a specified base must be raised in order to get a certain value.*

Exponential equation *An equation that contains one or more exponential expressions*

Natural logarithm *A logarithm written with base e, written as ln.*

Exponential regression *A statistical method used to fit an exponential model to a given data set.*

LIST THE SECTION HEADINGS:

Exponential Functions, Growth, and Decay

Inverses of Relations and Functions

Logarithmic functions

Properties of Logarithms

Exponential & Logarithmic Equations & Inequalities

The Natural Base, e

Transforming Exponential & Logarithmic Functions

Curve Fitting with Exponential & Logarithmic Models

FIGURE 4.4   Survey Strategy Guide Example for Algebra II

Students interact with the teacher as she/he thinks aloud while modeling the Survey Strategy. As readers become more proficient with surveying, they complete a Survey Strategy Guide to keep them engaged and aware of their strategy use. Figures 4.4 and 4.5 show two variations of Survey Strategy Guides, each for a different content area. When teachers explicitly use this strategy with students, it becomes a skill that students automatically use before reading any text.

PROCEDURE

1. Select a piece of appropriately leveled text.
2. Think aloud while noticing and discussing the following significant features of the text:
   a. Pages in the selection
   b. Heading of the section
   c. Main idea noted near heading
   d. Opening paragraph under the heading
   e. Subheadings within the section

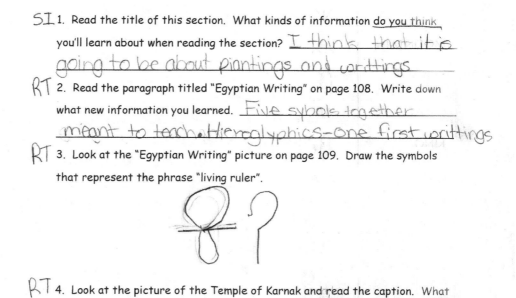

SI 1. Read the title of this section. What kinds of information do you think you'll learn about when reading the section? I think that it is going to be about piantings and writtings

RT 2. Read the paragraph titled "Egyptian Writing" on page 108. Write down what new information you learned. Five sybols together meant to teach. Hieroglyphics—one first writtings

RT 3. Look at the "Egyptian Writing" picture on page 109. Draw the symbols that represent the phrase "living ruler".

RT 4. Look at the picture of the Temple of Karnak and read the caption. What features of Egyptian architecture do you notice? Hieroglyphics, huge pillars, High windows, stars on roof, and very colorful

FIGURE 4.5   Survey Strategy Guide Example for Social Science

f. Pictures, maps, diagrams, plus their captions
g. Highlighted or italicized vocabulary within the text
h. Conclusion paragraph at the end of the selection
i. Expectations for questions to be answered or task to be completed after reading is finished

3. Throughout the process, encourage the students to respond and think aloud. (Survey Strategy Guides can also be completed as appropriate.)
4. Over time, allow students to work in small groups or with a partner to practice the Survey Strategy and to fill out the Strategy Guide. As students are working, the teacher monitors students closely, elicits information from students and completes a class Survey Strategy Guide for all to see.
5. As appropriate, have students use the Survey Strategy and complete the guide for each new section they are asked to read.

VARIATIONS   This strategy can have unlimited variation due to the vast differences in text that students are exposed to. For example, because of variation in text type, a survey of narrative text in a literature class would be very different from a survey of expository text in an agricultural mechanics class. However, the basic premise is the same for both—allow students to be exposed to a teacher who leads by modeling, giving explicit instruction in how to survey that particular piece of text.

Conclusion

The above examples of the K-W-L Chart (and its variations), the Text Box/Bag Activity, and the Survey Strategy and Guide are all documented effective methods to help students *activate* and *build* background knowledge about a topic before they read the selected text. There are many strategies that will help students develop their comprehension by activating and building background knowledge; this chapter describes procedures for a few of the most commonly practiced ones.

USE GRAPHIC ORGANIZERS

Graphic organizers are visual representations that help students organize ideas from text. Research findings indicate that graphic organizers can be effective tools to support comprehension for all students, including those who are at risk for academic failure (Kim, Vaughn, Wanzek, & Wei, 2004; Marzano, Pickering, & Pollock, 2001) or have been diagnosed with a learning disability (Kim, et al., 2004).

How do graphic organizers support comprehension? Studies suggest that they work to aid readers in remembering information. Graphic organizers commonly ask students to list categories of concepts and assist students in connecting, synthesizing, and comparing ideas. By asking students to focus on a small number of important concepts, graphic organizers capitalize on the capacities of short-and long-term memory.

Graphic organizers are most effective when they match the structure of the text or the content of instruction. Content area text has different structures and each corresponds with appropriate types of graphic organizers. For example, while a **Venn Diagram** might work well for a text that compares and contrasts, it would not work as well with a descriptive piece. Figure 4.6 shows which type of graphic organizers work best with which text structure.

Text Example	Text Structure	Purpose	Appropriate Graphic Organizers
History of Jazz	Sequential	Describe the events in order	MAIN IDEA/DETAIL INFERENCE
World Religions	Descriptive	Give details about a person, place, thing, or idea (nouns)	MAIN IDEA/DETAIL COMPARE/CONTRAST MATRIX INFERENCE
Atomic Bombings at Hiroshima and Nagasaki	Cause/Effect	Explain why something happens	OUTCOME INFERENCE
Substance Abuse	Persuasive	Convince reader to believe a point of view	EVIDENCE GUIDE INFERENCE
Styles of Artists: Impressionism (Monet) and Fauvism (Matisse)	Compare/Contrast	Show similarities and differences	COMPARE/CONTRAST MATRIX VENN DIAGRAM INFERENCE
Global Warming	Problem/Solution	Explain a problem and its solutions	EVIDENCE GUIDE INFERENCE

FIGURE 4.6   Graphic Organizers for Increasing Comprehension of Texts with Different Structures

Graphic organizers can be used to support comprehension before, during, and after reading content area text.

1. **Before Reading.** Use to introduce important information, to solicit prior knowledge from students, and to make predictions.
2. **During Reading.** Use to record important information, to show connection within the content, and to confirm and refute predictions.
3. **After Reading.** Use to review content as a basis for organizing writing and making connections to other content areas.

Graphic organizers can be used across all content areas to help teachers model and then provide subsequent practice with reading, extracting, and recording information in a visual representation or framework.

History

Much history text is written in a sequential, descriptive, problem/solution, or cause/effect structure. The authors aim to convey why historical events transpire, the order of those events, and to give a description of the people, places, and ideas surrounding them. Main Idea/Detail Graphic Organizers are especially useful in this content area. Outcome and Inference Graphic Organizers are also essential as students seek to continually determine the events that lead to an outcome and the subsequent effects that ensued. In addition, students who are analyzing various theories for events (e.g., the end of the dinosaur era or the assignation of JFK) will find Evidence Guides helpful.

Science

Science textbooks are structured to describe and explain causes and effects, and problems and their solutions. Main Idea/Detail and Compare/Contrast Matrix Graphic Organizers are well suited to science text that describes. For example, students in chemistry class learning about various chemical bonds (e.g., covalent, ionic, hydrogen) need to record information in a format that can help them understand the concept and the differences between them. Health teachers frequently use Inference and Outcome Graphic Organizers when reading about the effects of smoking, drinking, or drugs.

Mathematics

Teachers of various math classes will find Main Idea/Detail Graphic Organizers essential, as mathematics text frequently lists a sequence of steps that must be undertaken to solve equations. Compare/Contrast Matrices are also vital as students engage with their text to compare the similarities or differences of solving different types of problems. For example, Algebra II students must comprehend how to add, subtract, multiply, and divide complex numbers on a complex plane.

Language Arts

Middle school literature and high school English teachers integrate many of the graphic organizers shown in Figure 4.6, because the text structure of readings varies from lesson to lesson. For example, eleventh-grade English students reading *1984* by Orwell (1949) use Main Idea/Detail Graphic Organizers as they come to know the various characters within the events of the text. Consequently, an Evidence Guide is useful in a lesson sequence where students must analyze excerpts of the text of the Watergate tapes and draw conclusions about the events that transpired.

Electives

Visual and performing arts teachers will find it helpful to use Compare/Contrast Matrices when reading and understanding details about various composers. World language teachers find Main Idea/Detail Organizers helpful when learning about a new subculture from the language area they are studying.

This section describes the use of the following graphic organizers: Main Idea/Detail, Outcome, Evidence Guide, and Compare/Contrast Matrix. Each of these graphic organizers is useful with a specific type of text. Another visual, the Inference Graphic Organizer, can be used with various text types. All of these graphic organizers provide students with a way to organize information they learn by reading the text.

Main Idea/Detail Graphic Organizer

The Main Idea/Detail Graphic Organizer is best used with text that is sequential or descriptive in nature. Many expository textbooks, such as those in science and social science, follow this structure. The purpose for using this graphic organizer is to provide a framework for students to record the main idea and details that can be found within each paragraph as they read the text. It gives students a road map that they can use to chart the course before reading and a study guide or writing support to use after reading. Figure 4.7 on page 66 shows a Main Idea/Detail Organizer where a student recorded information about the Chinese Emperor Shi Huangdi.

PROCEDURE

1. Choose an appropriately leveled piece of text that covers the content, and be sure the text is either summative or descriptive in order to match the structure of the Main Idea/Detail Graphic Organizer.

2. Give all students a copy of the Main Idea/Detail Graphic Organizer that they can fill out, and prepare a copy for the overhead or Interwrite board. Have students survey the paragraphs that need to be read for the assignment, and number them on their graphic organizer sheet. (This task can be difficult for struggling readers, as many still do not know where a paragraph ends and where it begins or how to count how many paragraphs are within a section to be read.)

3. Model reading one paragraph at a time and recording significant details from the text. These details should be recorded in note format.

4. When details for that particular paragraph have been recorded, think aloud with students to determine the main idea of the paragraph. (Often, the main idea can be found in the topic sentence, so be sure to direct students to search for it there. In more complex text, students may have to summarize the details to find the main idea.)

5. Students will then fill out the graphic organizer as the teacher models it on the overhead or Interwrite board.

6. As students become more proficient with using this graphic organizer, have them begin to work in small groups or pairs under guided practice. Students complete one paragraph at a time, and then the class comes together to share the details and main idea before moving on to the next paragraph.

7. After much modeled and guided practice with this graphic organizer, allow the students to practice independently, but continue to frequently check student progress.

Teacher Tool

A blank Main Idea/Detail Graphic Organizer (TT9) is located in the Teacher Tools Appendix.

VARIATIONS   There are many different variations of this graphic organizer that can be created based upon the structure of the text and what the students need to achieve. For example, with younger students, the boxes within the organizer may need to be made bigger so students have ample space to write the details. With older students, the boxes can be made smaller, and more paragraphs can be noted on a single page. Also, the teacher will have to decide if the students are to record all details within each paragraph or only significant ones that directly relate to the topic being studied.

Outcome Graphic Organizer

The Outcome Graphic Organizer is best used with text that follows a cause and effect structure. This type of text often has many subheadings and is most commonly seen in the sciences and social sciences. Its purpose is to record significant details from the text and then to note the outcome of

Learning Log

Use the Main Idea/Detail Graphic Organizer in the Learning Log Appendix (LL3) to build your understanding of how to use various graphic organizers with text. At the same time you will be practicing how to use this useful comprehension strategy.

Paragraph	Main Idea	Details
5	Shi Huangdi – the builder	• builds large things • didn't think of dieing in the Great Wall • most builders of great wall convicts or disliked people • builders died constructing Great Wall • each stone cost a human a life • older wall built parallel to Great Wall • older wall rebuilt by his peasants
6	Shi Huangdi – extravagent death life	• his death was extravagent • buried with 6,000 soldiers • dubbed "Terra Cotta Soldiers" • soldiers: archers, infantry, charioteers, horses • supreeme quality detailed soldiers • solid arms, legs, and hollow body
7	Shi Huangdi – dead man	• three different tombs • no identical soldiers • sculptures represent standard of art • soldiers armed with bronze weapons • a revolution when rebels broke into vaults • died before tomb was complete • pilled dead fish on him to hide smell not ready for empire
8	Shi Huangdi – tomb undiscovered	• 1974 peasants found tomb of soldiers • tomb different from emperors made it • soldiers covered 3 miles • pyramid with him inside in center • nobody discovered tomb today

FIGURE 4.7   Main Idea/Detail Graphic Organizer Example for World History

each new subsequent set of details. Figure 4.8 shows an Outcome Graphic Organizer that was used by a student to record outcomes learned from a text about climbers on Mt. Everest.

PROCEDURE

1. Determine that the structure of a content-based leveled section of text is cause and effect.
2. Create an Outcome Graphic Organizer like the one shown in the example to match the length of the selection to be read.
3. Make copies of the organizer for all students and prepare, one for the overhead or Interwrite board.
4. After pre-reading, model and read aloud one section of the text at a time and record specific details (in note form) on the chart. Students should copy the model on their individual graphic organizers.

Teacher Tool

An Outcome Graphic Organizer (TT10) can be found in the Teacher Tools Appendix.

Section	Details	Outcome
Danger Ahead	frostbite Avalanche Snowstorms Crevasse fall lack of O_2	climb the last 1,100 ft higher
Months of Struggle	steep cliffs with rushing rivers rickety bridge of rocks & bamboo heavy rain swarms of hornets	they kept on going
The Death Zone	less O_2 O_2 tubes clogging up by ice 40 foot high rock wall	they didn't stop they kept on going
To The Top	struggled the peak they were climbing was conquered & they were on the top	They finally made it

FIGURE 4.8 Outcome Graphic Organizer Example for Text with Subheadings for Literature

5. When the details have all been recorded, think aloud with the class and generate the outcome from that particular section of text. Record this on the organizer.
6. Gradually, allow students to work with the graphic organizer in small groups and partners as a guided practice activity.
7. After modeling and guided practice, provide students with independent opportunities to use this graphic organizer and to become comfortable with its application.

VARIATIONS A variation of the Outcome Graphic Organizer can be used when the cause and effect text isn't neatly divided into subheaded sections. In this case, guide students to note outcomes after each paragraph separation. In Figure 4.9 a student recorded outcomes from a newspaper article about a boy who saved his school bus from crashing when his bus driver had a heart attack.

Teacher Tool

A template for an Evidence Guide (TT11) can be found in the Teacher Tools Appendix to copy.

	Details	Outcome
Paragraphs 1-4	• Riding on bus to school • driver fell unconcis & took control of bus	They were o.k. because he took control of the bus.
Paragraphs 5-8	• Only a small amount of people were hurt • He took it not serious but the others children took it really serious.	Aparently he took it as a small thing but really he was a hero.
Paragraphs 9-12	• driver had a stroke • called in for help	People would come to help soon.
Paragraphs 13-end	• bus driver told them what to do before hand • grandpa also provided information	They would be safe if there was an accident.

FIGURE 4.9 Outcome Graphic Organizer Example for Text without Subheadings for Newspaper Article

Another variation is to use this type of organizer with text that is narrative and includes a problem and solution within the story structure. In this case, students can still complete an Outcome Graphic Organizer at the end of each chapter where they note significant details about that chapter and the outcome thus far. This is extremely helpful for struggling students who tend to forget, from one day to the next, what they have read about in their narrative books. Rereading the details and outcomes noted on this graphic organizer can act as a pre-reading activity before they move on to the next section.

Evidence Guide Graphic Organizer

Evidence Guide Graphic Organizers are best used with texts that have a persuasion or problem-solution structure. These organizational patterns can be found in nearly all content areas. Use of this graphic organizer requires students to understand the theories being shared and to collect relevant evidence in support of and against each argument. Students often read several different text passages, including primary sources, textbooks, and novel excerpts. For students who are interested in mystery and crime scene investigation, this organizer is especially motivating. In Figure 4.10, a science class studying forensics read about and tried to comprehend the mystery of the Iceman's death.

Theories	Supporting Evidence	Evidence Against
-murdered by arrowhead (leader) (robber → leader)	-arrowhead in shoulder -no scar hole was there -cut artery (minutes)	-tools laid around -objects still there
-drowned (hypothermia)	-freeze-dried -crawling away/reaching -no water in body	-arrowhead in back-death
-fell backwards into arrowhead	-arrowhead in back -bow and quiver out	-laying on belly -tools were laying around him -front rib cage
-human sacrafice	-53 tattoos-shamon -tools laid all around -mountains	-no arrow going in back -arrow would be somewhere else

I think that he was murdered, and he broke his ribs from ice pressure I think that he was murdered because someone had something against him.

FIGURE 4.10 Evidence Guide Graphic Organizer Example for Science

PROCEDURE

1. Select a content area that is controversial, seems to have uncertainties about it, or is open for debate.
2. Find a few appropriately leveled passages of text that will provide students with varying points of view.
3. Model the reading of some of those passages, using vocabulary and fluency strategies noted in the previous chapters.
4. Brainstorm and record on the organizer the possible theories plus supporting and opposing evidence. As with other graphic organizers, the Evidence Guide can then be used later as a reference for studying for a test or writing an essay.
5. As appropriate, the teacher moves students through guided practice and into independent practice.

VARIATIONS   The variations with this type of graphic organizer are many. It can be used with persuasive text and text that encourages the reader to solve a mystery, problem, or analyze something controversial. The theory column can easily be renamed to state "points of view," "possible solutions," or "different concepts."

Compare/Contrast Matrix Graphic Organizer

The rationale behind the Compare/Contrast Matrix Graphic Organizer is to help students extract details from the text and organize them into a logical chart to use later when they are studying or writing an essay. This graphic organizer is best suited to text that is full of details and requires the student to learn many facts about different people, places, or events. The Compare/Contrast Matrix in Figure 4.11 shows a comparison of China's first dynasties. By recording information

DYNASTY	DATE	FOUNDER	LOCATION	SOCIAL CLASSES	ADVANCEMENTS
XIA	Around 2200 BC	Yu the Great	Along Huang He		channels to drain water major waterways of north China
SHANG	1500s BC		Northern China	Royal Family/Nobles Warrior Leaders Artisans Farmers Slaves	China's first writing system Bronze containers Axes, Knives & ornaments from Jade War chariots, powerful bows, bronze body armor Calendar
ZHOU	1100s BC	leaders of a people known as the Zhou	from an area west of Shang Kingdom to Chang Jiang	King Lords and Warriors Peasants	importance of family & social order mandate of heaven new political order ruling through lords

FIGURE 4.11   Compare/Contrast Matrix Example for World History

on this type of organizer, this student was able to clearly see the similarities and differences between these three dynasties.

PROCEDURE

1. Select an appropriately leveled text that covers the content needing to be taught and follows the text structure of either being compare/contrast or so detail-rich that using the matrix will help organize the information.
2. Create a graphic organizer, similar to that shown in Figure 4.11, with headings for the major concepts on the vertical and horizontal axes.
3. After activating and/or building background knowledge, read the text with students using vocabulary and fluency modeling strategies, and think aloud often to record details from the text in the appropriate places on the matrix.
4. As with other graphic organizers, gradually allow students to work in small groups and partners with guided practice until they are prepared to complete such a matrix independently.

Teacher Tool

The Compare/Contrast Matrix (TT12) is located in the Teacher Tools Appendix.

VARIATIONS   This type of graphic organizer has unlimited variations and can be adjusted to fit any passage that must be covered. The traditional format of this graphic organizer is the Venn Diagram, which uses two overlapping circles to compare and contrast two concepts. The Venn Diagram has proven to be effective in helping students improve comprehension (Boyle, 2000). However, as students progress into more advanced levels of text and concepts, the Venn Diagram cannot possibly house all of the information students must record in note format. Also, often there are more than two concepts to be compared. The matrix is more useful than the Venn Diagram for learners who are making complex comparisons.

Inference Graphic Organizer

The last graphic organizer to be discussed in this section can fit all types of text—sequential, descriptive, cause/effect, persuasive, problem/solution, and compare/contrast. The Inference Graphic Organizer is the most critical of all graphic organizers because it moves students beyond just recording information from the text to helping them make inferences about what they have read. Research shows that students who are proficient readers are able to make inferences about what they have read (Pressley & Afflerbach, 1995). Therefore, it is critical that all content teachers embed Inference Graphic Organizers into their regular reading routines so that all students can continue to develop this skill.

This graphic organizer is designed to help the student record details they have learned from reading the text; then, students spend time reflecting on what they already know about that concept in order to make a reasonable inference (D(*details*) + K(*known*) = I(*inference*)). Connecting the details learned to the known allows readers to activate their schemata and make sense of new information. Figure 4.12 shows an example with inferences made after a student read an article about the life of a young boy growing up in modern India.

PROCEDURE

1. Select a piece of text at the appropriate level.
2. Create a graphic organizer similar to the one shown in Figure 4.12.
3. Make copies of the organizer for each student, plus one for the overhead or Interwrite board.

	Details from the Text +	What You Know =	Inference (SI)
Clothing	wear sairis stitched clothes, + Dhotis with pants more modern many colors + more variety	wear saris + Dhotis, cotton stitched clothes + young girls had more color women more restricted	modern yet original - traditional mixed with new or modern
Sports	lot of outside games/ sports - soc., ten, hoc. cricket - pop. chess - Indian Grand master yoga + martial arts	chess came from India board games	more modern games board still really into games for entertainment +ia
Religion	All caste celebrated Holidays 3 national holiday 80% are Hindu acceptance of other religion religion very important strong family value	types of religions - Hindu - Buddism - Jainism	religion verys important very involved with other religions + other religious holidays
Food	Herbs + spices rice and wheat black pepper + hot chilli pepper from Portuguese	spices native to India spicy food	India has very natural food.
Language	Hindi largest number of speakers 2 linguistic families Indo - Aryan - 74% Dravidian 24% 21 other languages	Hindi official language of India english used in business	In India it would be hard because there are many different langues
M.A.D.	listen to classical music pop. music filmi + folk music modern film folk dances bhangra of the Punjab	Sanskrit poems + lit. theater based on hindu myth, medieval romances + news of social + political events	India has modern films and old music and dances

bihu of Assam
Bollywood most profitable film industry
literature first spoken
18R written

FIGURE 4.12   Inference Graphic Organizer Example for Social Science

4. After activating and building background knowledge, model vocabulary and fluency strategies while reading the text aloud to the class.
5. After reading each text section:
   a. record details from the text on the organizer
   b. think aloud, verbalizing prior knowledge about that topic and record that knowledge
   c. think aloud, verbalizing a reasonable inference about that subheading or concept
6. Complete the reading and record on the graphic organizer one section of the text at a time.

OBSERVATION	INFERENCE

Elements
    Lines-ripple on the pond
 	
    Color-value-light reflections
	Monet used art elements to create a peaceful scene of a pond. A light wind could have been felt as he sat by the pond, and the dim light illuminated the lilies so that they could be seen as connected to the water.

Subject Matter
    Pond-area with trees, lilies, and water
 	
    No surrounding terrain, water is complete subject
	Monet chose to focus on the pond scene to accentuate its natural beauty and did not take into account the environment directly surrounding the pond. He concentrated on bringing the pond, itself, to life so that it could be appreciated for its beauty.

Technical Qualities
    Broken-color technique
 	
    Scene created by brushstrokes to show shadows
	The painting technique used here by Monet is part of the Impressionistic Era; painters used this broken-color technique to create a scene of light and atmosphere.

FIGURE 4.13   Observation/Inference Chart Example for Visual Art

7. As appropriate, allow students to have guided practice opportunities with partners or small groups and return to share recorded thoughts at the end of each subheaded section.

8. Finally, move the students to independent practice with this graphic organizer.

When using an Inference Chart, remember that modeling is extremely important. Struggling readers can improve their ability to make an inference when provided explicit instruction in this area (Paris, Wasik, & Turner, 1991).

VARIATIONS   One variation of this Inference Graphic Organizer is the Observation/Inference Chart described by Nokes (2008). This organizer is divided into two sections, one for observations and the other for inferences. Figure 4.13 shows a sample of the Observation/Inference Chart. Students record their observations and subsequent inferences, linking them with an arrow. Like the Inference Graphic Organizer, it provides a framework for teachers to model and teach how to make inferences. However, it is limited in that students cannot record their own ideas to see how the connection can be made. The Observation/Inference Chart may be more appropriate for older and more proficient readers, but more research must be done in this area.

Teacher Tool

Blank Inference (TT13) and Observation/Inference Graphic Organizers (TT14) can be found in the Teacher Tools Appendix.

Conclusion

The above graphic organizers, Main Idea/Detail, Outcome, Evidence Guide, Compare/Contrast Matrix, and Inference are all effective in helping students create a framework for understanding the different types of text, as noted above. Research has shown that graphic organizers can be effective in helping students categorize, connect, synthesize, and remember information.

PAUSE and REFLECT 4.2

Several graphic organizers have been presented in this section. Choose a piece of text that you are planning to use with your students and determine which graphic organizer could support that text. Use Figure 4.6 to support your decision.

SUMMARIZE

Teaching students to summarize what they have read has also been shown to lead to increased comprehension (Brown, 2002). When summarizing, students discern the difference between more and less important ideas in the text. They generalize and attempt to state the main idea, usually in writing. Beyond aiding with comprehension, summarizing has been classified as one of the 11 elements of writing instruction effective in helping adolescents develop writing proficiency (Graham & Perin, 2007). While summaries are most often written, they can also be oral or visual (Neufeld, 2005). Text can also be summarized in the form of notes.

Strategies that help students summarize content can be used in all content areas. However, in each of these content areas, the focus and the content of the summary must be closely linked to the structure of the discipline.

History

World history students studying the fall of the Third Reich should be able to summarize the most important factors leading to the collapse. The study of the founding of the American government lends itself to summary writing—as students seek to concisely recap the major events leading to the First Continental Congress.

Science

A Written Summary in chemistry would be necessary when reporting on the details of a laboratory experiment—including the instruments used, calculations determined, and procedure used. Agricultural Science II students can summarize the events of the county fair and the steps they went through in obtaining, caring for, and showing their animals.

Mathematics

Summarizing in math is essential if students are to build schema from one lesson to the next. For example, algebra students would find value in providing a Written or Oral Summary of graphing the inverse of a function prior to the lesson on graphing the inverse of relations and functions. Taking notes in mathematics where the student records the central concept, explanation, example, formula, and a diagram can also prove helpful as a summarization strategy (Shanahan & Shanahan, 2008).

Language Arts

Almost every language arts lesson or unit lends itself to many summary opportunities. Students can summarize pieces of literature, short stories, and poems.

Electives

Physical education teachers can require students to orally summarize the rules of a game before play. World language students in Spanish can participate in "El Dia de los Muertos" at a nearby community center, and then summarize the events they experienced.

The following strategies are examples of how to teach students to create Written, Oral, and Visual Summaries and use Cornell Notes.

Written Summaries

Written Summaries are shortened versions of the text prepared by the reader that share the gist of the passage. They can vary in length from multiple sentences (Figure 4.14), to a paragraph (Figure 4.15), to an essay for summaries of longer pieces of text (Figure 4.16). Written Summaries are not a

using the definition of the derivative

$$f'(x) = \text{Rate of change of } f \text{ at } x = \lim_{h \to 0} \frac{f(x+h) - f(x)}{h}$$

When taking the derivative of a function we must use the definition of the derivative which is represented as $f'(x) = \lim_{h \to 0} \frac{f(x+h) - f(x)}{h}$. The first step to using this definition is to find $f(x+h)$ which is done by plugging $(x+h)$ in wherever there is an x in the function. Once you have found $f(x+h)$ you must find $f(x)$ which is just the original function. Next, you will subtract $f(x)$ from $f(x+h)$ and divide by h. When finished with this step some factors should cancel out leaving you with a simplified problem. The last step is to plug 0 in for h to solve for $f'(x)$. Once you have plugged zero in you should be left with an equation that only has an x and y variable and this is the equation that represents the derivative or the slope of the function you were first given.

FIGURE 4.14   Summary Multiple Sentence Example for Calculus

retelling of the events read about, but rather the reflections of the writer sharing the major sequential details and main idea. Summaries should note the title and author of the text.

PROCEDURE

1. Select an appropriately leveled piece of text covering the content area.
   a. Decide how often summarization will occur—after each subheading, section, chapter, or at the end of the book. (When working with less proficient readers, it is best to model summarization after reading only small chunks of text. Over time, students will be ready to summarize longer portions of text.)
   b. Decide whether the summary will be multiple sentences, a complete paragraph, or an essay.
2. Activate and build background knowledge about the topic being studied and then read the section of text, modeling fluency and vocabulary strategies. Students can be engaged in

El Dia de los Muertos is a very important day in the country of Mexico. This is when they celebrate those who have passed. They stay up late and eat sweets and talk about those people. Also, they place many flowers on their loved ones graves. The celebration of El Dia de los Muertos helps define the culture of Mexico's people.

FIGURE 4.15   Summary Paragraph Example for World Language

In the book *Goodbye Doesn't Mean Forever*, by Lurlene McDaniel, Melissa Austin learns to live life to the fullest because anything can happen. Melissa has leukemia, but she is in remission and doing very well. She has lots of support from her best friend, Jory Delaney, her brother, Michael Austin, and her mom, Mrs. Austin. Even though Melissa is ill, she still works hard toward her goals. She is not the kind of person to give up hope.

Melissa's chemotherapy treatment stops working. She goes back to the hospital and discovers she is very unhealthy. Her leukemia has come back. The doctors decide that Melissa needs a bone marrow transplant. They hope that the healthy bone marrow will kill the cancerous cells.

Melissa gets the bone marrow transplant from Michael. After a while, the doctors think that Melissa is rejecting the transplant. Suddenly, Melissa's illness turns completely around, and she accepts the transplant. She feels great and the leukemia starts going away. Melissa's family and friends are very happy that she is doing well.

Melissa discovers she has meningitis. Her body is not completely healed, so she is not very strong. Her heart is damaged from the leukemia. Mrs. Austin, Michael, and Jory are all very worried and sad. They know Melissa is a fighter, but her body is very weak.

Melissa dies after a long fight with cancer. Before she goes, she gives her personal journal to Jory. She also writes letters to her mom, brother, and Jory about what she wants them to do. They will always remember Melissa because they think she is strong, caring, and inspirational. When Melissa discoveres she has meningitis, she knows she is going to die, but she isn't scared because she has faith in God.

FIGURE 4.16   Summary Essay Example for English

using graphic organizers during the reading so that they can later use their notes to help them write.

3. Think aloud with students to discuss what details they have learned from the reading.
4. Then conduct a **Write Aloud**, guiding students to complete a summary a few sentences long about the section they have read.
   a. Students begin by writing a topic sentence (TS) that includes the title of the section or chapter, the author, and the main idea.
   b. They then write at least two significant details, each written in a separate sentence. The multiple sentence summary concludes with a supported inference (SI) about the topic. It is helpful to begin this sentence with the words "I think. . ." so that students will be prompted to use this sentence to share their reflections on this piece of text.
   c. Finally, write a conclusion sentence (CS) that restates the main idea.
5. As appropriate, begin to complete shared writing summaries and then move students to guided and independent practice, as was determined to be successful by Pearson (1985).

Figure 4.17 on page 78 shows an example of a student's independent summary written after reading the section, "Words for the Wise," about life in ancient Egypt. The example includes the pre-reading activity, vocabulary strategy, and note taking area.

VARIATIONS   As noted above, there are many variations to Written Summaries, such as length and how much text to read before beginning the writing. One variation that can be used when creating Written Summaries is to have students record their summaries in a notebook that acts as a running summary record of the textbook itself. This running summary is beneficial in social science classrooms where reviewing the textbook prior to an exam can become a daunting process. The continued Written Summary becomes a study guide for exams, noting the main ideas of the chapter in summary. Students can also compose Written Summaries on computers or post them on a blog for the teacher to review.

Oral Summaries

Students can also practice constructing Oral Summaries. With an Oral Summary, students learn how to verbally summarize sections of text.

PROCEDURE

1. Select a section of text or book to be read aloud to the class.
2. Read the text aloud.
3. Engage in a Think Aloud as model of how to create an Oral Summary of the text passage.
4. Read the subsequent paragraph aloud.
5. Have students turn to a partner and share an Oral Summary of the segment of text.
6. Have students read the next paragraph independently or with a partner.
7. Again, have students turn to a partner and share an Oral Summary of the text.

 *Learning Log*

Use the Summary Paragraph Template in the Learning Log Appendix (LL4) to deepen your knowledge about summarizing. At the same time, you can practice how to use the strategy described.

VARIATIONS   Many teachers also use Oral Summaries to share about new books they have brought into the classroom for the students to read. This is referred to as a **Book Talk**, and the main purpose is to grab the students' interest to make them want to read the book (Keane, 2005). With increased proficiency, students can give book talks about the books they have chosen to read independently.

Visual Summaries

The purpose of the Visual Summary is to create a visual picture, storyboard, diagram, or PowerPoint® slide show that summarizes what has been learned from the reading of the text. The

Before you read this section, make a prediction about this section.

What people do for work or a living.

Sub-title Heading

Words for the Wise   *boys work with their families

*scribes do different jobs for different people.

*5 years of schooling→how to make ink,paper,& how to write

*prayed to different gods for different reasons

*_____

Responsive Writing:

TS In the section "Words for the Wise" Kathy Welmore tells about going to school to become a scribe.

D A scribe is someone who earns a living by writing and reading skills.

D With five years of schooling you learn how to make ink, paper from papyrus, and how to write.

SI I think that going to school to be a scribe would be hard for me.

Vocabulary

Scribe   * a person who write and reads for a living

hiroglyphics * writing system in which pictures or symbols are used to represent words or sounds.

FIGURE 4.17   Summary Guided Practice Example for Social Science

use of visual images to summarize requires a different way of thinking about literacy (Flood, Lapp, & Bayles-Martin, 2000). For example, designing magazine covers (Assaf & Garza, 2007) to summarize what has been read is motivating because it allows readers to use visual images to connect, synthesize, and understand the big picture of the text.

The Visual Summary is not to be confused with a graphic organizer. Visual Summaries show the important information and main idea learned through a visual representation. Figure 4.18 shows

FIGURE 4.18   Visual Summary Example for Social Science

an example of a visual picture created by a student to summarize Table XI on marriage from the Roman Law of the Twelve Tables.

Since we know that proficient readers visualize what they read as they construct meaning from text (Pressley & Afflerbach, 1995), students need opportunities to see visual summarization modeled and have time to practice it across the content areas. Visual Summaries can be used to summarize a concept, a section of text, or an entire book. Students who struggle with visualizing what they have read may find it helpful to use Visual Summaries at the end of each chapter that has been read. This practice allows them to record a visual picture about the major event in that chapter and refer to it as they move forward in their reading. Figure 4.19 shows a Visual Summary that a student completed at the end of their home reading for literature each night. The student also included a two-sentence summary, an assignment to help this student develop Written Summary skills.

PROCEDURE

1. Select an appropriately leveled piece of text covering the content area, and activate and/or build background knowledge with the class.
2. Read a section of the text, using fluency and vocabulary strategies. Be sure that all students have a blank piece of paper for the Visual Summary.
3. When finished reading, think aloud about the key points and main idea.
4. Conduct a **Draw Aloud** by drawing a visual representation that summarizes the reading. Remind students not to focus on their actual drawings, but on the visual message to be conveyed. (If appropriate, teachers can do their best to integrate art strategies into the modeling of Visual Summaries.)
5. As students' proficiencies increase, allow them guided opportunities to practice in small groups, with partners, and finally move them to independent practice.

VARIATIONS   One variation is to have students create Visual Summaries for a younger audience. This activity allows the adolescent learner an opportunity to practice the Visual Summary and provides a literacy learning opportunity for a younger learner. For example, a physics teacher may

FIGURE 4.19 Visual Chapter Summary Example for Literature

ask her students to write and illustrate simple picture books that explain concepts. In one class, students created picture books on the physical science concepts of force and gravity and shared them with second-grade elementary students at a nearby school. The second-grade students were able to read about concepts they had been studying about in science, and the high school students demonstrated that they understood the concept through the use of a Visual Summary.

Cornell Notes

Text can also be summarized in the form of notes. This type of summarizing is referred to as **note making,** not to be confused with **note taking,** which involves recording thoughts shared during a lecture. Several studies have been completed on the effectiveness of making notes, and the results have shown that students who learn and practice it as a strategy, specifically Cornell Notes, have increased engagement with and understanding of concepts within the text (Yamamoto, 2007). Note making must be explicitly taught to students so that they learn to determine which details are important to record as notes (Marzano, et al., 2001). After modeling, the teacher gradually leads students through guided and independent practice. Students then refine and review notes before a test.

The note making summary strategy called Cornell Notes was first introduced by Walter Pauk, a professor at Cornell University in the 1940s (Pauk & Owens, 2007). Over time, it has been used widely across disciplines. It is one of the key strategies taught to students in Advancement Via Individual Determination (AVID), a school program that helps prepare students in the academic middle for the rigors of college (Nelson, 2007). It can be used with any type of expository text, but it is also helpful when reading detail-rich text.

PROCEDURE

1. After selecting the appropriate leveled content area text, use pre-reading strategies to help students activate their prior knowledge about the concept.
2. Prepare notepaper with students and be sure to have a blank copy for the overhead or Interwrite board. Divide the top two-thirds of the paper vertically into two sections labeled "Subheadings" and "Notes." Students can easily make this on their own by folding a lined sheet of paper in half (vertically). The bottom third of the paper should be separated from the top with a horizontal line and labeled "Summary."
3. Read the section of text, modeling fluency and vocabulary strategies.
4. Record subheadings within on the text in the left-hand column.
5. Think aloud with the students to record significant details about the topic in the column directly across from the subheading. The Think Aloud and recording phase of this step is critical; before practicing it independently, students must watch this strategy being modeled repeatedly.
6. Review the subheadings and notes together, and write aloud a summary in the bottom section of the page. Use the same strategies noted above in the Written Summaries section.

Figure 4.20 on page 82 shows Cornell Notes created during guided practice while reading a social studies textbook section entitled "The Geography of Early Kush."

VARIATIONS   One variation is called Continual Cornell Notes. Students divide part of their papers in half, vertically, and take notes on a particular section of text. When they finish one section of notes, they draw a line and write the summary. They then write the next section's notes directly under that summary. This variation allows students to adjust the amount of paper needed for note making and to move from one section to the next without needing another piece of paper.

Sometimes texts are not neatly divided into headings. If this is the case, the teacher models how to determine the main idea to record on the "Subheading" side of the notes.

Conclusion

Teachers can help support student comprehension with Written, Oral, and Visual Summaries. In addition, Cornell Notes help students record key points from the learning and engage in summary writing.

PAUSE and REFLECT 4.3

Students can summarize in almost any content area. Consider one type of summary strategy that you could integrate into your current content lessons to build comprehension.

ASK AND ANSWER QUESTIONS

Over the last few decades, the role of questioning in reading comprehension has changed. Once just used for assessment, research illustrates the positive effects of learning to *generate* and *answer* questions about a text. When students *generate* questions before, during, and after reading, they engage deeply with the content and monitor their comprehension (Nokes & Dole, 2004). Second, when students learn about how to *answer* different types of questions about a text, they become more able to differentiate between information that is explicitly stated in the text and ideas that are inferred from the text (Raphael, 1986).

Asking and answering questions about a text can help students build comprehension across all content areas.

Geograpy & Early Kush	-South of Egypt along the Nile -today called Nubia
The land of Nubia	NE Africa -fertile land -gold, stone, and copper
Early civilization in Nubia	-ag-summer & winter crops -wheat, barley, other grains -cattle/livestock -capital/Kerma -people are priests and artisans
Egypt rules Kush	Kush had supplies of raw meat & slaves -they sent materials to Egypt
Egypts conquest of Kush	-Kush got wealthy from and got stronger armies -rulers of Egypt got scared -Egypt attacked around 1500 BC -Ramses the Great made more palaces in Kush territory
Effects of the conquest	Kush was Egypts territory for 450 years -many people settled in Kush
A change in power	-the Kushite regained power -Kush became a city again

FIGURE 4.20   Cornell Notes Example for Social Science

History

Most history textbooks contain lesson, chapter, and unit questions that prompt readers to reflect upon the reading. Often the types of questions that are asked are varied. For example, a U.S. history textbook might contain the following: "Find two sentences in the above passage that are irrelevant. What makes them irrelevant to the passage about the Transcontinental Railroad?" The next question might ask, "Why do you think the economic mood of the time affected people's attitude toward the railroad's progress?" Students must be explicitly taught how to differentiate between these two types of questions so that they will know how to hone in on details in the text and make inferences about concepts the author implied.

Science

After students read about reproductive systems in their life science books, they will likely bring many questions with them to the class discussion. Teachers who tap into these wonderings will more readily engage students with the text, as they help these teenagers find answers to their questions about reproduction.

Mathematics

Students in advanced mathematics classes must learn to generate questions prior to reading about a new or partially familiar concept as they seek to determine the real-world application of the concept. For example, Algebra II students learning about function tables and graphs could inquire how this concept can be applied in business and finance to connect to their learning of the stock market in their economics class.

Language Arts

All literature lends itself to opportunities where students can ask questions before, during, or after reading the text. In addition, students must be explicitly taught about various types of questioning strategies in order to understand whether information can be found in or must be inferred from the passage being read.

Electives

In world language courses, students have questions about both language and culture. For example, students may believe that "Cinco de Mayo" commemorates the day that Mexico declared its independence from Spain. While reading a passage in their Spanish I books describing the day (in English), a teacher can prompt students to generate questions and dispel their misconceptions.

The following section describes two instructional practices that focus on questioning. The first (SQ3R: Survey, Question, Read, Recite, Review) uses student-generated questions to guide reading. The second (QAR: Question Answer Relationship) teaches students to think strategically about the relationship between the type of question asked and how to compose an answer.

SQ3R (Survey, Question, Read, Recite, Review)

The SQ3R strategy gives students a purpose for reading by having them formulate questions that they answer while reading. SQ3R is a well-known and popular reading and study strategy. The components of this strategy reflect many of the behaviors that are engaged in by expert readers (Pressley & Afflerbach, 1995). SQ3R allows students to be aware of a purpose for reading, overview the text, read selectively, and review what is read. While there have been few studies of the effectiveness of SQ3R, Topping and McManus (2002) give SQ3R partial credit for engaging students in a difficult middle school science curriculum. Figure 4.21 shows an example of SQ3R in a high school technology class. As they read about online computer access, students first generated questions from the subheadings, and then they noted details.

PROCEDURE

1. Select the appropriately leveled text that covers the content needing to be taught.
2. Survey. Think aloud and model for students how to skim the text to determine the structure or organization of the chapter. This might include reading the introduction, looking at headings, reading the summary, or reading the questions at the end of the chapter.
3. Have each student prepare a sheet of lined paper folded vertically (trifolded) so that the paper is divided into three columns; label them "Headings/Subheadings," "Questions," and "Notes."
4. Question. Model with students how to turn each heading/subheading into a question. Students should record these questions in the question column and leave enough space

Heading	Question	Notes
Online Bill Pay	How does online bill paying work?	Money is taken directly out of your checking account and sent to pay the bill. You can also set up automatic payments for monthly bills.
Transfer Funds	Can funds be transferred from one account to another?	Money can be easily transferred from a checking account into a savings account and back again. Money can be transferred as you need it or set up as a regularly scheduled transfer.
View Transactions	How can transactions be viewed?	You can go online at any time to see deposits, withdrawals, bills paid, and transfers made. You can see your account balance at any time.

FIGURE 4.21   Survey, Question, Read, Recite, Review Example for Technology

underneath so that they have ample space in the note column to keep the questions and notes aligned. A good rule of thumb is to leave two to three blank lines per paragraph for each section. For example, if the subheading has been turned into a question and the text passage underneath it is four paragraphs long, skip eight to twelve lines before students write the question for the next subheading.

5. Read. Read the section together, modeling fluency and vocabulary strategies. Stop often to think aloud while reading.
6. Recite. Give an oral summary when finished with that section. Then, write aloud notes that will give an answer to the question. Students should record this answer in their notes, as well as other significant details that will help them better understand.
7. Repeat this process for each section of the text.
8. Review. After completing the passage, think aloud to show students how to go back and review all of the headings/subheadings, questions, and notes from the reading.
9. Gradually move students to more guided, and then independent practice with this questioning strategy.

VARIATIONS   One variation of SQ3R is to have students only divide their paper into two sections as opposed to three. This provides students with more space to record notes; label the sections "Questions" and "Notes."

Another variation is to provide strategy cards for students that remind them of the steps involved in this process (survey, question, read, review, recite). Included can be reminders about what to do for each section. These cards can be used as bookmarks in student's textbooks if the strategy is used often enough.

QAR (Question-Answer-Relationship)

The purpose of the QAR strategy is to help students identify the relationship between questions and answers (Raphael, 1986). Without the QAR strategy, when students answer questions, they usually rely on their prior knowledge, or they rely on the text, but they rarely make connections between the two. QAR teaches students to identify and then answer questions that can either be found "in the book" or "in their heads." Answers "in the book" are either *Right There* or *Think and Search*. *Right There* questions can be found in single sentences in the book, and *Think and Search* questions can be pieced together from different sections of text. Answers "in your head" can either be called *Author and You* or *On My Own*. *Author and You* questions ask students to make an inference based on prior knowledge and details from the text. *On My Own* answers can be crafted without even reading the text. The purpose of QAR is to teach students how to identify the different

Label	Type of Question	Definition	Example
RT	Right There	The answer can be found right there in the text. You can point to it.	When was the Declaration of Independence ratified?
I	Author and You/Inference	The answer can be found by making an inference from what you know and what has been learned from the details in the text. (K + D = I)	Why do you think the patriots were so eager to join the Boston Tea Party?
TS	Think and Search	The answer can be found in the text, but you must look and perhaps search in more than one spot to piece it together.	How long did the Revolutionary War last?
OYO	On Your Own	The answer comes from your own knowledge and thoughts. You do not have to read the passage in order to answer this type of question.	Would you have joined the patriots in their fight against England?

FIGURE 4.22   QAR (Question-Answer-Relationship)

types of questions so that they can more effectively answer them. QAR helps students understand which information is present in the text and which information requires inference. Figure 4.22 is a QAR chart that may help in understanding its structure.

PAUSE and REFLECT 4.4

Consider Figure 4.22 in connection with questions presented in your content area. Find and label (or generate) one example of each of the four types of questions about a topic you are planning to teach (Right There, Think and Search, Author and You, and On Your Own).

PROCEDURE

1. Choose a content area passage of text that is appropriately leveled.
2. Activate and build background knowledge and read aloud, modeling fluency and vocabulary strategies. Encourage the use of graphic organizers or summarization during and/or after reading.
3. Think aloud while reading the questions with students and label the questions with the QAR categories noted in Figure 4.22.
4. Write aloud while modeling how to respond in writing to the questions.
5. Move students away from modeling, into guided and independent practice with QAR until students become proficient.

Figure 4.23 is an example of QAR in action. Tenth-grade students in a health class were reading about the childhood obesity epidemic.

VARIATIONS   To simplify QAR, one variation is to initially introduce students to two question categories rather than three. For example, students can label questions as either being RT (*Right There*) or I (*Inference*). Another variation of QAR is to ask students to categorize a question even without answering it. Just the act of practicing to identify the types of questions can be beneficial.

Learning Log

Use Learning Log (LL5) to deepen your understanding of how to ask and answer questions to improve comprehension. You will also get additional practice with the QAR strategy.

But how is it that we have gotten to this point...that obesity is escalating around the world?

One explanation is that the "toxic food environment" that renders high-fat and sugar-laden products has become more available. The scientific research of the 1800's brought about changes in production and preservation of food. In 1903, trans fat was patented which allowed food to stay fresh longer and have a more desirable texture. This was a benefit for the food industry because it allowed them to provide more desirable products; consumers could now purchase items that would stay fresh longer. Research has shown, however, that trans fat is directly correlated with heart disease, diabetes, cancer, low birth weight, obesity, and immune dysfunction. Therefore, the benefits it provided are being outweighed by the negative effects. In addition, the supermarket promoted the selling of standardized foods and products which were sold as processed items, preserved with salt and fat. By 1980, Americans increased their caloric intake from 2,600 to 3,200 per person, per day; this is almost twice the amount of calories that adults need to survive. Most of the excess calories were added from snack foods and sodas; further escalating the obesity epidemic. For example, a McDonald's Happy Meal (cheeseburger, small French fries, and 8oz chocolate milk) is 700 calories, with 27 grams of fat, 45 mg cholesterol, 1060 mg sodium, 88 grams carbohydrates, 31 grams sugar and 26 grams protein. This "toxic food environment" has changed the food eaten by humans significantly over the past 100 years.

> What foods have contributed to the obesity epidemic? _I_
> _fast foods, snack foods & soda_
>
> What was the benefit of trans fat? _RT_
> _food could stay fresh longer & have a better texture_
>
> Why did the caloric intake increase in the 1980's? _TS_
> _more snack food & soda were consumed_
>
> Why do experts say that we live in a "toxic food environment"? _OYO_
> _Because the food we eat is full of toxins that can harm our bodies._

FIGURE 4.23 QAR Example for Health

Conclusion

SQ3R and QAR are both effective strategies for helping students better comprehend text. When used systematically, they help students generate and answer questions before, during, and after reading.

PAUSE and REFLECT 4.5

Since we know that generating and answering questions can be beneficial, how will you begin to adapt your lessons to incorporate these strategies?

MONITOR COMPREHENSION

Research tells us that proficient readers track or monitor their understanding and that they apply strategies as needed (Pressley, 2002). As they read, these readers constantly ask themselves, "Does that make sense?" Then, when they realize their comprehension is faltering, they apply strategies (such as rereading) to increase their understanding. The ability to monitor one's own comprehension is thought to be the first step toward becoming a strategic reader (Baker, 2002).

Self-monitoring is one of the reading practices that will be useful to students into adulthood, as they approach new and unfamiliar texts (Willingham, Winter 2006/2007). To be able to monitor comprehension, students must become self-regulated, meta-cognitive thinkers who are able to reflect on their own thought processes. In order to reach this goal, students must be given authentic practice embedded in the content areas.

History

If they are to make sense of the text, students in all types of history classes —from studies of geography to U.S. government— must monitor their comprehension while reading. Because these curricula are cyclic throughout a student's academic career, new concepts and details are continually being built upon one another. Hence, students must fit the new knowledge into their existing understanding, question as they read, and compare current ideas they have with new contradictory details. For example, students reading a section of their world history textbooks on Cuba's policies and involvement in Africa in the 1960s and 1970s must be encouraged to ask themselves questions and reread. They must be encouraged to think deeply about the inconsistencies between this text and others read previously, such as the excerpt from *Conflicting Missions* (Gleijeses, 2003), a text that they read the day before. By monitoring their comprehension in this way, students will build a more accurate and detailed understanding of the content concept.

Science

Science textbooks are laden with details to help readers build a complex knowledge of concepts. It is critical that students monitor their comprehension while they are engaged in the reading process as concepts develop throughout a section, chapter, or unit. Students in a physical science class, for example, must be given opportunities to regulate their reading about "pressure" in order to build a full understanding of the concept so that they can build upon this knowledge as they learn about "calculating pressure" and "buoyant force."

Mathematics

Similarly, students in mathematics classes must continually monitor their reading to continue to build extended understanding of concepts. Teachers of Algebra I must ensure that their students are monitoring their comprehension as they read about "greatest common factors" (a review from previous math learning) before they move on to subsequent lessons on "factoring $x^2 + bx = c$," "factoring $ax^2 + bx + c$," and "factoring special products."

Language Arts

It is also essential that language arts teachers embed monitoring strategies into their teaching. Students can then practice these techniques when they independently read novels for their literature classes.

Electives

Teachers of electives can support students in learning how to monitor comprehension. For example, during warm-up stretches, physical education teachers can easily model how they think about text as they read aloud a brief article from *Sports Illustrated*. In agricultural mechanics, teachers can encourage students to monitor their comprehension as they read from direction manuals and learn the "how to" for certain projects.

The two strategies presented in this next section—Interactive Think Aloud and Comprehension Monitoring Strategy Guide—teach students to monitor their understanding as they read. By modeling them, guiding student practice, and supporting independent practice, teachers can help all readers use the strategies of the most proficient readers.

Interactive Think Aloud

In Interactive Think Aloud (Lapp, Fisher, & Grant, 2008), the teacher literally *thinks aloud*, modeling how to monitor her own comprehension. The goal is for students to watch the proficient reader model this strategy, then practice while the teacher guides them, until students eventually gain control over their own comprehension. When they are ready, they will be able to engage in self-monitoring as they independently attempt to understand challenging text. The Interactive Think Aloud occurs while the teachers or students (chorally) read and stop as necessary to think aloud. Figure 4.24 shows an example dialogue from an Interactive Think Aloud that centered on a high school economics text.

Teacher: I see from the title that this text is about supply. Can anyone give me a definition for supply (without looking at the book)? Clay?

Student (Clay): I know that it means how much of something is available, like "supplies are limited" when I was trying to get concert tickets.

Teacher: Okay, so it includes how much of something is available. I'm wondering if the word has a different meaning when we're talking about economics. Let's see:

(The class chorally reads from their textbook.)

> *Supply in economics relates to the ability and willingness of a seller to produce goods and services for consumers. Suppliers experiment with selling different amounts of goods at different prices to determine the highest value they can receive in exchange for the product.*

Teacher: Talk to your partner and come up with a one-sentence definition of supply.
(Students talk to their partners.) Take a look at the definition in the text, and see if you agree with it.
Okay, so it involves both the willingness and the ability of sellers to produce and offer goods. Now I'm wondering what "willingness and ability" mean, so let's read on:

(The class again chorally reads from the textbook.)

> *The ability of the seller to produce a product is determined by the cost of production and whether or not the seller has the financial resources necessary; in other words, can he provide a product? The willingness of the seller refers to the seller's eagerness to sell a product if it has a large margin of profit. Does he choose to provide a product?.*

Teacher: Can anyone think of a time when you might be willing to produce the good, but you are unable to produce it? Lisa?

Student (Lisa): I guess that you could want to make a reality TV show, because they are popular. But actually making one would be another thing. Then, you'd have the desire, but not the ability, right?

FIGURE 4.24 Interactive Think Aloud Example for Economics

PROCEDURE

1. Choose text that is at the appropriate instructional level and meets the content area need.
2. Before teaching, carefully read the text, thinking about one's own reading processes, noting the text structure, unfamiliar vocabulary, text features, and concepts that are essential to comprehending the text.
3. The teacher should begin by introducing the text and using either an *activating* or *building* background knowledge strategy.
4. All students should have a copy of the text that is being used, preferably one where they can highlight/underline and make notes.
5. The teacher begins by thinking aloud while reading.
   a. Model how to address the text structure, unfamiliar vocabulary, text features, and new concepts.
   b. Model how to note comments within the body of the text. Highlight or underline certain concepts and write margin notes where thoughts have been shared.
   c. With time and practice, encourage students to share their thoughts aloud. (In many classrooms, this interactive time is one of open discourse; the students are free to share aloud without raising their hands, as long as they are mindful of taking turns appropriately as the discussion progresses.)
6. As students become more proficient in thinking aloud, they work in pairs or small groups with the teacher monitoring comprehension.

VARIATIONS   The procedures for this strategy will vary based upon the subject area and the text type. In some classrooms where teachers desire more physical activity during Think Aloud discourse, the teacher can have three "thought cards" (numbered 1, 2, 3) and three "comment cards" (numbered 1, 2, 3) that circulate around the room. When a student wishes to speak, he takes a card, which shows the order in which students are waiting to share a thought or make a comment about a section of text.

Comprehension Monitoring Strategy Guide

Like the Interactive Think Aloud, the Comprehension Monitoring Strategy Guide helps students develop comprehension monitoring during reading. When students use the Comprehension Monitoring Strategy Guide, they must continually monitor their comprehension. (Figure 4.25 shows an example.) It helps less proficient readers ask themselves the question, "Does that make sense?"

To construct a Comprehension Monitoring Strategy Guide, a teacher selects seven to ten statements from the text. She or he then converts these to false statements and types them on a handout for students to refer to while reading. The teacher guides students to look for and correct these false statements while reading.

Studies have seen some success with strategies of this type. Ghent (2008) used a similar strategy with college students reading a biology text. Students who were asked to correct false statements as they read comprehended the material better than other students who read the text segment twice. Although more research is needed, Ghent concluded this type of "false correction" is successful because it continually forces the reader to infer meaning from the text in order to answer the question or correct the false statement as the reading progresses.

PROCEDURE

1. Choose a text that is at the appropriate instructional level and meets the content area need.
2. Select seven to ten critical concepts or details from the text that can be turned into false correction statements. (Some can be left correct so that students will not assume all of them

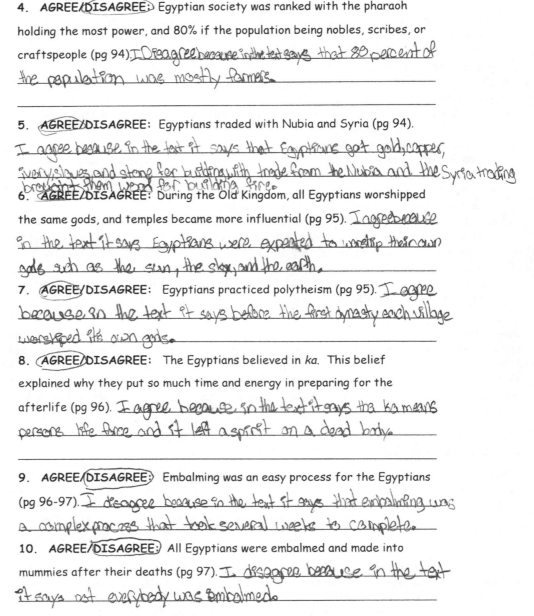

4. AGREE/DISAGREE: Egyptian society was ranked with the pharaoh

holding the most power, and 80% if the population being nobles, scribes, or

craftspeople (pg 94) I Disagree because in the text says that 80 percent of

the population was mostly farmers.

5. AGREE/DISAGREE: Egyptians traded with Nubia and Syria (pg 94).

I agree because in the text it says that Egyptians got gold, copper,

ivory, slaves and stone for building with trade from the Nubia and the Syria trading

brought them wood for building fire.

6. AGREE/DISAGREE: During the Old Kingdom, all Egyptians worshipped

the same gods, and temples became more influential (pg 95). I agree because

in the text it says Egyptians were expected to worship their own

gods such as the sun, the sky, and the earth.

7. AGREE/DISAGREE: Egyptians practiced polytheism (pg 95). I agree

because in the text it says before the first dynasty each village

worshiped its own gods.

8. AGREE/DISAGREE: The Egyptians believed in *ka*. This belief

explained why they put so much time and energy in preparing for the

afterlife (pg 96). I agree because in the text it says tha ka means

persons life force and it left a spirit on a dead body.

9. AGREE/DISAGREE: Embalming was an easy process for the Egyptians

(pg 96-97). I disagree because in the text it says that embalming was

a complex process that took several weeks to complete.

10. AGREE/DISAGREE: All Egyptians were embalmed and made into

mummies after their deaths (pg 97). I disagree because in the text

it says not everybody was embalmed.

FIGURE 4.25   Comprehension Monitoring Strategy Guide Example for Social Science

should be recorded as "disagree.") Changes that highlight important ideas have the most impact. For example, a sixth-grade social studies text might read: "Like all early civilizations along the Nile, the people who lived in Nubia depended on agriculture for their food." The false correction statement might say, "The early civilizations that lived along the Nile River depended upon it for their food." This false correction statement could spur a discussion about how the Nile River provided the water to help crops grow, supporting agriculture. Or, students might discuss that the Nile River itself did not provide food, but the agriculture in the area did.

3. Type these statements—with the words "agree" and "disagree" in front of them. Type several blank lines after each statement so the students can record the correct concept. To increase engagement and independent use of the strategy, provide each student with a copy of the Comprehension Monitoring Strategy (CMS) Guide.

4. In order for CMS Guide to be effective, it is important that teachers model how to use them. Using the Interactive Think Aloud strategy with students, teachers model reading a small section of text at a time and comparing that with the false correction statement. Students record why this statement is or is not correct as the teacher models it on the overhead, board, or Interwrite board.

5. As students become more proficient with the strategy, they can practice completing the CMS Guide with small groups or partners. Eventually, students will be able to complete them independently.

VARIATIONS   A variation of the CMS Guide is to turn some of the false correction statements into statements that are true, yet use different language to explain the same concept. For example, a CMS Guide social science example states: "Many Egyptian pyramids were built during the Old Kingdom." This could have actually stated: "The Egyptians first built tombs during the Old Kingdom, but many were built during later time periods." The student would need to circle *Agree* because the statement is true. The concept was just explained in a different way.

Another variation of the CMS Guide is the Imposter Strategy. First discussed by Curran and Smith (2005), this strategy aims to strengthen comprehension monitoring by embedding contradictory ideas into reading passages and having students critically question the text in order to become a more active reader. Kane (2007) found fault with this strategy in that it alters the text the teacher is providing the students and creates too much uncertainty for students about the passages they read. Instead, Kane (2007) suggests using authentic texts as they are, so that teachers can model comprehension monitoring strategies as they come across ambiguities in the text, such as logic problems. The Imposter Strategy can help students further develop comprehension monitoring if they are already critical readers. However, for less proficient readers, it requires significant scaffolding and Think Aloud modeling.

Conclusion

The Interactive Think Aloud and the Comprehension Monitoring Strategy Guide are both effective in helping students practice and build meta-cognitive awareness of their own reading. Other strategies of this type are currently being developed and studied. Further research is critical to test strategies that can help students become more active, self-monitoring readers.

Learning Log

Use Learning Log (LL6) to practice using the Comprehension Monitoring Strategy Guide while you read the next section and learn how to use multiple reading strategies to improve comprehension.

PAUSE and REFLECT 4.6

Consider the Interactive Think Aloud and the Comprehension Monitoring Strategy Guide. Can you think of ways that you could integrate these strategies into your teaching to help students better comprehend the content you are trying to teach while extending their meta-cognitive awareness?

USE MULTIPLE READING STRATEGIES

Researchers and educators have argued about the relative value of single and multiple strategy instruction. If several strategies (predict, clarify, summarize, question) are taught simultaneously, students might not be able to do any of them well. Over time, however, students also need practice using multiple strategies together. Through proper modeling and introduction of each strategy, this concern can be addressed (Block, Schaller, Joy, & Gaine, 2002).

Multiple strategy instruction refers to those instructional practices that teach several reading strategies simultaneously (NICHD, 2000). These instructional practices mirror the reality of strategic reading. They ask students to learn a flexible repertoire of strategies that they can apply when reading challenging text. Multiple strategy methods give students explicit strategies to help scaffold their comprehension monitoring and should be fostered across the content areas.

History

To comprehend world history, government, and U.S. history texts, students must use multiple reading strategies if they are to expand content competency. For example, when learning about the Jefferson Era, U.S. history students can activate and build their background knowledge about Jefferson, use graphic organizers while reading about the Louisiana Purchase, summarize Jefferson's policies, and ask and answer questions about what brought about the War of 1812. By using multiple strategies, students will better understand this period in American history and how it has impacted us today.

Science

Comprehension will also increase if students use multiple reading strategies in science. In one example, a sixth-grade science teacher designed a sequence of lessons about civil engineering, encouraging the use of multiple reading strategies. Her students had to synthesize several passages of text about bridge design, as they sought to understand the different types of bridges— "suspension," "beam," and "arch." Students then decided which type of structure would be the strongest to build.

Mathematics

Mathematics classes provide a setting for lesson sequences that encourage the use of multiple reading strategies. To be successful, students must reflect on their background knowledge about a concept, summarize the new computational processes, and monitor their comprehension along the way. This is especially critical for Algebra II students who have had a year-long hiatus from algebra while they learn geometry. When they begin to relearn radical expressions during Algebra II, they must reflect back into their prior knowledge to then extend their learning in this area.

Language Arts

Literature and English teachers will find that the predominately fictional text of this content area also lends itself well to the use of multiple reading strategies by students. For example, while reading *Romeo and Juliet*, students can engage in the use of multiple strategies as they seek to follow the story plot and understand the depth of the characters.

Electives

It is essential for vocational education teachers to structure lessons so that students can use multiple reading strategies. Some students may have a passion for hands-on building in automotive, wood, or metal shop classes, but they may struggle with text directions. Integrating strategies will help foster students' understanding and stimulate their reading comprehension skills.

Two instructional practices are Reciprocal Teaching and PLAN (Predict, Locate, Add, Note). Both of these allow students to experience multi-strategy models to better prepare them for the rigors of independent comprehension.

Reciprocal Teaching

Reciprocal Teaching is a systematic way of monitoring comprehension in small groups (Palincsar & Brown, 1984). After teacher modeling, student groups engage with a text and apply four strategies—predicting, clarifying, questioning, and summarizing. Studies show that students who receive training make lasting gains in reading comprehension performance as indicated by their scores on multiple-choice comprehension tests over time (Palincsar & Brown, 1984). Research also indicates that Reciprocal Teaching can be used as a base for engaging in a wider array of literacy skills and inquiry in various subject areas. As students become accustomed to the process, the scaffold of Reciprocal Teaching falls away. Students continue to use the process, but they also begin to engage in more complex forms of discourse such as argumentation and explanation (A. L. Brown & Campione, 1992).

PROCEDURE

Teacher Tool

A Reciprocal Teaching Organizer (TT15) is available for you to copy from the Teacher Tools Appendix.

1. Choose text that is appropriately leveled and divided into several sections, by paragraph or subheading.
2. Activate and/or build background knowledge before the actual reading begins.
3. Put students into mixed-ability cooperative groups of four. Each group of four chooses a learning leader or the teacher assigns a leader.
4. Students *predict* about the first section of text. Predictions can be based on headings, charts, and graphics. Students can use the Survey Strategy to help them during this time.
5. The group reads the first section of text silently or chorally, stopping frequently to *clarify* confusion of words, sentences, paragraphs, or ideas. Use the "Interactive Think Aloud," "Comprehension Monitoring Strategy Guides," or "Cornell Notes" described in this chapter.
6. When finished reading, the discussion leader facilitates the group to *summarize* what has been read. "Written, Oral, and Visual Summaries" previously described can be used to guide this process.
7. In addition, she/he asks the group to *question* themselves to see if they can answer *Right There* and *Inference* questions about the text as were described with "QAR" in this chapter.
8. The group then repeats the cycle with the next section of text.

VARIATIONS   There are different ways Reciprocal Teaching can be structured to help support student learning of multiple reading strategies. One way to model the strategies is through a fishbowl, in which the teacher works with a small group, while other students observe. During the fishbowl, the teacher can act as a learning leader and model appropriate conversation and group behaviors.

Another is the use of predetermined student roles— predictor, clarifier, questioner, summarizer. This ensures that each student has an opportunity to participate and also that each is held accountable.

Strategy cards can also be used to aid recall of the key components of each individual strategy. Prompts for each strategy, along with the headings "predict, clarify, summarize, and question" can be printed out on cards and fastened together with binder rings for each student to hold.

Lastly, students can use a Reciprocal Teaching Organizer like the one shown in Figure 4.26, to help them record their predictions, note areas for clarification, summarize, and ask and answer questions.

Predict

I think…

we will learn about

- *Sources*
  - *Contaminates*
  - *Smog*
- *Solutions*
  - *Prevention*
  - *Control*
  - *Cleaning*

of air pollution

Question

Factual

Who? *Monitors air pollution*
What? *Can be done about it*
When? *Will we reach a point of hazardous air quality*
Where? *Are the cleanest places to live*

Interpretive

Why? *Don't people stop polluting our air*
How? *Can it be controlled*

Air Pollution

I thought…

Air pollution wasn't as bad as it is described here

The main point is…

- *air contaminates pollute our air*
  CO-carbon monoxide
  Pb-lead
  NO-Nitrogen oxides
  VOC-Volatile organic compounds
  PM-Particulate matter
  SO_2-Sulfur dioxide
- *photochemical smog adds to the problem*
  Hydrocarbons + Sun + O_2 + CO + NOx →
  O_3 + NO_2 + irritants + CO_2 + H_2O

When I read, I realized…

Something must be done about air quality in the USA

Summarize

Clarify

FIGURE 4.26   Reciprocal Teaching Organizer Example for Chemistry

PLAN (Predict, Locate, Add, Note)

The PLAN strategy guides students in using concept mapping to identify information that is known and information that is new from the text (Caverly, Mandeville, & Nicholson, 1995). The PLAN strategy is built upon research showing that concept maps and graphic organizers are beneficial for science instruction (Stoddart, Abrams, Gasper, & Canaday, 2000). Research about this strategy shows that it effectively helps students comprehend text in science classrooms (Radcliffe, Caverly, Hand, & Franke, 2008; Radcliffe, Caverly, Peterson, & Emmons, 2004). Figure 4.27a shows the PLAN concept map for physics and 4.27b shows the completed map at the end of the lesson.

Before the Lesson (shows prediction based on headings)

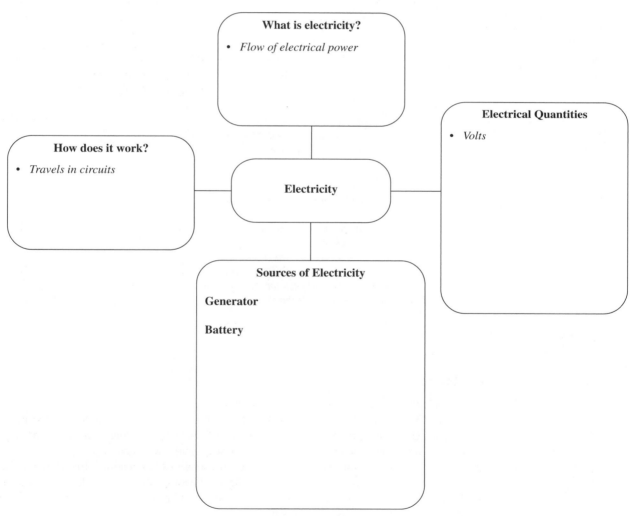

FIGURE 4.27a   PLAN Strategy Example for Physics

After the Lesson (shows concepts located, added and noted after reading)

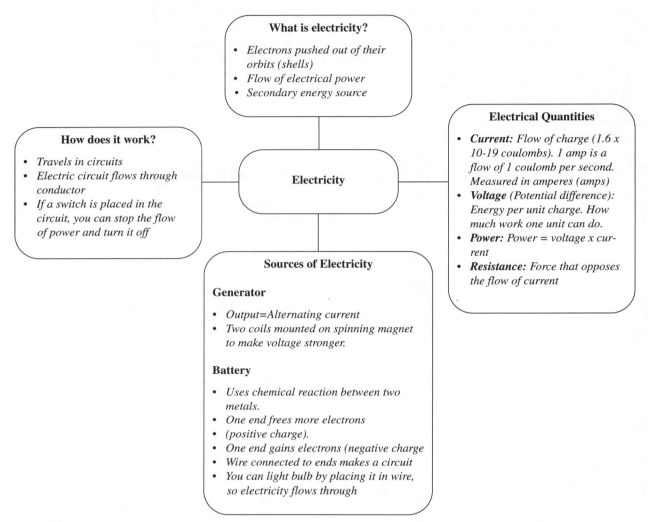

What is electricity?

- *Electrons pushed out of their orbits (shells)*
- *Flow of electrical power*
- *Secondary energy source*

How does it work?

- *Travels in circuits*
- *Electric circuit flows through conductor*
- *If a switch is placed in the circuit, you can stop the flow of power and turn it off*

Electricity

Electrical Quantities

- ***Current:*** *Flow of charge (1.6 x 10-19 coulombs). 1 amp is a flow of 1 coulomb per second. Measured in amperes (amps)*
- ***Voltage*** *(Potential difference): Energy per unit charge. How much work one unit can do.*
- ***Power:*** *Power = voltage x current*
- ***Resistance:*** *Force that opposes the flow of current*

Sources of Electricity

Generator

- *Output=Alternating current*
- *Two coils mounted on spinning magnet to make voltage stronger.*

Battery

- *Uses chemical reaction between two metals.*
- *One end frees more electrons*
- *(positive charge).*
- *One end gains electrons (negative charge*
- *Wire connected to ends makes a circuit*
- *You can light bulb by placing it in wire, so electricity flows through*

FIGURE 4.27b

PROCEDURE

1. Select a content area appropriately leveled text passage.
2. *Predict:* Students use text clues (such as title, graphics) to predict content and structure of the text. Using this preliminary understanding of the text, they construct a concept map that visually links the content. They label their concept maps with headings.
3. *Locate:* On the concept map, students place a check next to headings that they have some knowledge of. They place a question mark next to headings they have little knowledge about.
4. *Add:* While reading the text, students add words and phrases to the concept map, to explain the unknown and confirm the known.
5. *Note:* After reading, students revise the map, engage in a discussion, or perform another task that is relevant to the content.

VARIATIONS   PLAN is very versatile in that it can be used as a supportive strategy whenever students are learning new content. For example, it can be used to scaffold student learning during a science lab. First, students *predict* what they will discover. Next, they *locate* on a concept map what is known and not yet known. While engaged in the experiment, they add to the map. Then, after completing the experiment, they can note new knowledge on the map and discuss their findings (Radcliffe, et al., 2008).

Conclusion

Reciprocal Teaching and PLAN are both effective in providing readers opportunities to practice simultaneously using different reading strategies to improve comprehension. Teachers can use multiple strategy instruction in all content areas to help under-prepared, and even proficient readers read more strategically.

 *Learning Log*

Revisit the K-W-L Strategy Chart found in the Learning Log Appendix (LL2) to increase your comprehension and practice implementing the final step of this effective comprehension strategy described earlier in this chapter.

PAUSE and REFLECT 4.7

Students need practice with multiple strategy use in the context of the content areas. Consider how you may be able to use Reciprocal Teaching or PLAN with a content concept that you are preparing to teach.

Chapter Summary

This chapter describes numerous instructional strategies that teachers can embed into content area teaching to help students increase their comprehension and deepen conceptual knowledge. Best instructional practices focus on activating and building prior knowledge, using graphic organizers, summarizing, asking and answering questions, monitoring comprehension, and using multiple strategies (Boardman, et al., 2008). By embedding these strategies into content area reading, teachers guide students in strategic reading that is sustained, intentional, and deepens content knowledge. The ultimate goal of comprehension strategy instruction is for students to independently use and adapt these strategies to different contexts.

This chapter began with a description of Austin, a reader who was motivated, fluent, and had a strong vocabulary; however, his comprehension was not yet proficient.

How can a teacher respond? By integrating knowledge of reading comprehension strategies described here, with an understanding of the learner, teachers can make an informed decision about the type of instruction that would be beneficial. Applying instructional strategies thoughtfully, in a sequence of assessment, reflecting, planning, and instruction, will help to foster content literacy. And Austin will carry the ability to read strategically into a successful future.

PAUSE and REFLECT 4.8

List the six goals of comprehension instruction. Can you think of ways that you could improve your content instruction by integrating some of the strategies described in this chapter?

Resources

Bjork, C. (1987). *Linnea in Monet's Garden*. New York: R & S Books.

Bradbury, R. (1953). *Fahrenheit 451*. New York: Ballantine Books.

Gleijeses, P. (2003). *Conflicting missions: Havana, Washington, and Africa 195–1976*. University of North Carolina Press.

Orwell, G. (1949). *1984*. New York: Signet (1981).

References

Afflerback, P., Pearson, P. D., & Paris, S. (2008). Clarifying differences between reading skills and reading strategies. *The Reading Teacher, 61*(5), 364–373.

Anderson, R. C., & Pearson, P. D. (1984). A schemata-theoretic view of basic processes in reading. In P. D. Pearson, R. Barr, M. L. Kamil, & P. Mosenthal, (Eds.), *Handbook of reading research* (pp. 255–291). New York: Longman.

Arnold, R. A. (2007). *Economics: New ways of thinking*. St. Paul, MN: EMC Publishing.

Assaf, L., & Garza, R. (2007). Making magazine covers that visually count: Learning to summarize with technology. *The Reading Teacher, 60*(7), 678–680.

Baker, L. (2002). Metacognition in reading comprehension. In C. C. Block & M. Pressley (Eds.), *Comprehension instruction: Research-based best practices* (pp. 77–95). New York: Guilford Press.

Block, C. C., Schaller, J. L., Joy, J. A., & Gaine, P. (2002). Process-based comprehension instruction. In C. C. Block & M. Pressley (Eds.), *Comprehension instruction: Research-based practices* (pp. 42–61). New York: Guilford.

Boardman, A. G., Roberts, G., Vaughn, S., Wexler, J., Murray, C. S., & Kosanovich, M. (2008) Effective instruction for adolescent struggling readers: A practice brief. Portsmouth, NH: RMC Research Corporation, Center on Instruction.

Boyle, J. (2000). The effects of a venn diagram strategy on the literal, inferential, and relational comprehension of students with mild disabilities. *Learning Disabilities: A Multidisciplinary Journal, 10*(1), 5–13.

Brown, A. L., & Campione, J. (1992). *Fostering a community of learners. Progress report prepared for the Andrew W. Mellon Foundation*. University of California, Berkeley.

Brown, R. (2002). Straddling two worlds: Self-directed comprehension instruction for middle schoolers. In C. C. Block & M. Pressley (Eds.), *Comprehension instruction: Research-based best practices* (pp. 337–350). New York: Guilford.

California Department of Education. (2000). *Strategic Teaching and Learning: Standards-based instruction to promote content literacy in grades 4-12*. Sacramento, CA: CDE Press.

Cambourne, B. (2002). The conditions of learning: Is learning natural? *The Reading Teacher, 55*(8), 758–762.

Caverly, D., Mandeville, T., & Nicholson, S. (1995). PLAN: A study reading strategy for informational text. *Journal of Adolescent and Adult Literacy, 39*, 190–199.

Curran, M., & Smith, C. (2005). The imposter: A motivational strategy to encourage reading in adolescents. *Journal of Adolescent and Adult Literacy, 49*(3), 186–190.

Flood, J., Lapp, D., & Bayles-Martin, D. (2000). The role of visual media in literacy education. In M. A. Gallego & S. Hollingsworth (Eds.), *What counts as literacy: Challenging the school standard* (pp. 62–84). New York: Teacher's College Press.

Fuhler, C. J., Farris, P. J., & Nelson, P. A. (2006). Building literacy skills across the curriculum: Forging connections with the past through artifacts. *The Reading Teacher, 59*(7), 646–659.

Ghent, C. A. (2008). *Effectiveness of false correction strategy on science reading comprehension*. Graduate School of the University of Maryland.

Graham, S., & Perin, D. (2007). Writing next: Effective strategies to improve writing of adolescents in middle and high schools. A report to the Carnegie Corporation of New York. Washington, DC: Alliance for Excellent Education.

Kane, S. (2007). Does the imposter strategy pass the authenticity test? *Journal of Adolescent & Adult Literacy, 51*(1), 58–64.

Keane, N. J. (2005). *Using Literature in the middle school classroom*. Columbus, OH: Linworth.

Kim, A., Vaughn, S., Wanzek, J., & Wei, S. (2004). Graphic organizers and their effects on the reading comprehension of students with LD: A synthesis of research. *Journal of Learning Disabilities, 37*, 105–118.

Lapp, D., Fisher, D., & Grant, M. (2008). You can read this text—I'll show you how: Interactive comprehension instruction. *Journal of Adolescent & Adult Literacy, 51*(5), 372–383.

Marzano, R. J. (2004). *Building background knowledge for academic achievement: What works in schools*. Alexandria, VA: Association for Supervision and Curriculum Development.

Marzano, R. J., Pickering, D., & Pollock, J. E. (2001). *Classroom instruction that works: Research-based best practices for increasing student achievement*. Alexandria, VA: Association of Supervision and Curriculum Development.

Massey, D. D. (2007). "The Discovery Channel said so" and other barriers to comprehension. *The Reading Teacher, 60*(7), 656–666.

National Institute of Child Health and Human Development (NICHD)(2000). *Report of the National Reading Panel: Teaching children to read: An evidence-based assessment of the scientific research literature on reading and its implications for reading instruction*.

Nelson, J. (2007). AVIDly seeking success. *Educational Leadership, 64*(7), 72–74.

Neufeld, P. (2005). Comprehension instruction in content area classes. *The Reading Teacher, 59*(4), 301–312.

Nokes, J. D. (2008). The observation/inference chart: Improving students' abilities to make inferences while reading nontraditional texts. *Journal of Adolescent & Adult Literacy, 51*(7), 538–546.

Nokes, J. D., & Dole, J. A. (2004). Helping adolescent readers through explicit strategy instruction. In T. L. Jetton & J. A. Dole (Eds.), *Adolescent literacy: Research and practice* (pp. 162–182). New York: Guilford Press.

Ogle, D. M. (1986). K-W-L: A teaching model that develops active reading of expository text. *The Reading Teacher, 39*(6), 564–570.

Palincsar, A. S., & Brown, A. L. (1984). Reciprocal teaching of comprehension-fostering and monitoring activities. *Cognition and Instruction, 1*(2), 117-175.

Paris, S. G., Wasik, B. A., & Turner, J. C. (1991). The development of strategic readers. In R. Barr, M. L. Kamil, P. Mosenthal, & P. D. Pearson (Eds.), *The handbook of reading research* (Vol. II, pp. 609–640). Mahwah, NJ: Erlbaum.

Pauk, W., & Owens, R. (2007). *How to study in college* (9th ed.). Boston, MA: Houghton-Mifflin.

Pearson, P. D. (1985). Changing the face of comprehension instruction. *The Reading Teacher, 38*, 724–738.

Pressley, M. (2002). Metacognition and self-regulated comprehension. In A. E. Farstrup & S. J. Samuels (Eds.), *What research has to say about reading instruction.* (pp. 291–309). Newark, DE: International Reading Association.

Pressley, M., & Afflerbach, P. (1995). *Verbal protocols of reading: The nature of constructively responsive reading.* Hillsdale, NJ: Erlbaum.

Radcliffe, R., Caverly, D., Hand, J., & Franke, D. (2008). Improving reading in a middle school science classroom. *Journal of Adolescent & Adult Literacy, 51*(5)598-6408.

Radcliffe, R., Caverly, D., Peterson, C., & Emmons, M. (2004). Improving textbook reading in a middle school social studies classroom. *Reading Improvement, 41*, 145–156.

Raphael, T. (1986). Teaching question answer relationships, revisited. *The Reading Teacher, 39*(6), 516–522.

Shanahan, T., & Shanahan, C. (2008). Teaching content area literacy to adolescents: Rethinking content area literacy. *Harvard Educational Review, 78*(1), 41–59.

Spires, H. (1992). Effects of schema-based and text-structure-based cues on expository prose comprehension in fourth graders. *Journal of Experimental Education, 60*(4), 307–320.

Stoddart, T., Abrams, R., Gasper, E., & Canaday, D. (2000). Concept maps as assessment in science inquiry learning—A report of methodology. *The International Journal of Science Education, 22*(12), 1221–1246.

Topping, D. H., & McManus, R. A. (2002). A culture of literacy in science. *Educational Leadership, 60*(3), 30–33.

Willingham, D. T. (Winter 2006/2007). How we learn: Ask the cognitive scientist. *American Educator* (pp. 39–44).

Yamamoto, M. (2007). *Cornell notes in a science classroom: Question formulation as a means of cognitive engagement.* (Masters thesis). University of California: Davis, Davis, CA.

CHAPTER 5

Strategies to Initiate and Sustain Motivation

"Where on earth have you been?" yelled Jake's mom as he came in through the door at 11 P.M.

Jake, a senior at Valley High School, was usually really good about letting his mom know where he was going after football practice, but today he ignored the cell phone calls she had made to him and never called to let her know where he was.

"I was hanging out with my friends." Jake replied. He knew he was avoiding going home to his mom and having to answer her questions about his progress report.

"Your teacher called today to let me know that you didn't pass government on your progress report. Do you know what that means? You'll go on academic probation and not get to play. You know what will happen to your future if those recruiters from the university can't watch you play! Jake, you know how important this is. What is going on?" his mom asked.

"The reading for that class is stupid. I have to read a section in my book every week. They're like 40 pages with hecka tiny print. Then, I've gotta answer questions about it. It counts for half of my grade. It's *#!*."

"How many assignments did you complete?" inquired Mom.

"Well I did the first two and then figured out how I could participate in the class and sound like I had read if I just paid attention instead of taking my usual pre-practice power nap. As far as the assignments, I haven't read much except for those first few weeks. Mom, you should see what we have to read. In class we are learning about famous law cases that forever changed the civil rights of Americans— like Brown vs. Board of Education, but the book spends most of the chapter talking about other garbage and barely talks about what we are learning. If the book was actually interesting and had something to do with what we are talking about in class, I'd read it."

"Jake, this is ridiculous. You are a good reader, and you are failing history. I am going to set up a meeting with your teacher tomorrow."

"Go ahead, Mom, but it isn't going to change anything. Mrs. Stephens has been teaching at that school for a hundred years, and she isn't going to change the reading now. Just forget it. Who cares about it anyway?"

"I care," said Jake's mom, "and you should too."

Jake exemplifies many middle and high school students who are proficient in their vocabulary, fluency, and/or comprehension skills, yet who are unmotivated to read, and as a result, fail to pass content area classes and further develop their literacy.

Conversely, there are other students who struggle to be proficient in each or all of these literacy skills. As a result, they too are not motivated to practice reading because they already feel defeated. They avoid reading tasks and miss opportunities to practice reading strategies, develop reading skills, and learn from content text. This vicious cycle must be stopped.

Research continues to show that there is a clear, positive, and complex relationship between motivation and reading comprehension (Guthrie & Wigfield, 2000). It is therefore imperative that teachers use strategies, like those described in this chapter, to motivate students to read and help them move toward becoming more literate.

As was explained in the previous chapters, studies have shown that it is important to use and teach vocabulary, fluency, and comprehension strategies and skills while students are engaged with text. Under these conditions, students have the desire to make sense of the context, and they are more likely to monitor comprehension and apply strategies (Alvermann, 2002). However, teachers of adolescents often find themselves wondering how to help students become engaged in reading. This chapter focuses on strategies to initiate and sustain motivation for adolescents.

Motivation is a process by which a goal-directed activity is both initiated and sustained (Schunk, Pintrich, & Meece, 2008). The emphasis on goals is especially important in relationship to learning, because goals provide a reason to act. With literacy, three related motivational constructs, *value of reading*, *self-concept*, and *interests* impact reading performance.

VALUE OF READING Students' motivation is determined by their values, needs, and goals. If a literacy task closely matches these, then the student is more likely to engage in the task. When the task does not match needs and values, a student may become a **reluctant reader**—a reader who is capable of reading, but, when faced with a particular task, chooses not to. Research has shown that many adolescent males lack this **value of reading** related to school subjects (Newkirk, 2002).

SELF-CONCEPT **Self-concept** involves a student's perceptions of his or her own competence (Schunk, et al., 2008). Researchers in the area of motivation find that students develop self-concepts about academics in general and about specific domains like reading. Self-concept differs from self-esteem in that self-concept is a cognitive understanding of competence, and self-esteem is an emotional reaction or evaluation of oneself.

If I know I can read well, I have a high self-concept as a reader.

If I feel good about myself for being a good reader, I have high self-esteem.

INTERESTS Interest can be defined as the liking and willful engagement in an activity (Schraw & Lehman, 2001). There are two types of interest: personal interest and situational interest (Krapp, Hidi, & Renninger, 1992). **Personal interest** is an enduring characteristic of an individual, while **situational interest** refers to the contextual features that make some task or activity interesting. For any task to be enduring, it needs to move from one of situational interest to personal interest. However, when asked about reading at school, many adolescent readers will cite lack of interest as a reason why they could, but don't read (Lenters, 2006). Lenters concludes that by making instruction relevant to students we help them switch from situational to personal interest.

Teachers cannot control all of the factors that contribute to student engagement. However, they can control certain elements of the context. Researchers and educators who specialize in motivation for reading have made numerous suggestions for teachers. These suggestions may not "create" motivation with every learner, especially reluctant adolescents. However, they can help to create an environment in which students are engaged in the learning process. And if a student experiences engagement, he may become more engaged in future reading experiences.

Research suggests that adolescent learners will become more motivated if teachers can work toward these three instructional goals:

1. Foster student control and choice,
2. Encourage collaboration, and
3. Ensure mastery of content and literacy skills.

Literacy Component	Goals of Instruction	Strategies for Instruction
Motivation	Foster Student Control and Choice	• Socratic Seminars • WebQuests
	Encourage Collaboration	• Learning Clubs • PALS (Peer Assisted Learning Strategies)
	Ensure Mastery of Content and Literacy Skills	• Scaffolded Reading Experiences • CORI (Concept-Oriented Reading Instruction)

FIGURE 5.1 Motivation Strategy Summary Chart

The strategies described in this chapter, outlined in Figure 5.1, will help teachers meet these goals.

FOSTER STUDENT CONTROL AND CHOICE

Allowing students to have some control over their learning is a central component in fostering motivation. Students who perceive more control over their reading or writing are more engaged in literacy activities (Reeve, Jang, Carrell, Jeon, & Barch, 2004). In one study, teachers were trained to support students' autonomy during instruction. They accomplished this by offering students choices about what tasks to perform. Researchers found that students in autonomy-supportive classrooms were more engaged in instruction than students in classrooms where student autonomy was not supported.

Why is student control so important? During adolescence, students are constantly examining their identities. They are negotiating between many roles and multiple life contexts. Reading allows adolescents to explore and form their identities (Richardson & Eccles, 2007); they are drawn to texts that can help them learn about who they are and who they hope to become. Having some autonomy is important in this developmental process.

In addition, as adolescents begin to form an identity, any support of this identity will help motivation that is more internally focused. If reading can focus on an area that is important to a student's identity, like that of being a swimmer or a musician, a close connection can be made between reading and the student's sense of self. By carefully considering ways to foster control and choice, reading (and all academics) can become integrated into a student's identity, rather than being excluded from it. This is more favorable than the alternative, in which a teen feels that the context of school does not reflect or support his identity. That lack of perceived control over school tasks can lead to decreased motivation and behaviors that can be interpreted as illiterate (Reed, Schallert, Beth, & Woodruff, 2004).

Unfortunately, adolescent students often are given less control and choice over school tasks than they experienced in elementary school. Teachers of older students are focused on instructing sometimes as many as 150 students each day, and the idea of allowing control and choice sounds overwhelming. The answer lies in finding a balance between instruction that is overly teacher-centered and overly student-centered (Fillman & Guthrie, 2008). Fillman and Guthrie (2008) and other educators offer suggestions for promoting student control and choice. Three of the most important are to encourage ownership of text, provide options in learning from text, and seek student input into the curriculum.

ENCOURAGE OWNERSHIP OF TEXT In school, students expect content area reading to be assigned and controlled by the teacher. In this context, the teacher, not the student, is the "owner" of the text and the reading experience. One way that students can gain ownership is by being allowed to choose which text to read. When possible, allow students to search magazine articles, Web sites, and zines for text passages that will help them better understand the content.

It is not always possible to allow students to choose the text. In this case, students can gain ownership by making choices within the text that they are reading. For example, when given a text with multiple sections, individual students or small groups can focus on one area of the text. When individuals or groups of students focus on one aspect of the text, they gain ownership of their specific area of expertise. The structure of such an activity is often called "jigsaw" (Aronson, 1978). In a jigsaw activity, a student becomes an expert and exchanges knowledge with a peer.

Even choices that seem simple may be effective. Fillmore and Guthrie (2008) tell an anecdote of a math teacher whose students did not complete homework on word problems. To respond, he gave them a choice of doing the odd or the even problems. He found that even this simple choice led to 90 percent of his class completing the problems. Many even read all the problems in order to decide which set, odd or even, they preferred.

PROVIDE OPTIONS IN LEARNING FROM TEXT.   Another way to foster control and choice is to allow students to choose how they approach text and display their understanding. This can vary from the way they approach the reading, to the support strategies they use while reading, to the product they create when the reading is complete. When students make sense of text and express their understanding in a new way that makes sense to them, they "transform" the text (Douglass & Guthrie, 2008). Reading comprehension strategies, like those described in Chapter 4 (e.g., Outcome Graphic Organizers, Cornell Notes, Comprehension Monitoring Strategy Guides, and Evidence Guide Graphic Organizers), can be used to help students transform the text from words that are read on a page to a format that they produce while reading. Similarly, when the reading and transformation of text are completed, students can take ownership of their "new" text in whatever format they have created (e.g., Written Summary, Visual Summary). This new text can serve as a valuable assessment of student content and literacy learning.

SEEK INPUT INTO THE CURRICULUM.   Given the ever-increasing demands placed on teachers, allowing students input into the curriculum sounds impossible. However, students can give input into which topics to study most deeply and how those topics will be addressed and assessed. Allowing students to choose topics will help them to explore their interests and assist in the process of developing their identities as they move into adulthood.

Student control and choice can be integrated across all content areas. In each content area, there are different choices of texts that can be used to enhance instruction and allow for student ownership of the reading. For example, social science teachers can provide supplementary reading material for students who have a particular interest about a topic; journal entries written by Meriwether Lewis and William Clark are readable texts that complement student understanding about the Louisiana Purchase. Articles in popular science magazines, such as *Scientific American*, serve as texts to support concepts learned in chemistry and physics.

Student control and choice can also happen in all content areas as students extract and record information gained from text. Teachers who guide student practice with comprehension strategies can later give students the freedom to select which strategies to use when working independently. For example, students in an eighth-grade U.S. history class use Cornell Notes, Written Summaries, or Graphic Organizers to record their notes. When it comes time to take the test, the teacher allows them to use their notes. This approach gives students the opportunity to find which strategies work best for them as they make meaning from text.

Lastly, students in all areas can give teachers input into the curriculum so they feel they have control and choice. For example, after seven 4-H sheep died, students in an agricultural science class asked to study about diseases that affect sheep. In another case, a teacher asked eighth-grade U.S. history students what they wanted to learn about the 2008 presidential election. The teacher then planned for learning that met the standards and the students' interests.

Resource

Teachers may want to have students search Teen Life: Magazines and E-zines at http://www.dmoz.org/Kids_and_Teens/Teen_Life/Magazines_and_E-zines/

Of many motivating instructional strategies, two in particular, Socratic Seminars and WebQuests, best illustrate how reading can occur during lessons to promote student choice and control.

Socratic Seminars

Socratic Seminars are based on an ancient mode of discourse attributed to Socrates. The premise is that by engaging in systematic inquiry through Socratic discourse, one can discover the truth. Teachers use this method to engage students in critical thinking, reading, and discussion (Coke, 2008).

Socratic Seminars have a number of identifying characteristics. First, a Socratic Seminar focuses on one central theme. The topic of inquiry has multiple perspectives and enough depth to pull students into layers of meaning. Second, a Socratic Seminar involves a reading or sets of readings. Students must complete the background reading before engaging in the seminar. Third, the Socratic Seminar is rich with dialog. Finally, students have control over the direction of inquiry.

Resource

Resources on Socratic Seminars can be found at: http://www.webenglishteacher.com/socratic.html.

In a Socratic Seminar, the teacher serves as a facilitator and a member of the group. Students serve as leaders who are in charge of designing questions, preparing material, and leading the discussion. The discussion that occurs is intended to be open, with many voices offering ideas supported with evidence from reading. This approach is different from the more familiar **Initiation-Response-Evaluation** approach (IRE) in which a teacher asks a question, a student answers, and the teacher evaluates. Because facilitating the discussion takes some skill, teachers can become trained in how to enact Socratic Seminars in their classrooms.

PROCEDURE

Plan

1. Decide on a leader or leaders for the seminar. The leader can be the teacher, but is often a student or group of students.
2. The leader (in collaboration with the class) chooses a guiding question for the discussion. Before the seminar, students generate other related questions.
3. The leader assigns a reading that relates to the guiding question. While reading, students engage in a during-reading activity, such as making notes of their responses as they read. The notes from the reading can serve as a "ticket" into the Socratic Seminar—if students don't do the reading, they can observe but not engage in the dialog (Coke, 2008). Another option is to have students read and write some important questions before coming to class; questions connecting the text to self, world, other texts.

Teach

1. Begin with students sitting in a circle.
2. Students establish goals. For example, they might decide that every point needs to refer back to the text.
3. Students begin talking. The leader serves as a facilitator, making sure that the conversation is focused on the questions and that any established ground rules are respected.
4. Encourage dialog in the following ways:
   a. Ask **open-ended questions**. Open-ended questions are those without obvious answers. Open-ended questions require more thought than closed questions.
   b. Give students time to think about the answers; this is also known as **wait time**.
   c. Encourage students to respond to each other and build on ideas of previous speakers.
   d. The leader will need to help the group decide when to explore the answer and when to move on. The leader can encourage exploration by asking for clarification, textual support, and contributions from others. To move on, the leader can summarize, revisit a previous idea, or ask a new question.

The Socratic Seminar allows students to experience choice and control. Students help choose the questions and direct the seminar. This choice and control allow students to have a voice in what they study and to proceed in a way that is meaningful to them. In addition, by connecting the text to their discussion, students have an opportunity to explore the text and take ownership of it during their dialog. The teacher does not interpret the text for the students.

VARIATIONS   Steinbeck and Cook (2001) describe a variation of Socratic Seminars as part of a unit on social security. In their adaptation, the seminar had several student leaders, each who lead during a different question. Changing leaders encouraged more students to practice taking on a leadership role. Students in the seminar were all encouraged to participate. The leaders called on students, and students could choose to pass.

Socratic Seminars often work best with groups of 12 to 15 students, therefore, some modifications will need to be made for the average middle and high school class. One modification is to create a fishbowl with two concentric circles. The inner group engages in the seminar, and the outer group observes and records the group process. Then, after the discussion, the two groups come together and debrief both the content and the process of the seminar. Another option is to conduct two Socratic Seminars within the classroom once the students are adept at using the strategy.

WebQuests

A WebQuest is another example of an instructional method that, when used thoughtfully, can give students choice and control over the learning process (Dodge, 2001). In a WebQuest, the learner engages in an online inquiry about a particular topic. The concept was developed in 1995 by a team of teachers and university faculty from San Diego State University. Beginning in 1996, San Diego State began building a database of WebQuests. At the time this book was written, there were over 2,500 available on the site. In addition, the site links new users to a series of YouTube videos that explain how to use WebQuests in the classroom (Dodge, 2001).

Resource

The San Diego State University WebQuest page is located at http://webquest.org/

Some key characteristics are present in every WebQuest. They focus on a relevant, real-life task, and they require students to use the web to achieve a goal. The process requires thinking; it is not one in which students follow a pre-determined procedure.

WebQuests can be found on the Internet or a teacher may choose to create one. Many teachers choose to use existing WebQuests and make adaptations to them that suit their classroom (Ikpeze & Boyd, 2007). Following are the procedures for conducting a WebQuest.

PROCEDURE

1. Plan
   a. *Choose a task.* To be effective, the task must be complex enough to engage students' thinking and exploration. Within each task, there are sub-tasks that provide necessary content knowledge.
   b. *Organize the process.* Write directions for how students should progress through the task.
   c. *List the resources.* Develop a list of teacher-approved Web sites for student reference. Each of these Web sites should be user-friendly.
   d. *Design an evaluation.* Plan an assessment method so that students will understand the expectations of a WebQuest. Many WebQuests include a rubric.
2. Teach
   a. *Introduce.* Introduce students to the topic or scenario in which they will be engaged. Discuss the teacher-developed rubric or help students create a class rubric for evaluation. Teach or review necessary computer navigation skills. Show students the start page of the WebQuest and where to find particular links.

   b. *Guide*. Help students navigate through the WebQuest so that they can meet the instructional goal.

   c. *Debrief*. After the WebQuest, engage in reflection and discussion about learning. Discuss ways in which the WebQuest fits with the context of the larger unit or course goals.

   d. *Evaluate*. Engage in evaluation of the WebQuest itself and the assessment of student learning.

Resource

A full description of "Water Safari"can be found at the Peace Corps Coverdell World Wise Schools Site http://www.peacecorps.gov/wws/educators/enrichment/africa/lessons/MSgeog04/index.html

For example, a WebQuest called "Water Safari, A Journey of Life" was designed for middle school students to explore water as a resource in seven African countries (Ray, 2000). The WebQuest was created in partnership with the Peace Corps and makes use of the Peace Corp's "Water in Africa" Website. During the WebQuest, student teams work approximately 45 minutes for seven days to conduct research on the relationship between humans and water resources. The outcome is a formal report that will help the Peace Corps develop a video to train volunteers in Africa.

In studies of WebQuests, findings suggest that students learn about the same amount of content as they do with other instructional methods. Research does, however, suggest that students are more motivated when engaging in WebQuests than when they engage in more traditional forms of instruction (Abbit & Orphus, 2008). While there is not a clear explanation for why they are more motivated, one explanation could be the amount of choice and control that they experience in the WebQuest. As they navigate, students are constantly making choices about which text to read. From the keyboard, they are directing their own learning and using electronic texts to complete the task at hand.

Resource

Critters! is available free of charge at http://www.agentmodeler.org.

VARIATIONS   A close relative to the WebQuest is a computer simulation, in which students learn important concepts while making choices about how to apply those concepts to significant situations. One such example, *Critters*! (Latham & Scully, 2008), gives students the opportunity to learn about genetics and adaptations. Rather than navigating to different Web sites, students have control and choice within the simulation itself.

Conclusion

Control and choice are important for adolescent learners. Autonomy has been found to be especially important when guiding English learners in the reading process. From their study of English learners, Short and Fitzsimmons (2007) found that students should be offered choice of text, of task, and of partner. This means that they have input into what they read, what they do with the reading, and who they work with. If teachers can provide lessons and units of study that encourage ownership, provide options in learning from text, and seek input into the curriculum, students will be more willing to engage in learning. Socratic Seminars and WebQuests, as described above, are dynamic examples of these aspects in action.

PAUSE and REFLECT 5.1

Consider the three suggestions for promoting student control and choice. How can you integrate Socratic Seminars and/or WebQuests into your teaching so that your students are motivated to learn content and expand their literacy?

ENCOURAGE COLLABORATION

Collaboration is another instructional practice that supports motivation. When students engage in social interactions around a text, they develop a sense of belonging and are more willing to continue when the text is challenging (Wenzel, 2005). Additionally, interaction fosters the use of oral language—an important component to building fluency with language. In the classroom, teachers can build collaboration by providing opportunities for collaborative reasoning, building reading partnerships, and scaffolding social interactions (Antonio & Guthrie, 2008).

PROVIDE OPPORTUNITIES FOR COLLABORATIVE REASONING   An authentic way to create collaboration is for students to work together using text to solve problems. For collaboration to be successful, students must have an authentic set of tasks that require reasoning. In the context of collaborative reasoning, the text becomes a source of information and can lead to discussion and debate.

In addition, research has shown that successful group work is that which combines individual accountability with group accountability (Johnson & Johnson, 1975). Each individual in the group takes on a role, either assigned or self-selected, and meets the goal of that role. As a group, a process is assigned or agreed upon so that students understand expectations.

BUILD READING PARTNERSHIPS   Another form of collaboration is reading partnerships. When all students in a class examine a text or read aloud with a partner, all of the students are participating. This image is different from that of a classroom in which just one person at a time is reading or talking about the text.

Partnerships differ depending upon the goals of the activity. If the goal is fluent reading, then less proficient readers can be paired with more proficient readers, as was described in Chapter 3. This pairing is especially effective for English learners because they can read aloud or examine and discuss the text without speaking to the whole class. Besides partnering with someone in the class, students can read with someone outside of class (a parent, sibling, or uncle). If the focus is on making meaning from text, students benefit from hearing perspectives of their peers and/or family.

SCAFFOLD SOCIAL INTERACTIONS   To be effective, student collaborations require guidance and modeling. This means that control over collaboration will gradually become the responsibility of the students, in a way similar to the scaffolding pattern used when introducing students to a new reading strategy (Pearson & Gallagher, 1983). For example, in the beginning, the teacher might make most of the decisions, such as choice of topic, role assignments, and duties of group members. But once students and the teacher have established norms for interaction, students can take over more of the decision making (Antonio & Guthrie, 2008). In guiding students toward collaboration, it is important to remember that choice and control are important. Students all bring to the classroom patterns of language and interaction. Scaffolding allows the teacher to observe these patterns and ensure that the culture of communication is built by every voice in the classroom.

Collaboration occurs naturally in every discipline every day. Historians defend their interpretations of the past. Scientists use the scientific method to conduct inquiry and share results with their peers. Artists engage in peer review of their work and discuss the meaning of imagery. These real-world applications of collaboration can serve as models for designing collaboration in the classroom. Indeed it is possible to integrate collaboration into every content area.

Many classes provide perfect opportunities for students to engage in open discussions and collaborative reasoning. In a sixth-grade classroom, students learning about early man engaged in reading partnerships to research about the probable cause of death for the Iceman. Eighth-grade students learning about early settlement of America worked to determine "Who really discovered America: Native Americans, Christopher Columbus, Lief Erikkson, or Bjarni Herjulfson?" Students in a home economics course successfully worked together to read from their text about "Consumer Information." They collaborated as they completed a month-long nutritionally balanced meal plan for a family of four, staying within a specified budget. As these students collaborated together, they were motivated to learn new content.

Two instructional methods, Learning Clubs and Peer-Assisted Learning Strategies (PALS) are strong examples of engaging adolescents through collaboration.

Learning Clubs

A Learning Club (Casey, 2008) is an example of an instructional strategy that encourages students to engage in discussion and collaborative reasoning. Learning Clubs are grouping systems that organize students around active learning events. They evolve in response to students' literacy needs. Learning Clubs have grown out of a tradition of book clubs, of which "literature circles" (Daniels, 2002) are the most widely known.

Teachers build the context for the Learning Club, including areas of inquiry, structures of groups, types of student involvement, and possible outcomes. Some key features of a Learning Club are student selection of text, temporary groups, and regular meetings to discuss the text. The Learning Club is not tied to a single piece of literature. Rather, it includes multiple texts, such as magazines, Web sites, and videos.

Learning Clubs are not imposed from outside the classroom; rather, they are developed in the classroom, from the teacher listening and responding to student interests and needs. Casey (2008) has seen these clubs develop when groups of students share the same interests and wish to learn more. The program requires that the teacher is able to balance content, pedagogy, and student needs. Because a Learning Club is developed in an individual classroom context, it cannot be neatly packaged. However, there are some suggested steps to take for enacting a Learning Club.

PROCEDURE

1. Consider possible topics and how these topics are connected to students' experiences and grade level standards.
2. Introduce the topics to students, using a **Topic Talk**. The Topic Talk includes some information about the topic, including its importance and impact on the community.
3. Identify texts that students will need and make sure that they represent multiple difficulty levels. (Chapter 7 will detail how to check the difficulty level of texts).
4. Decide which roles students might assume in their groups and the "job description" for each role.
5. Schedule time for students to engage in reading, researching, and discussion. Depending upon students' needs, guide them toward appropriate strategies for finding, synthesizing, and recording information.
6. Consider ways that students can demonstrate their understandings, and design assessment activities that meet group objectives. Teachers often provide a menu of choices, so that students have a tangible project on which to focus.
7. Help students make connections between the literacies used in their Learning Clubs and literacies used out of school.

In her article, Casey (2008) describes how a seventh-grade teacher, Sharon, uses Learning Clubs in her classroom. In one example, students are placed in groups, focusing on using strategies to help them learn vocabulary. Together, this group of struggling students creates an image to help them understand the concept "parallel lines." In the course of the discussion, one of the students showed parallel using his hands, and he says that they look like railroad tracks (Casey, 2008).

Learning Clubs provide space for students to engage in collaborative reasoning and discussion. These interactions are not instant—it takes time for students to feel safe with these interactions. It is the teacher's responsibility to build a safe classroom environment by encouraging students to share and defend their opinions. The teacher must also remember that students' opinions should not be judged as either right or wrong. Learning Club students should be encouraged to question and explore. Learning should be scaffolded—moving from using common class texts (earlier in the year) to allowing more flexibility in groups' choices of text (later in the year).

VARIATIONS   Learning Clubs often extend into a rich, thematic unit. At a local high school, teachers in a tenth-grade biology class used Learning Clubs to teach about the biodiversity of the local community watershed. Students learned about watersheds as part of their content curriculum. They were so fascinated by having one behind their school that they asked to extend their learning. Teachers listed students' interests on related topics—endangered birds, local fish, native plants, and the Sacramento River system. Students selected a group that interested them most and read from many sources to collect information. Collaborative groups produced a comprehensive flyer and presented the information they learned to local businesses to encourage them to Adopt-a-Watershed in their community. These students were able to work collaboratively, participating in open discussions and reading partnerships using content area text.

PALS (Peer-Assisted Learning Strategies)

Peer-Assisted Learning Strategies (PALS) pairs readers together to promote fluency and comprehension (McMaster, Fuchs, & Fuchs, 2006). There are five characteristics that distinguish PALS from other paired reading activities.

1. During PALS, more proficient readers are paired with less proficient readers, and all students are paired. (Teachers can determine students' proficiency levels in reading by following the guidelines that will be outlined in Chapter 6.)
2. There is a high level of verbal interaction. Students both read and respond orally with their partners.
3. The teacher shows students how to use responses and feedback in their conversations.
4. Roles switch, so that each partner plays the role of tutor and tutee.
5. PALS includes a set of three activities that students are trained to use independently (McMaster, et al., 2006):
   • reading with retell—students read aloud and summarize their reading.
   • paragraph shrinking—students summarize the content of their reading in 10 words or less.
   • prediction relay—students make a prediction, read, then confirm or disconfirm the prediction.

PROCEDURE

Prepare

1. Before class, create a list of students ranked in reading proficiency from highest to lowest. Split the list in half, and pair the strongest reader from the top half with the strongest reader from the bottom half. Continue pairing until all students have a partner.
2. Choose readings that are appropriate for the less proficient reader in each pair.
3. Model for all students how to engage in the paired interaction.

Teach

1. Partner reading with retell.
   a. Partner A begins by reading from the text for about 5 minutes. (The more fluent reader should read first to model fluent reading.)
   b. Partner B reads the same piece of text. When he comes to a word that he doesn't know, partner A helps pronounce the word, and partner B repeats it.
   c. After partner B rereads the text, he summarizes it.
2. Paragraph shrinking. Students continue to read orally, but they stop at the end of each paragraph and give an oral summary.
   a. Partner A asks partner B to identify the most important idea in 10 words or less.
   b. If the summary misses the mark, partner A asks B to skim the paragraph and try again.

Resource

The PALS method has a set of scripts that students can use for training. These can be purchased at the Web site: http://kc.vanderbilt. edu/pals/teachmat/ Reading_Materials.html.

3. Prediction relay. Students make predictions about the texts. They then read to check for the accuracy of their predictions.

    a. Students A and B each make a prediction about the upcoming text.

    b. Students A and B each read one-half page of text.

    c. Student A checks for prediction confirmation.

    d. Student B summarizes in 10 words or less.

In experimental studies, PALS has improved the reading achievement of a wide range of learners: those who struggle with reading, those who are proficient readers, and learners with reading disabilities. To date, most research has been conducted with students in kindergarten through grade six. However, studies with high school students have also shown positive learning and motivational effects. In a study comparing students from PALS and non-PALS classes, students' beliefs about reading were different in PALS and non-PALS classes (Fuchs, Fuchs, & Kazden, 1999). After participating in PALS, students felt that they worked hard to become a better reader and that their teacher had helped them significantly. In addition, significantly more students in the PALS classes reported that they enjoyed helping other students.

In this example of collaboration, students are participating in a highly structured interaction about text. Partnerships are created so that peers support each other in the reading process. Interdependence is created because each member of a pair must listen to her/his partner's reading and responses and actively provide feedback. A specific set of statements can guide this student interaction.

VARIATIONS   Most variations with this method involve the nature of rewards for participation. Each pair can be placed on one of two teams in the class. As pairs participate in activities, students earn points and record them on a scorecard. Every week, all pairs report the points earned to the teacher. In some classrooms, the class awards the "winning team" with recognition and applause. In other classrooms, each week the names of the two people in the pair are listed on the board with "High Scoring Pair." The high scoring pair write their names on slips of paper that are entered in a monthly drawing for a $10 prize (Fuchs, et al., 1999). Another option is for high school students to earn PALS dollars, redeemable for community-donated CDs, sports apparel, or school supplies. Teachers who choose the PALS strategy will need to decide whether and how to use the rewards.

Teachers may also vary in how long they require each partnership to last. In elementary schools, pairs usually work together for about four weeks. But in high schools, teachers prefer to have students switch partners more often, even daily. These teachers report that high school students seem to prefer having an option to work with different peers. In addition, a higher absence rate in some schools makes it difficult to have one pair stay together for long periods of time (McMaster, et al., 2006).

Conclusion

Opportunities to collaborate are important for adolescent learners. When students engage in open discussions under the guidance of a teacher, students become more adept at working with others. In addition, they gain knowledge from the content area because they are motivated to participate. Encouraging collaboration is a win-win situation for everyone, student and teacher alike. Learning Clubs and PALS are just two examples of how a teacher can encourage collaboration in middle and high school content area classes.

PAUSE and REFLECT 5.2

Reflect upon the three things teachers can do to promote collaboration in middle and high school classrooms. How might you be able to use Learning Clubs and/or PALS in your content area to motivate the students you teach?

ENSURE MASTERY OF CONTENT AND LITERACY SKILLS

In order to be engaged in reading, students must both *be* competent and *feel* competent. They need to be readers who seek meaning in text, and they need to feel confident in their abilities.

Competence can be created with instructional practices that foster a mastery orientation (Douglass & Guthrie, 2008). Research suggests that each student has a specific orientation to learning from text. This orientation may be performance-oriented, mastery-oriented, or some combination of the two. A **performance orientation** means that the student is engaged in reading to complete a task or "make the grade." A **mastery orientation**, on the other hand, means that a student is focused on making meaning from text; the purpose of reading is to increase conceptual understanding. While research shows that both orientations may lead to success in school, students with a mastery orientation are more likely to comprehend what they read.

To choose to engage in reading in the classroom, students need to feel successful. Success is related to students' perceived **self-efficacy** or their confidence in reading. If students learn strategies for effective reading, they experience success and develop a greater sense of self-efficacy (Bandura, 1997).

Five teaching practices can help to increase student mastery: provide mastery goals, match students with appropriate text, help students set goals and record progress, scaffold and re-teach, and reward effort over performance (Douglass & Guthrie, 2008; Yudowich, Henry, & Guthrie, 2008).

PROVIDE MASTERY GOALS   Motivation can be increased if the goals of instruction are focused on learning rather than completing tasks. With all of the demands on instructional time, it is easy to see how reading can become just another task on a long list of things to do. Teachers find themselves making a statement like "Your job today is to read pages 368–379 and answer the questions on page 380." In contrast, **mastery goals** focus on guiding students toward finding meaning in their text. The teacher provides the goal of the lesson, chapter, or unit prior to beginning instruction. These goals link to content standards learning, but are also connected to the real-world application of the skill, as well as literacy. With mastery goals in mind, the reading assignment might sound like this: "We are going to learn about the rise of democracy in ancient Athens when we practice fluently reading from 368–379 today. It is critical that we understand how the direct democracy they created paved the way for the representative democracy we have in the United States today."

MATCH STUDENTS WITH APPROPRIATE TEXT   One of the difficulties with middle school and high school textbooks is that they don't often match the reading level of the students. When students read, many quickly become frustrated, which leads to disengagement and decreases their confidence with informational text. For example, a textbook written at a tenth-grade reading level is not appropriate at-home reading for a student who reads at the fifth-grade level. In this case, there are ways to carefully scaffold student vocabulary, fluency, and comprehension of text through well-planned lessons and teacher or peer support as was described in Chapters 2, 3, and 4.

One way to avoid this predicament is to provide texts that are at the students' reading levels. (Text levels will be further discussed in Chapter 7.) Consider providing text at various reading levels. Web sites provide lists of trade books that also focus on science and social studies content areas.

Resource

For science, see the National Science Teachers Association at www. nsta.org/ostbc. For social studies, see www. socialstudies.org/resources/ notable. Using these types of text allow students to deepen literacy and master content.

HELP STUDENTS SET ATTAINABLE GOALS AND TRACK PROGRESS   To achieve a feeling of mastery, students need to be able to set and meet goals. In the opening vignette, Jake is not able to achieve the goal set for him in independent reading from his history textbook. Students must be given the opportunity to take ownership of their goals. Rather than the teacher charting and evaluating progress, students must be involved in setting appropriate goals about their reading and learning. How much should I read? How will I be held accountable? Jake was not given the opportunity to do this. Instead, his teacher *owned* his goal and *tracked* his progress; he (and his mother, unfortunately) simply received the news. His teacher could have recognized his lack of engagement with the reading and worked to help him divide the task into manageable segments, monitoring his progress along the way.

All students need feedback on their progress as readers. By acknowledging students' growth in their ability to read in the content area, teachers can validate the importance of content literacy. Opportunities for feedback also allow students and teachers to monitor learning and adjust goals when needed. For example, seventh- and eighth-grade middle school students record fluency and comprehension data at the end of every cluster assessment in language arts, and they graph and analyze the changing results.

SCAFFOLD AND RE-TEACH   Mastery requires that failure is met with renewed commitment to learning. If a student does not understand the reading or the concept, teachers must provide opportunities to relearn the material and scaffold where appropriate.

REWARD EFFORT OVER PERFORMANCE   Mastery also requires effort. As Donald Kendall once said, "The only place where 'success' comes before 'work' is in the dictionary." Our schools tend to reward performance, but to instill a mastery orientation, students need to be praised for setting manageable goals and working until they achieve those goals. This is especially important in assigning independent reading to students.

Teachers of adolescent learners have a double challenge—to ensure that students gain mastery in their content area and become more literate. In each content area, effective teachers focus on mastery goals and provide students with text that they can read. The latter is especially important in social science and science classrooms where the majority of the content learning comes from the textbook. If teachers know the reading proficiency level of all of their students and the reading level of the text, they can readily see which students will need scaffolded instruction and/or supplemental materials. Chapter 7 describes how to choose texts that students can effectively understand.

While many instructional strategies can build and support mastery goals, this chapter focuses on two approaches that incorporate many of the above recommendations. These approaches are Scaffolded Reading Experiences and Concept-Oriented Reading Instruction.

Scaffolded Reading Experiences

One way to motivate students is to engage them in Scaffolded Reading Experiences (SRE). The term "scaffolding" was first applied to education by developmental psychologists who studied the interaction between parents and children as they learned language (Wood, Bruner, & Ross, 1976). Scaffolding occurs when an individual provides structure to help a learner accomplish something that would otherwise be too difficult. In reading, it refers to support before, during, and after reading with text that is at the student's instructional level.

SRE includes attention to both techniques (a teacher's actions) and application of strategies (a reading behavior of students) (Boiling & Evans, 2008). Pre-reading techniques help to prepare and motivate students for reading by connecting or building prior knowledge and establishing a purpose or mastery goal for reading. During-reading activities focus on comprehension of the text, and teachers employ techniques to help students stay focused, transform text, and comprehend. Post-reading includes strategies to investigate the reading, learn from it, and make extensions.

PROCEDURE

1. Consider the students, the text, and the purpose for reading; plan a lesson that will make learning relevant.
2. Plan pre-reading activities. (Recall those that were described in Chapter 2—"Pre-Teaching Vocabulary" and Chapter 4—"Activate and Build Background Knowledge.")

3. Plan during-reading activities. (Refer back to "Guided Fluency Development Instruction" and "Repeated Reading" in Chapter 3, and "Comprehension Monitoring Strategy Guide" in Chapter 4 for strategy ideas.)

4. Plan post-reading activities. (See "Written, Oral, and Visual Summaries" in Chapter 4 for more ideas.)

5. Teach the lesson, including scaffolding techniques and strategies for pre, during and post-reading.

Massey and Heafner (2004) describe some pre, during, and post-reading strategies that are effective in teaching content reading while teaching students about the U.S. Revolution. For pre-reading, teachers engage students in the List-Group-Label strategy (Chapter 2) to help them connect to background knowledge and set a purpose for reading. During reading, students complete a Cause/Effect Graphic Organizer (Chapter 4) in which they describe the causes and effects of the revolution. After reading, they engage in Reciprocal Teaching (Chapter 4), a technique in which students ask the teacher questions, the teacher responds and then asks students higher-order questions about the text. These three activities are appropriate for reading history texts because students are learning how to apply their prior knowledge to the text, think about causal relationships, and ask questions that evaluate and synthesize the text's content.

One of the key factors in Scaffolded Reading Experiences is to ensure that over time, students become more independent and able to support their own reading. In order for gradual withdrawal to occur, teachers need to be explicit about the uses of the reading strategies, focusing on them as tools for learning, rather than just tools for teaching (Conley, 2008).

SRE builds motivation in several ways. With pre-reading activities, the reading is made relevant to students from the start. Throughout the pre, during, and post-reading phases, students are guided toward making meaning as they are rewarded for their effort, and they have several opportunities to transform the text. Opportunities for supporting and reteaching occur naturally during the scaffolding process, in which student comprehension is checked and rechecked.

VARIATIONS   SRE is a very flexible method. It allows teachers to make choices based upon factors, such as student needs. Each pre, during, or post instructional scaffold creates a new variation on the SRE model.

Concept-Oriented Reading Instruction (CORI)

Another instructional approach that promotes competency is Concept-Oriented Reading Instruction (CORI), a collaborative project between the University of Maryland and Frederick County Public Schools.

Resource

More information can be found about Concept-Oriented Reading Instruction at the University of Maryland Web site: http://www.cori.umd.edu/.

CORI was originally designed by Allan Wigfield and John Guthrie to promote both reading strategy instruction and science inquiry. While this method originated in elementary school, it is now taking shape with adolescents in a program called "REAL: Reading Engagement for Adolescent Learners." This new program has been used mostly in upper elementary and middle school grades, yet the concepts are relevant to secondary instruction. Its four components are: reading strategy instruction, science inquiry activities, motivational support, and reading-science integration.

In one example, the CORI method was used in a classroom with 25 seventh graders on a two-week module focused on weather (McPeake, 2009). During the unit, the students focused on comprehension monitoring (identifying main ideas and details, making inferences) and science content goals (weather conditions, severe weather). Also, built into each lesson were motivation supports, such as mastery goals for reading.

To foster a mastery orientation, the unit included opportunities for students to build both reading competency and science knowledge. Reading fluency was one of the emphases of the unit. On several occasions, the teacher modeled how to read informational text with appropriate expression. In pairs, students then read aloud, focusing on proper intonation and phrasing.

The unit also gave students many opportunities to become experts with the content. Details about the clouds, wind, and air temperature were learned about through a carefully scaffolded sequence of lessons. For the first 70-minute lesson, students learned about wind. They began with a "wind walk" in which students went outside to observe the wind and write answers to questions. They first observed how the wind changed things in the environment. They made initial predictions of wind speed, followed by more accurate judgments using the Beaufort Wind Scale. Each student then compared and contrasted their data with a classmate (McPeake, 2009).

How did this lesson connect to reading? As they engaged in this "wind walk," they used a weather atlas and applied the wind scale. When they completed the wind walk, the teacher engaged them in a guided reading activity about wind, including such concepts as local wind, prevailing winds, and the interaction between wind and temperature. The teacher modeled how to identify the main idea. When students were ready, they read their textbook section in teams, identified important ideas, and entered them on a chart.

This lesson included many opportunities to build a mastery orientation. Students' learning was scaffolded, progressing from a relevant, shared experience (wind walk) to reading and learning from the text. Students transformed the text by finding the main idea and writing it on a chart. The end goal was making meaning, rather than merely completing a reading and answering questions from a textbook.

CORI has shown to lead to positive effects on both reading comprehension and motivation. CORI has a positive impact on engagement in reading and decreased negative dispositions, such as avoidance of reading (Guthrie, Mcrae, & Klauda, 2007). In addition, using the CORI model led to significant gains in reading comprehension test scores and use of reading strategies. These findings hold true for upper elementary school; the effects of CORI are currently being tested with middle and high school students.

The CORI framework has four phases that teachers can use as they develop instruction.

PROCEDURE

1. *Observe and Personalize*. The teacher creates interest in the topic to be learned by making a connection between the topic and the real world.
2. *Search and Retrieve*. The teacher helps students learn more about the topic and answers questions that they might have. Students learn how to find information, decide which information is important, and organize their data.
3. *Comprehend and Integrate*. In the third phase, students learn how to use comprehension strategies to better understand the content. They learn to think deeply about what they've learned, connect it to what they know, solve problems, and write about their learning.
4. *Communicate to Others*. The purpose of the fourth phase is to teach students how to share their knowledge with a variety of audiences. They organize language to communicate it effectively through writing and speaking (Swan, 2004).

VARIATIONS   Although CORI began with science instruction, it can be used across subject areas. Each step—observe and personalize, search and retrieve, comprehend and integrate, and communicate to others—will look different depending upon the grade level and content area (Swan, 2004).The following section describes what the CORI model looks like in a tenth-grade class in world history.

Observe and Personalize: For a unit on World War II, the teacher invites a veteran to class. The veteran talks about his experiences landing on Omaha Beach and being one of the few in his troop who survived the climb up the steep and barren beach cliffs. He did this when he was the same age as some of the students sitting in the classroom—a point that allows students to create a personal connection with an historical event.

Search and Retrieve: As they continue their study about World War II, they *search and retrieve* by looking for relevant information on the Internet, in history books, and in history journals. Members of the class visit local retirement communities to interview local World War II veterans. They look for various sources that bring different perspectives to historical events of World War II.

Comprehend and Integrate: As they continue to study World War II, students learn the reading skills and strategies of historians. They read, synthesize, and critique different forms of texts. For example, the class reads an obituary of a Japanese-American man who, according to the article, was held at the Topaz Internment Camp. Based on their prior knowledge of internment camps, the students make some inferences about this individual's life. This is an opportunity to discuss the importance of how we use text clues together with prior knowledge to make inferences (Swan, 2004).

Communicate to Others: Within the World War II unit there are many authentic opportunities for students to communicate what they have learned. For example, students write reports and design visuals based on their interviews with World War II veterans. At a special event, they present their findings to the veterans' families.

In this example of CORI, students are given multiple opportunities to master both the content and the reading skills and strategies necessary to engage with history.

Conclusion

Both Scaffolded Reading Experiences and Concept-Oriented Reading Instruction are strategies that middle and high school teachers use to ensure mastery of content and literacy skills. As students become more competent both in literacy practices and in reasoning about the content, they will experience success, and their confidence will grow.

PAUSE and REFLECT 5.3

Consider the five teaching practices that can help promote mastery. How can you use Scaffolded Reading Experiences and/or Concept-Oriented Reading Instruction to ensure that your students will obtain mastery of the content and literacy skills you are teaching?

Chapter Summary

This chapter described instructional strategies that teachers use to initiate and sustain student motivation toward content reading. It suggests that engagement can be increased if teachers follow three principles during instruction: foster student control and choice during learning, encourage collaboration between students, and ensure mastery of content and literacy skills. The strategies described in this chapter are just a few examples of those that support these principles. Other strategies presented in Chapters 2, 3, and 4 also exemplify these motivational teaching practices. Figure 5.2 shows a matrix of the strategies presented in this text and their connection to the motivational goals of fostering student control and choice, encouraging collaboration, and ensuring mastery.

Figure 5.2 demonstrates that every strategy from Chapters 2, 3, and 4 can build student mastery of reading. Approximately half of the 40 strategies involve collaboration among students; half include a significant amount of student choice. By integrating what teachers learn from assessment of their students, they can use this master chart to choose appropriate motivational strategies that will meet the needs of their students.

Jake, introduced in the vignette at the beginning of the chapter, is not motivated to read for his government class, even though he is a capable reader. How can a teacher motivate him to read so that he is getting reading practice, passing government, and developing his literacy? By integrating motivational instructional strategies that address literacy and content, teachers can create a classroom environment where students like Jake become inspired to read and learn. Adolescents who are engaged with content reading become more knowledgeable about content concepts and more skilled and strategic at reading.

Strategy Name	Chapter	Motivational Principles		
		Choice	Collaboration	Mastery
Concept of Definition Map	2		X	X
Semantic Feature Analysis	2			X
Pre-Teaching Vocabulary	2			X
Vocabulary Rating Guide	2		X	X
List-Group-Label	2	X		X
Vocabulary Visits	2	X	X	X
Word Analysis	2		X	X
Contextual Redefinition	2	X		X
Dictionary Use	2			X
Personal Dictionary	2	X		X
Teacher Read Aloud	3			X
Generated Read Aloud	3	X		X
Guided Fluency Development Instruction	3		X	X
Adapted Retrospective Miscue Analysis	3			X
Repeated Reading	3	X	X	X
Wide, Independent Reading	3	X		X
K-W-L Strategy Chart	4	X	X	X
Text Box/Bag Activity	4		X	X
Survey Strategy and Guide	4	X	X	X
Main Idea/Detail Graphic Organizer	4			X
Outcome Graphic Organizer	4			X
Evidence Guide Graphic Organizer	4	X		X
Compare/Contrast Matrix	4			X
Inference Graphic Organizer	4			X
Written Summaries	4	X		X
Oral Summaries	4	X		X
Visual Summaries	4	X		X
Cornell Notes	4	X		X
SQ3R	4			X
QAR	4			X
Interactive Think Aloud	4	X	X	X
Comprehension Monitoring Guide	4	X	X	X
Reciprocal Teaching	4	X	X	X
PLAN (Predict, Locate, Add, Note)	4	X	X	X
Socratic Seminars	5	X	X	X
WebQuests	5	X	X	X
Learning Clubs	5	X	X	X
Peer-Assisted Learning Strategies (PALS)	5		X	X
Scaffolded Reading Experiences	5		X	X
Concept-Oriented Reading Instruction (CORI)	5	X	X	X

FIGURE 5.2 Strategies to Promote Student Choice, Collaboration, and Mastery.

PAUSE and REFLECT 5.4

List the three instructional goals teachers should work toward in order to motivate readers. How can you improve your content instruction by integrating some of the strategies described in this chapter?

Resources

Latham, L. G., & Scully, E. P. (2008). Critters! A realistic simulation for teaching evolutionary biology. *The American Biology Teacher, 70*(1), 30–33.

Ray, D. (2000). *Water safari, a* journey *of life. Water in Africa.* Washington, DC: Peace Corps Coverdell Office of World Wise Schools.

References

Abbit, J., & Orphus, J. (2008). What we know about the impacts of WebQuests: A review of research. *Journal of the Association for the Advancement of Computers in Education, 16*(4), 441–456.

Alvermann, D. E. (2002). Effective literacy instruction for adolescents. *Journal of Literacy Research, 34*(2), 198–208.

Antonio, D., & Guthrie, J. T. (2008). Reading is social: Bringing peer interaction to the text. In J. T. Guthrie (Ed.), *Engaging adolescents in reading* (pp. 49–64). Thousand Oaks, CA: Corwin Press.

Aronson, E. (1978). *The jigsaw classroom.* Beverly Hills, CA: Sage.

Bandura, A. (1997). *Self-efficacy: The exercise of control.* New York, NY: W.H. Freeman.

Boiling, C., & Evans, W. (2008). Reading success in the secondary classroom. *Preventing School Failure, 52*(2), 59–66.

Casey, H. (2008). Engaging the disengaged: Using learning clubs to motivate struggling adolescent readers adn writers. *Journal of Adolescent & Adult Literacy, 52*(4), 284–294.

Coke, P. K. (2008). Uniting the disparate: Connecting best practices and educational mandates. *English Journal, 97*(5), 28–33.

Conley, M. (2008). Cognitive strategy instruction for adolescents: What we know about the promise, what we know about the potential. *Harvard Educational Review, 78*(1), 84–106.

Daniels, H. (2002). *Literature circles: Voice and choice in book clubs and reading groups* (2nd ed.). Portland, ME: Stenhouse.

Dodge, B. (2001). FOCUS: Five rules for writing a great WebQuest. *Learning and Leading with Technology, 28*(8), 6–9.

Douglass, J., & Guthrie, J. T. (2008). Meaning is motivating. In J. T. Guthrie (Ed.), *Engaging adolescents in reading* (pp. 17–31). Thousand Oaks, CA: Corwin Press.

Fillman, S., & Guthrie, J. T. (2008). Control and choice: Supporting self-directed reading. In J. T. Guthrie (Ed.), *Engaging Adolescents in Learning* (pp. 33–48). Thousand Oaks, CA: Corwin Press.

Fuchs, L. S., Fuchs, D., & Kazden, S. (1999). Effects of peer-assisted learning strategies on high school students with serious reading problems. *Remedial and Special Education, 20*(5), 309–318.

Guthrie, J. T., Mcrae, A., & Klauda, S. L. (2007). Contributions of concept-oriented reading instruction to knowledge about interventions for motivation in reading. *Educational Psychologist, 42*(4), 237–250.

Guthrie, J. T., & Wigfield, A. (2000). Engagement and motivation in reading. In M. L. Kamil, P. B. Mosenthal, P. D. Pearson & R. Barr (Eds.), *Handbook of Reading Research* (Vol. III, pp. 403–422). New York: Erlbaum.

Ikpeze, C. H., & Boyd, F. B. (2007). Web-based inquiry learning: Facilitating thoughtful literacy with WebQuests. *The Reading Teacher, 60*(7), 644–654.

Johnson, D. W., & Johnson, R. T. (1975). *Learning together and alone: Cooperation, competition and individualization.* Englewood Cliffs, NJ: Prentice-Hall.

Krapp, A., Hidi, S., & Renninger, K. A. (1992). Interest, learning and development. In K. A. Renninger, S. Hidi & A. Krapp (Eds.), *The role of interest in learning and development* (pp. 3-25).

Lenters, K. (2006). Resistance, struggle and the adolescent reader. *The Journal of Adolescent and Adult Literacy, 50*(2), 136-146.

Massey, D. D., & Heafner, T. L. (2004). Promoting reading comprehension in social studies. *Journal of Adolescent & Adult Literacy, 48*(1), 26–40.

McMaster, K. L., Fuchs, D., & Fuchs, L. S. (2006). Research on peer-assisted learning strategies: The promise and limitations of peer-mediated instruction. *Reading and Writing Quarterly, 22*, 5–25.

McPeake, J. A. (2009). CORI in Middle School. Retrieved from http://www.cori.umd.edu/real/presentations.php.

Newkirk, T. (2002). *Misreading masculinity: Boys, literacy, and popular culture.* Portsmouth, NH: Heinemann.

Pearson, P. D., & Gallagher, D. R. (1983). Instruction of reading comprehension. *Contemporary Educational Psychology, 8*(3), 317–344.

Reed, J. H., Schallert, D. L., Beth, A. D., & Woodruff, A. L. (2004). Motivated reader, engaged writer: The role of motivation in the literate acts of adolescents. In T. L. Jetton & J. A. Dole (Eds.), *Adolescent Literacy: Research and Practice* (pp. 251–282). New York: Guilford Press.

Reeve, J., Jang, H., Carrell, D., Jeon, S., & Barch, B. (2004). Enhancing students' engagement by increasing teachers' autonomy support. *Motivation and Emotion, 28*, 147–169.

Richardson, P., & Eccles, J. (2007). Rewards of reading: Toward the development of possible selves and identities. *International Journal of Educational Research, 46*(6), 341–356.

Schunk, D. H., Pintrich, P. R., & Meece, J. L. (2008). *Motivation in education: Theory, research and applications* (3rd ed.). Upper Saddle River, NJ: Pearson, Merrill, Prentice Hall.

Schraw, G., & Lehman, S. (2001). Situational interest: A review of the literature and directions for future research. *Educational Psychology Review, 13*(23-52).

Short, D., & Fitzsimmons, S. (2007). *Double the work: Challenges and solutions to acquiring language and academic literacy for adolescent English language learners.* New York: Carnegie Corporation.

Steinbeck, J. E., & Cook, J. W. (2001). Understanding social security: A civic obligation. *The Social Studies, 93*(5), 209-221.

Swan, E. A. (2004). Motivating adolescent readers through concept-oriented reading instruction. In T. L. Jetton & J. A. Dole (Eds.), *Adolescent literacy: Research and practice* (pp. 283–303). New York: Guildford Press.

Wenzel, K. R. (2005). Peer relationships, motivation, and academic performance at school. In A. J. Elliot & C. S. Dweck (Eds.), *Handbook of competence and motivation* (pp. 279–296). New York: Guilford Publications.

Wood, D. J., Bruner, J. S., & Ross, G. (1976). The role of tutoring in problem-solving. *Journal of Child Psychology and Psychiatry, 17*(2), 89–100.

Yudowich, S., Henry, L. M., & Guthrie, J. T. (2008). Self-efficacy: Building confident readers. In J. T. Guthrie (Ed.), *Engaging Adolescents in Reading* (pp 65-86). Thousand Oaks, CA: Corwin Press.

CHAPTER 6

Assess—Learning About Students

Ms. Johnson, a first-year eighth-grade teacher, sat with a stack of student spiral notebooks. It was the second week of school, and she had tried a new strategy—Cornell Notes—with her U.S. history classes. Even though the notebooks were bulky, she had collected them from her fourth-period class to make sure that her students were taking notes that made sense.

She opened Ava's notebook and saw that the page was divided into the trademark sections of Cornell note taking—a column for subheadings on the left and a column for notes on the right. The notes were neat, and Ava had underlined essential vocabulary. At the bottom of the page was a concise summary, in Ava's own words. Ms. Johnson nodded silently as she flipped open the next notebook. She tilted her head, and her eyes followed Lao's slanted print. The first few lines were all there, but then there were gaps of several lines. The summary at the bottom had a couple of general ideas.

Ms. Johnson leaned back in her chair and stared at the ceiling. She had followed the steps for the instructional strategy. She used the overhead to model note taking, and then she asked students to try a couple of paragraphs with their reading partners. What happened? She looked back at her desk, and as she quickly flipped through the notebooks, she noticed the wide variation in student work. She knew that her students read at different levels, but she hadn't expected to see this much difference in their notes. It was time to find out more about her students' reading abilities so that she could help each one move forward as reader and learner.

In this vignette, Ms. Johnson recognized the importance of using data to inform instruction. After examining student work, she realized that she did not know enough about her students' needs as readers. Even when she used an instructional strategy and followed a step-by-step procedure, her students' performance varied greatly. The strategy requires that students read segments of the text and paraphrase the ideas. These two tasks require that students comprehend what they are reading in their eighth-grade textbooks. But can they all read grade level material? How proficient is each of them with grade level vocabulary? Are they fluent? What motivates them as readers? She knows she must answer these questions if she is to help them develop their literacy and their understanding of social science.

Chapters 2 through 5 described instructional strategies that build vocabulary, fluency, comprehension, and motivation. This chapter explains how to collect and compile data that will help teachers choose instructional strategies that meet the needs of their students.

USE DATA TO DRIVE INSTRUCTION

When using data to drive instruction, it is important to consider both the goals of assessment and the role of the teacher in the assessment process.

The Goals of Assessment

Assessments can be used in a number of ways to meet different classroom goals. Three types of assessment commonly used in reading are summative, formative, and diagnostic.

- **Summative** assessments test learning and occur at the end of a unit or course. The goal with summative assessment is to answer the question "Did the student learn enough?" (Stiggins, 2008). Unit, quarter, and year-end written exams are all summative assessments.
- The goal of **formative** assessments is to support learning. Formative assessments allow the instructor to evaluate what a student has learned so that instruction can be modified for subsequent lessons. They answer the question "How can I support learning?"(Stiggins, 2008). For example, a formative assessment in biology asks students to label a diagram with parts of an animal cell. Based on students' responses, the teacher knows which concepts to reteach.
- **Diagnostic** assessments uncover strengths and areas for growth. They can be thought of as a pretest—a way of measuring students before instruction to learn what instruction should include. Diagnostic assessments answer the question "What, specifically, does this student need?" In math, a teacher may give a diagnostic assessment before a lesson on units of measurement, to test whether students remember that when they square a numerical measurement, they also have to square the unit of measurement.

Standardized tests, such as the ones that public school students take annually, serve a summative purpose. They test the student's learning in relationship to grade level standards. Designed for accountability purposes, they show student growth from instruction. But, when the results are used thoughtfully, teachers can use standardized tests as one source of information to diagnose student needs and to guide future instruction. For example, students' standardized test scores from the previous year might give a teacher guidance about which areas of content or literacy need further attention.

The keys to success are to understand exactly what the standardized test is measuring and to use the results prudently. Too often these test scores have been used to place students in remedial classes. In one case study, a sixth-grade student was placed into a remedial class purely on the basis of her low standardized test score (Dennis, 2008). There, she received instruction that focused on the relationship between sounds and letters and did not have any opportunity to read meaningful material. The school's original placement decision was based upon limited information. However, after a few additional reading assessments, the teacher found that the student belonged with her peers in a sixth-grade classroom. Both this particular case and other research support the idea that struggling readers need to be present for the best instruction possible, with an expert teacher who can help the student improve reading in the context of real instruction (Allington, 2002).

The Teacher's Role in the Assessment Process

School districts and individual school sites have different approaches to conducting assessments, compiling data, and reflecting upon results. The teacher's responsibility for each of these components of assessment and reflection depends upon his or her role at the school. There are many different scenarios possible. At some schools, a literacy coach or another individual compiles data on all students and communicates student needs to teachers. At others, a content area teacher compiles this data for him or herself. At others, it is a joint effort among all school personnel.

Figure 6.1 is useful in thinking about one's own responsibility for assessment. The figure shows two continua, one running horizontally and one running vertically. The horizontal continuum represents the amount of responsibility that an individual has for *collecting* data and reflecting upon the results. The vertical continuum represents the amount of responsibility an individual has for *using* the data to improve instruction.

In Figure 6.1, Mr. Brown, a high school social studies teacher, is not responsible for collecting or interpreting literacy data for his students. A literacy coach and a reading specialist compile

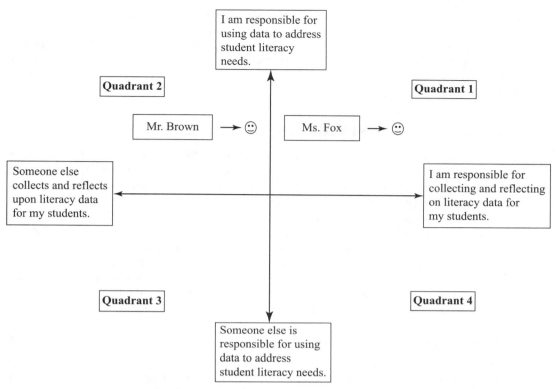

FIGURE 6.1   Continua Showing Varying Levels of Teacher Responsibility for Data Collection and Use

this data. However, he is responsible for using any data on hand to address the needs of his students in five periods of social science classes. Mr. Brown's role would place him on the continuum in Quadrant 2.

Ms. Fox, an eighth-grade language arts and social science teacher, is responsible for collecting all data for her students, reflecting upon that data, and sharing it with the science and math teachers. She is responsible for using this data to address the needs of her students; in addition, she provides content literacy support for her colleagues in mathematics and the sciences. Ms. Fox's role places her in Quadrant 1.

PAUSE and REFLECT 6.1

Students engage in many forms of assessment, including those constructed by the state, school districts, school sites, and teachers. What role do you play in assessing and addressing student literacy performance and development? In which of the quadrants in Figure 6.1 would you place yourself?

Each school's approach to data collection, storage, and access is different. Many have assessment models that work effectively. But for teachers to become actively engaged in literacy, all teachers need to have access to the data, participate in evaluating students' needs, and deciding appropriate instruction. In one middle school, a sixth-grade teacher volunteers to record data for all sixth-grade students. However, all sixth-grade teachers help compile the data and/or conduct assessments. Data for standardized assessments is housed electronically. While the teachers have access to *some* of the data, they work closely with the principal to access the additional data that they need. At that particular site, the faculty, administrators, parents, and students know that the data is being used to help students learn.

The extensive data generated from the educational system provide an overwhelming amount of information with little direction about how to use that data in the best interest of students. The LinC cycle helps literacy coaches and teachers use assessment data to plan instruction for middle and high school students.

COLLECT ASSESSMENT DATA: THE LinC CLASS PROFILE

To address the issues with organizing and using data, the authors created a Class Profile, shown in Figure 6.2. The Class Profile includes several categories of information: language proficiency, vocabulary, fluency, comprehension, and motivation. Each of the components in the Class Profile is essential to promote both content area knowledge and literacy development.

One common concern among content teachers is the availability of time in which to conduct assessments and record data. Fortunately, teachers who use the Class Profile are surprised that data is easier to collect than they had anticipated. Teachers, administrators, or literacy coaches complete some of these columns simply by transferring data from school and/or district test reports. To collect other data, teachers conduct quick assessments with a whole class of students. The following sections describe how to efficiently and effectively compile data. Recall Ms. Johnson's student Lao. In order to better understand the Class Profile, Lao's data will serve as an example.

English Language Proficiency

Growing proportions of students in U.S. classrooms come to school speaking a language other than English. In 2006, 20 percent of students ages 5 to 17 spoke a language other than English at home; 5 percent of students ages 5 to 17 spoke English with difficulty (Grigg, Donahue, & Dion, 2007). Understanding the student's language proficiency is important so that instruction can meet the unique language needs of the student. Two elements in measuring English language proficiency are the Home Language Survey and the English Language Development Assessment.

THE HOME LANGUAGE SURVEY   Public schools are required by federal law (Title VI of the Civil Rights Act of 1964) to identify students with limited English language proficiency. Each student's cumulative folder must contain a **Home Language Survey** that parents/guardians complete when their child enrolls at the school. For initial identification, most U.S. public schools use a form similar to that shown in Figure 6.3.

On the Home Language Survey, the parent or guardian lists the child's native language and the language(s) spoken by other household members. If the child's native language is not English, school personnel give the child assessments to determine her or his first (L1) and second (L2) language proficiency. For example, Jose, whose first language is Spanish, takes a test to measure his proficiencies in the Spanish language—reading, writing, speaking, and listening. He then takes a second assessment, an English Language Development Assessment, to determine his proficiency in English. This test classifies him as an EL student (**English Learner**) or as FEP (**Fluent English Proficient**).

THE ENGLISH LANGUAGE DEVELOPMENT ASSESSMENT   If the student is an English learner, an assessment determines the level of his or her proficiency in reading, writing, speaking and listening. This assessment battery measures the annual progress made by nonnative English speakers, grades K through 12, as they work toward becoming fully English proficient. The specific exam differs from state to state. Some states use the English Language Development Assessment (ELDA) built collaboratively by state educational leaders and the U.S. Department of Education. Another consortium of states administers assessments through a group named WIDA (World-Class Instructional Design and Assessment). Other states have designed their own assessments, like Colorado's test of English Language Acquisition (CELA).

Student	Language Proficiency			Vocabulary		Fluency			Comprehension					Motivation		
	L1	L2	Prof	Voc Stand	Cloze	Rate	Acc	Pros	Comp Stand	Inst Lv1	Strat			Self Con	Value Read	Interview/ Inventory
											G	PS	S			

FIGURE 6.2 Class Profile: A Chart for Recording Student Assessment Data

---

HOME LANGUAGE SURVEY

Student Name: _____ Grade: _____ Age: _____
School: _____
Parent/Guardian Name: _____

Fill this form out completely. This is to assist us in the assessment and placement of your child.

1. Which language did your child learn when he/she first began to talk?

   _____

2. Which language does your child most frequently speak at home?

   _____

3. Which language do you (the parents or guardians) most frequently use when speaking with your child?

   _____

4. Which language is most often spoken by the adults in your home? (parents, guardians, grandparents, or any other adults)

   _____

5. If a language other than English is indicated on any line above, does your child:

   Understand this language?   ____ Yes ____ No
   Speak this language?   ____ Yes ____ No
   Read this language?   ____ Yes ____ No
   Write this language?   ____ Yes ____ No

6. How many years of instruction has your child had in a language other than English?

   _____

_____   _____
Parent/Guardian Signature   Date

FIGURE 6.3   Sample Home Language Survey

Each of these exams attempts to categorize a student's English language proficiency. For example, Figure 6.4 describes each of the levels of English proficiency from the English Language Development Assessment (South Carolina Department of Education, 2009). The five levels are: Prefunctional, Beginning, Intermediate, Advanced, and Fully English Proficient. Moving from left to right on the chart (Figure 6.4), the student's comprehension and production of English increases in complexity.

Periodic evaluations determine if the student is ready to be re-designated into the Fluent English Proficient group. If the student is designated as Fluent, the district will no longer receive extra financial resources to aid this student's English language development; however, that student can still, like his grade level peers, benefit from carefully chosen instructional strategies.

PAUSE and REFLECT 6.2

Each state administers a test to assess English language proficiency. In your state, which assessment is conducted? Which performance levels are used, and what are the characteristics of students who perform at each level?

	Pre-Functional	Beginning	Intermediate	Advanced	Fully English Proficient
Listening	Understands: • some common words or key phrases, especially when contextualized • Generally unable to identify what the speaker intends to say	Understands: • simple and short statements, questions, and messages on familiar topics in school settings • key words, phrases, and cognates in content-area settings • simple, basic vocabulary of spoken English	Understands: • main ideas in short conversations • single step and some multistep directions • frequently used verb tenses and word-order patterns • a range of vocabulary from school-social environments • key academic terms	Understands: • speech in most school settings • main ideas and some supporting ideas in content-area settings • multistep directions • most of the basic forms of spoken English • a range of vocabulary and idioms, beginning to develop content area vocabulary	Understands: • a significant amount of content-area and school-social speech • main ideas, details, and nuances of meaning • a broad range of vocabulary
Speaking	• Repeats common phrases with simple structures • Can say a few common, everyday words • Is able to provide some basic information	• Uses familiar formulas or memorized phrases • Word order and grammatical mistakes may impede meaning • Little or no academic vocabulary	• Uses familiar speaking structures • May make errors in tense, agreement, pronoun use, and verb endings • Limited in vocabulary, especially academic vocabulary	• Can supply mostly coherent, unified verbal responses • Verbal errors usually don't impede understanding • Uses language to connect, tell, expand, and reason • Pronunciation occasionally interferes with communication	• Uses a variety of devices to connect ideas logically • Uses a range of complex and simple grammatical structures • Grammar and vocabulary are comparable to an English speaker • Pronunciation seldom interferes with communication

FIGURE 6.4 English Proficiency Levels from an English Language Development Assessment (ELDA). *Adapted from the South Carolina Department of Education (2009)*

(Continued)

	Pre-Functional	Beginning	Intermediate	Advanced	Fully English Proficient
Reading	• May identify isolated words, phrases, and cognates, especially when contextualized • Unable to identify ideas intended by writer • Does not understand how words and word order convey meaning in English	• Understands short, simple authentic texts • Has some understanding of narrative texts that are mostly below grade level • Relies heavily on visual cues and prior knowledge • Understands simple grammatical structures and everyday vocabulary	• Understands many authentic narrative and descriptive texts, especially below grade level • Comprehends content-area text with familiar content • Understands simple written directions, familiar verb tenses • Comprehends a wide range of vocabulary from school-social environments and some key vocabulary from content areas	• Understands most nonacademic and non-technical texts appropriate for grade level • Comprehends many content area texts, mostly on familiar topics • Understands relevant details and writer perspectives • Comprehends a wide range of vocabulary and idioms and is developing a wide range of technical, content-area vocabulary	• Understands a range of texts including literary and academic genres • Understands complex structures of written English • Has a wide range of vocabulary and idioms related to content areas and school-social environments
Writing	• Not yet functional in English writing • Can copy letters or words, but text does not transmit a coherent message • No evidence of appropriate text or sentence structure	• Writing is limited to typical, present-tense sentences or phrases and is likely to be repetitive • Writes with a limited vocabulary • Makes frequent errors in mechanics	• Demonstrates some use of discourse features and comprehensible use of sentence structure • Uses everyday vocabulary, but knows very few content specific words • May make frequent mechanical errors, particularly when expressing complex ideas	• Demonstrates mostly successful use of discourse features • Has sufficient vocabulary to express him or herself in writing, with some errors that infrequently affect comprehensibility	• Demonstrates almost completely appropriate use of discourse features such as word order • Uses complex sentence structures • Has a wide range of vocabulary that allows for precision • Uses writing conventions with some errors that do not affect comprehensibility

FIGURE 6.4 Continued

The evaluation of levels allows teachers to appropriately differentiate instruction and to meet state standards for English language development. According to the English Language Development Assessment, Lao is an English learner at an *Advanced* proficiency level. Based on that knowledge, the teacher is equipped to choose appropriate assignments for Lao. For example, if a science teacher is considering asking students to use the PLAN strategy (predict, locate, add, note) described in Chapter 4, she would conclude that his language proficiency would not interfere with his ability to locate important information in the text. The same assignment, however, might not be appropriate for a student whose English was at the Beginning or Intermediate levels of English proficiency.

In addition, results from the ELDA and other comparable tests help teachers choose appropriate formative assessments in the classroom. If a student who is at an Intermediate level of English proficiency writes a paragraph summary of a reading in science, the teacher should expect to find some grammatical errors that might interfere with the meaning of the summary. If a teacher knows this in advance, she might ask the student to engage in an alternative assessment that would measure knowledge of content. Chapter 8 describes how to use this information about language proficiency in planning for instruction.

ADD TO THE CLASS PROFILE—LANGUAGE PROFICIENCY On the Class Profile, enter data for each student's language proficiency, including first language (L1), second language (L2), and English proficiency.

1. Find the Language Proficiency section on the Class Profile. Record the primary language spoken by that student in the column marked *L1*.
2. In *L2,* record the second language (if any) spoken by the student.
3. Under *Proficiency*, record data from an English Language Development Assessment (if available). For example, if using levels of English proficiency shown in Figure 6.4, write Pre-functional (P-F), Beginning (Beg), Intermediate (Int), Advanced (Adv), or Fully English Proficient (FEP).

Figure 6.5 shows the Class Profile with Lao's data. He is an English learner whose first language is Hmong. The Class Profile shows "Hmong" in the L1 (first language) column and "Eng"(English) in the L2 (second language) column. When Lao took the ELDA, he tested at the *Advanced* level, so the abbreviation "Adv" appears in the Proficiency column.

Vocabulary

Assessing students' proficiency with vocabulary allows teachers to plan for instruction that helps students develop both content-general and content-specific vocabulary knowledge. Teachers have two readily available means to understand students' vocabulary proficiency: using existing standardized test data and conducting cloze assessments within the content area classroom.

STANDARDIZED MEASURES Typically, to measure vocabulary knowledge, teachers rely on data provided by state testing. For example, in California, students must demonstrate proficiency toward the Language Arts/Reading Standard of Word Analysis and Vocabulary Development (Reading 1.0). Each year, the California Standards Test (CST) assesses students' vocabulary proficiency, and the results become available to teachers and parents. A **standardized test** is one that is administered and scored in a consistent, predetermined manner.

Questions on these exams focus on two types of vocabulary knowledge—word knowledge out of context and word knowledge in context. For vocabulary out of context, the assessment gives a word and asks the student to choose the closest meaning. To test vocabulary knowledge in context, the test first gives a sentence, paragraph, or a passage that uses that word. Then the student identifies the closest word meaning. Figure 6.6 shows an example of these two types of vocabulary questions on a ninth-grade, standardized language arts test (California Department of

Student	Language Proficiency			Vocabulary		Fluency			Comprehension					Motivation		
	L1	L2	Prof	Voc Stand	Cloze	Rate	Acc	Pros	Comp Stand	Inst Lvl	G	Strat PS	S	Self Con	Value Read	Interview/ Inventory
Lao	Hmong	Eng	Adv	Basic	Frust	Low	Frust	25%	BBasic	6th	+	✓	–	40%	80%	Enjoys working with partner

FIGURE 6.5 Lao's Language Proficiency Data on the Class Profile

---

Sample 1. (Vocabulary out of context)

The word "glorify" most closely means

A. imagine
B. predict
C. examine
D. honor

Sample 2. (Vocabulary in context)

Read the following sentence:

First he stirred fresh mint leaves with sugar and secret ingredients in a small pot on the stove for a very long time, concocting a fragrant elixir of mint.

The word "concocting" means

A. examining
B. creating
C. imagining
D. tasting

FIGURE 6.6 Sample Vocabulary Items from a Standardized Assessment.   (California Department of Education, 2003)

Education, 2000). Experts in reading assessment recommend that vocabulary knowledge be tested in context because those items more closely resemble authentic reading tasks.

When assessment reports list vocabulary as a separate score, teachers can see students' scores and levels that rank them within the state's system. These data give teachers an indication of the student's vocabulary knowledge as measured on that particular exam. Figure 6.7 shows a sample of three seventh-grade-students' vocabulary data, including points possible, raw score, percent correct and ranked level. Many states in the United States have adopted consistent language to describe a student's proficiency level: Basic, Proficient, and Advanced. The definitions of these terms are:

- *Advanced:* Superior mastery of knowledge and skills that are fundamental for proficient grade level work.
- *Proficient:* Solid mastery of knowledge and skills that are fundamental for proficient grade level work.
- *Basic:* Partial mastery of knowledge and skills that are fundamental for proficient grade level work (National Center for Educational Statistics, 2008).

In addition, some states add the achievement levels "Below Basic" and "Far Below Basic." These two levels indicate that students have not mastered knowledge and skills that are fundamental for proficient, grade level work.

Student	Points Possible	Raw Score	% Correct	Level
Denise	11	8	73%	Proficient
Kia	11	7	64%	Basic
Chris	11	10	91%	Advanced

FIGURE 6.7 Sample Vocabulary Data from a Seventh-grade Standardized Test

In using data from standardized tests, it is important to remember the limitations of standardized testing. These data cannot give teachers a complete picture of the vocabulary that a student knows. In particular, standardized measures cover more content-general as opposed to content-specific vocabulary. Teachers need other measures to determine how proficient the student will be at reading content area text. One option is to conduct a Cloze Procedure.

THE CLOZE PROCEDURE   In the **Cloze Procedure**, a student reads a paragraph that has select words deleted. While reading, she fills in words that fit the context. Many teachers use modified versions of the Cloze Procedure to assess whether students will be able to understand the vocabulary in a content area textbook. This particular assessment measures words in context, following the recommendations of current experts in vocabulary assessment. Figure 6.8 shows an example of a Cloze Procedure to assess students' understanding of mathematics vocabulary.

Procedure

1. Select a paragraph of 5 to 7 sentences.
2. Type the passage.
3. Leave the first sentence, the last sentence, and all punctuation intact.
4. Remove words in a particular pattern, such as every seventh word. Do not remove proper nouns.
5. Prepare the passage by replacing words with blanks that are about 15 spaces long. In a "word bank" column on the paper, type the words that have been omitted from the text.
6. Ask students to read the entire passage.
7. Students try to fill in each blank, if possible, with the words from the "word bank."
8. To score, count how many words are replaced exactly with the ones that have been omitted.
   a. 60 percent = Independent level. The student can read and understand the vocabulary in the text without assistance.
   b. 45 percent to 59 percent = Instructional level. The student will need assistance with the vocabulary in the text.
   c. Less than 45 percent = Frustration level. The student is unlikely to understand the vocabulary in the text, even with help.

With the Cloze Procedure, the reader must be able to place grade level content-general and content-specific vocabulary in the context of a sentence. This process is similar to the one that students use when attempting to comprehend the meaning of content vocabulary within a new text passage. The cloze, when used in this manner, helps teachers understand whether the vocabulary in the text poses a particular problem for the student.

One variation of the Cloze Procedure is the **Concept Maze** (Ketterlin-Geller, McCoy, Twynman, & Tindal, 2006). In this procedure, the teacher removes words that represent key concepts from the content. For a high school passage of 350 words, about 16 words would be eliminated. As the sample in Figure 6.9 shows, each missing word has three options from which to choose; students choose the one that makes the most sense. The Concept Maze measures students' subject specific vocabulary knowledge (Ketterlin-Geller, et al., 2006).

ADD TO THE CLASS PROFILE—VOCABULARY   Transfer scores for both vocabulary measures—the standardized test and the Cloze Procedure—to the Class Profile.

1. Under the *Standardized (VocStand)* column, record whether the student is: Advanced (Adv), Proficient (Prof), Basic, Below Basic (BB) or Far Below Basic (FBB).
2. Under *Cloze* record the results of the Cloze Procedure. Based on the Cloze Procedure, record if the vocabulary from the text is at the student's Frustration (Frust), Instructional (Inst), or Independent (Ind) level.

Figure 6.10 shows Lao's vocabulary data on the Class Profile. For the standardized vocabulary test, Lao reached a *Basic* level of proficiency. When the teacher used the Cloze Procedure

Resource

A free cloze generator is available from the Osaka Institute of Technology via the Web site http://www.oit.ac.jp/ip/~kamiya/mwb/mwb.html.

Directions: Use the vocabulary in the Word Bank to complete the paragraph.

Word Bank

called   equivalent   careful
equations   operation

What is an Equivalent Equation?

In an equation, the two sides need to balance. So, to solve an equation, you must be _____ to keep
                                                                                    1
that balance by performing the same _____ on each side of the equation. When two _____ have
                                     2   3
the same set of solutions they are _____ equivalent equations. For example, the equations x = 5 and
                                   4
x − 5 = 0 are _____.
              5
They have only one solution—the number 5.

Answers:

1. careful
2. operation
3. equations
4. called
5. equivalent

FIGURE 6.8 Cloze Procedure Example with the First Sentence Intact and Every Ninth Word Removed

with an unfamiliar eighth-grade social studies passage, Lao placed 40 percent of the words in the correct blanks. This means that the vocabulary in the text is at Lao's *Frustration* level. Together, these data suggest that Lao will require help in how to figure out the meaning of unknown words, especially when facing the unfamiliar vocabulary in his textbook.

Directions: The paragraph below has four words missing. Under each blank space there are three possible choices. Circle the word that best completes the sentence.

Forming Equivalent Equations

In an equation, the two sides need to _____. So, to solve an equation, you must be careful
                                      1. reduce, balance, solve
to keep that balance by performing the same _____ on each side of the equation. When
                                            2. operation, number, subtraction
two equations have the same set of solutions, they are equivalent. For example, the equations x = 5
and x − 5 = 0 are _____. They have only one _____ —the number 5.
                  3. irrational, inverse, equivalent   4. slope, ratio, solution
Answers:

1. balance
2. operation
3. equivalent
4. solution

FIGURE 6.9 Concept Maze Example with Four Content Vocabulary Words Removed

Student	Language Proficiency			Vocabulary		Fluency			Comprehension					Motivation		
	L1	L2	Prof	Voc Stand	Cloze	Rate	Acc	Pros	Comp Stand	Inst Lvl	Strat G	Strat PS	Strat S	Self Con	Value Read	Interview/ Inventory
Lao	Hmong	Eng	Adv	Basic	Frust	Low	Frust	25%	BBasic	6th	+	✓	–	40%	80%	Enjoys working with partner

FIGURE 6.10 Lao's Vocabulary Proficiency Data on the Class Profile

Fluency

Many elementary and some middle schools conduct school-wide assessments on fluency several times per year. Assessment of fluency is less likely in middle and high school. However, as explained in Chapter 3, fluency is an important component of becoming a proficient reader. Assessing student fluency enables teachers to focus instruction on teaching students to read with appropriate rate, accuracy, and prosody. Fortunately, teachers can assess fluency with grade level materials by conducting a Curriculum-Based Measurement, or CBM.

Resource

Generate grade level reading materials for Curriculum-Based Measurement at the Intervention Central Web site: http://www. interventioncentral.org/htm docs/tools/okapi/okapi.php.

CURRICULUM-BASED MEASUREMENTS   One of the most common ways of assessing reading fluency is with a **Curriculum Based Measure** (CBM). A CBM is an assessment system created with items that represent the grade level curriculum (Dudley, 2005). To measure reading fluency, teachers ask students to read aloud a series of short, grade level passages. While students are reading, teachers assess students' rate, accuracy, and prosody.

Teachers who use CBMs can create them or purchase them as part of a published reading program. Any content area teacher can conduct this quick assessment to learn how well students will be able to read and understand the content area textbook.

Procedure

1. From the content area text, select at least one grade level passage, 250 words or more. (If there is time, choose three grade level passages to calculate an average score).
   a. The student and teacher each need a copy of the text. The student reads from one copy, and, on the other copy, the teacher notes accuracy and prosody (see #2).
2. Have the student read aloud from the text passage for one minute.
   a. Note prosody. While listening, make mental or written notes regarding the student's intonation, phrasing, and expression. For example, if the student does not pause for a period, put an "x" through it to show that it was omitted.
   b. Note accuracy. While listening, note errors that the student makes (omissions, additions, and miscues).
3. Score reading rate.
   a. Count how many words the student read in one minute and count how many errors were made.
   b. Subtract the number of errors made from the number of words read to determine *words correct*. The *actual rate* is the number of words read correctly in one minute.
   c. Compare the results with the rate norms shown in Figure 6.11. These norms represent data collected from thousands of students in grades 1 through 8. (There is no data available for students just beginning first grade. In grades 9 through 12, norms are approximately the same as for eighth grade.) (Hasbrouck & Tindal, 2005). Grade levels are listed on the left-hand column. The second column shows a percentile number. The columns labeled "Fall," "Winter," and "Spring" show the norms for the words per minute. For example, in the fall, if a seventh-grader is reading 180 words per minute, she is in the 90th percentile—she reads more fluently than 89 percent of eighth-graders.
      i. To compare a student's rate, look at the area of the chart representing her or his grade level. Find the student's words per minute (WPM) and the corresponding percentile.
      ii. Decide whether the WPM is at, above, or below grade level. WPM in the 50th percentile range is at grade level. For the purposes of the Class Profile, scores below the 50th percentile are "Low" and above the 50th percentile are "High." For example, an eighth-grader reading at grade level would read somewhere between 133 and 151. Above 151 would be considered "High" and below 133 would be considered "Low."
4. Score reading accuracy.
   a. Divide "words correct" by "number of words" and multiply by 100 to determine the percentage correct.

Grade	Percentile	Fall WPM	Winter WPM	Spring WPM
1	90		81	111
	75		47	82
	50		23	53
	25		12	28
	10		6	15
2	90	106	125	142
	75	79	100	117
	50	51	72	89
	25	25	42	61
	10	11	18	31
3	90	128	146	162
	75	99	120	137
	50	71	92	107
	25	44	62	78
	10	21	36	48
4	90	145	166	180
	75	119	139	152
	50	94	112	123
	25	68	87	98
	10	45	61	72
5	90	166	182	194
	75	139	156	168
	50	110	127	139
	25	85	99	109
	10	61	74	83
6	90	177	195	204
	75	153	167	177
	50	110	140	150
	25	98	111	122
	10	68	82	93
7	90	180	192	202
	75	156	165	177
	50	128	136	150
	25	102	109	123
	10	79	88	98
8	90	185	199	199
	75	161	173	177
	50	133	146	151
	25	106	115	124
	10	77	84	97

FIGURE 6.11 Fluency Norms for Students in Grades 1 through 8.   Data from Hasbrouck, J. & Tindal, G. (2005). *Oral Reading Fluency: 90 Years of Measurement* (Tech Rep. No. 33). Eugene, OR: Behavioral Research and Testing, University of Oregon. Cited with permission

Prosody	Proficient (4)	Basic (3)	Below Basic (2)	Far BB (1)	Total
Intonation	Voice matches text interpretation	Some appropriate voice	Lacking intonation and voice adjustment, but volume control	Quiet voice without intonation	/ 4
Expression	Correct tone of voice matching punctuation	Voice sounds like natural language	Voice similar to natural language, but no expression	Reads words to just get them out	/ 4
Phrasing	Reads to commas, breathes at periods	Reads phrases, but runs-on	Reads two and three word phrases	Reads word by word	/ 4
				Total Points	/12
				Total Percent Score	%

FIGURE 6.12   Prosody Proficiency Rubric

b. Use the following guidelines (Pikulski, 1990) to determine if the accuracy in reading the passage is at the student's Independent, Instructional, or Frustration level.
  i. 97 to 100 percent = **Independent level:** The student can read the text without assistance.
  ii. 90 to 96 percent = **Instructional level:** The student can read the text with some assistance.
  iii. Less than 90 percent = **Frustration level:** Even with assistance, the student will have difficulty reading the text.

5. Score prosody.
  a. Consult the descriptors on the prosody proficiency rubric in Figure 6.12.
  b. Use the rubric to score each component: intonation, expression, and phrasing.
  c. Add the total score (out of 12) and convert number to a percent.

ADD TO THE CLASS PROFILE—FLUENCY   On the Class Profile, record the fluency scores for rate, accuracy, and prosody.

1. Record Rate. Based on the reading rate score, record whether students are at grade level (At), above grade level (High), or below grade level (Low).
2. Record Accuracy. On the Class Profile, record whether students read the text at an Independent (Ind), Instructional (Inst) or Frustrational (Frust) level.
3. Record Prosody. On the Class Profile, record the prosody score, a percentage that represents the number of points out of 12 possible.

Figure 6.13 shows Lao's rate, accuracy, and prosody. Fluency assessments show that Lao reads at a *Low* rate. When he reads the text, his accuracy places him at the *Frustration* level. In addition, his prosody assessment revealed that he has difficulty with expression, in particular his intonation.

If a student reads a grade level passage at a rate that is below grade level, it can be interpreted a few ways. Usually, low rate means that the student cannot decode the words in the text. This interpretation is especially true if it is paired with a low accuracy score.

If the accuracy happens to be high, but the rate is still below grade level, the student might be reading more slowly in order to be more accurate. High accuracy and a slow pace is only troublesome in a context in which a slow pace can hinder how much text they can process in a period of time, such as during a timed test. Figure 6.14 shows other combinations of high and low fluency.

In the case of Lao, his fluency scores show that his rate, accuracy, and prosody are all below grade level. These data suggest that he will benefit from instruction in fluency.

Learning Log

Use a student's fluency data in the Learning Log Appendix to practice how to calculate reading rate and accuracy. (LL7)

Student	Language Proficiency			Vocabulary		Fluency			Comprehension						Motivation		
	L1	L2	Prof	Voc Stand	Cloze	Rate	Acc	Pros	Comp Stand	Inst Lvl	G	Strat PS	S	Self Con	Value Read	Interview/ Inventory
Lao	Hmong	Eng	Adv	Basic	Frust	Low	Frust	25%	BBasic	6th	+	✓	–	40%	80%	Enjoys working with partner

FIGURE 6.13 Lao's Fluency Data on the Class Profile

Results say. . .			What it means. . .
Rate	Accuracy	Prosody	
High	High	High	Fluency OK
Low	Low	Low	Fluency needs improvement in all areas.
Low	High	High	May want to help improve rate. Only important in time-critical situation.
High	High	Low	Focus instruction on prosody: read more slowly, noting punctuation.
High	Low	Low	Fluency needs improvement; stress accuracy, not speed.

FIGURE 6.14 Interpretation of Fluency Assessment Results

Comprehension

In assessing reading comprehension, it is important to attend to both reading skills and reading strategies. **Reading skills** are automatic and uncontrolled actions that result in decoding and comprehension. **Reading strategies**, on the other hand, are deliberate actions made in an effort to make meaning from text (Afflerbach, Pearson, & Paris, 2008).

Collecting comprehension data is the most critical piece in knowing how to support students in their literacy development and their understanding of subject matter. Three possibilities for data collection are: standardized tests, informal reading inventories, and/or self-report surveys.

STANDARDIZED MEASURES As described above state standardized measures assess reading comprehension, usually once each year. For comprehension items, students read a passage, and then answer questions. Passages represent different genres and text forms, such as stories, informational essays, and poetry. Figure 6.15 shows sample items from the tenth grade language arts exam from the Massachusetts Comprehensive Assessment System (Massachusetts Department of Education, 2009). This particular question asks students to make a conclusion based upon information in the passage. The specific reading skill or strategy assessed depends upon state standards and will differ at various grade levels.

The data from this annual statewide assessment show the comprehension score for each student. The state divides the scores into text types: narrative and expository. The score for

---

Passage excerpt from "Don't Burn Out: The New Science of Being Cool"

Paragraph 2:
Our natural defenses against the heat are remarkably effective. Blood, our first level of protection, cools muscles and organs by carrying body heat to the skin's surface where it dissipates. But if the air temperature is higher than 82 degrees or if exercise spikes our body temperature, our core won't be adequately cooled. To keep from overheating, the body turns on its sprinklers, the backup cooling system we call sweating. Perspiration that evaporates off the skin has a cooling effect; so the hotter it is outside, the more your body will be cooled.

What does paragraph 2 reveal about the human body?

A. It regulates its temperature well.
B. It uses perspiration for heating and cooling.
C. It cools quickly if it has a high surface area.
D. It functions poorly in hot and humid conditions.

FIGURE 6.15 Sample Reading Comprehension Passage and Item. (Massachusetts Department of Education, 2009)

expository, or content area text, gives teachers an indication of students' proficiency levels with content area text. The names of achievement levels vary by state, but expect to see some or all of these descriptors: Advanced, Proficient, Basic, Below Basic, and Far Below Basic.

Data from these standardized assessments are a starting point for understanding students' needs. However, additional data help teachers discover if their students are able to comprehend grade level text. For example, based on the standardized test results, Lao's reading comprehension is at a *Basic* level. Conducting an Informal Reading Inventory will help to clearly identify his strengths and areas for growth.

INFORMAL READING INVENTORIES   An **Informal Reading Inventory** is an individually administered battery of assessments designed to determine a student's reading instructional needs. Informal Reading Inventories allow educators to understand student reading proficiency to a level of depth greater than standardized tests. In most schools, the reading specialist will conduct this type of assessment. However, in some schools, especially rural and charter schools, this responsibility might fall to the teachers. Even if a reading specialist is available, teachers may choose this type of assessment in order to learn more about students who seem puzzling or are severely at risk.

Informal Reading Inventories include leveled sets of passages designed to measure student comprehension. Teachers can test students' proficiencies in reading narrative versus expository text, and can monitor how prior knowledge impacts students' understanding of the text. In the QRI (Leslie & Caldwell, 2011), an example of an Informal Reading Inventory, the examiner first gives a word list assessment, then she or he uses the results of this assessment to choose an appropriate passage for students to read. After answering prior knowledge questions, students read the passage aloud, retell the passage, and answer comprehension questions.

Each portion of the assessment has implications for instruction. Reading aloud gives the examiner an opportunity to check for reading fluency. Using the test materials, educators identify patterns in miscues. If, for example, the reader is constantly skipping words, an instructional plan might include reading more slowly and tracking words while reading.

The retelling gives the teacher clues about whether the student understands the structure of narrative text (plot, characters, setting, theme) or informational text (e.g., descriptive text with main ideas and details). After reading, a student might retell the main ideas but have trouble remembering the details. This student would benefit from strategies such as graphic organizers to use during reading.

The comprehension questions reveal whether students are more proficient with literal, explicit questions or implicit, inferential questions. The comprehension questions help determine whether students need to work on making inferences as they read. Depending upon how the assessment is administered, students can be asked to think aloud as they read, which would indicate their use of strategies. The results help teachers identify students' reading levels, specifically what level they can read independently, with some assistance, or what level is frustrating.

Results from a QRI conducted with Lao indicated that sixth-grade text is at his *Instructional* level. This finding means that, even with support, Lao may be frustrated by his eighth-grade text. In addition, the QRI data show that Lao has trouble remembering the details of expository texts; he also has difficulty answering implicit comprehension questions—questions that require him to go beyond a literal understanding of the text.

SURVEY OF STRATEGY USE   Another important aspect to assess is the reader's use of reading strategies. To assess whether students are aware of reading strategies, teachers use a survey called the Metacognitive Awareness of Reading Strategies Inventory, or MARSI (Mokhtari & Reichard, 2002). **Metacognition** refers to one's own knowledge about one's thinking (Flavell, 1976). Designed for adolescents and adults, the MARSI measures a reader's awareness of and their perceived use of reading strategies. For each item, the participant reads a statement, like "I preview the text to see what it's about before reading it." The participant then rates her or his use of that strategy on a scale of one to five, with one meaning "I never or almost never do this" and five defined as "I always or almost always do this." The Teacher Tool Appendix includes the complete MARSI survey.

Teacher Tool

The Metacognitive Awareness of Reading Strategies Inventory (MARSI) (TT 16) can be found in the Teacher Tools Appendix.

Strategy Subgroup	Strategies Used
Global Reading Strategies	Setting purpose, predicting and confirming predictions, previewing texts, using context clues, deciding what to read closely, using text structure
Problem-Solving Strategies	Reading slowly and carefully, adjusting reading rate, paying close attention to reading, pausing to reflect, visualizing, reading text out loud, considering meaning of words
Support Reading Strategies	Taking notes, paraphrasing, rereading, asking self questions, using reference materials, underlining, discussing reading, writing summaries

FIGURE 6.16   Subgroups of Strategies Measured on the MARSI (Metacognitive Awareness of Reading Strategies Inventory).   (Mokhtari & Reichard, 2002)

The 30 items on the survey are designed to measure three types of strategies: 1) Global Reading Strategies, 2) Problem-Solving Strategies, and 3) Support Reading Strategies (see Figure 6.16). A **Global Reading Strategy** is a tool that readers use to aid comprehension when reading any text, such as having a purpose in mind while reading. A **Problem-Solving Strategy** (such as rereading) is one that is used to correct comprehension. And a **Support Reading Strategy** (such as note taking) assists the reader as she or he reads the text.

Once students have finished the survey, the teacher can use the score sheet with its step-by-step directions and guide students through the scoring process. The overall average score indicates how often students report using strategies when reading academic materials. The subscores reveal which group of strategies are the strongest for students, and which are areas for potential growth and instructional focus. In Lao's case, his mean score for Global Strategies is 4.0, which means that he often uses this particular group of reading strategies: prediction, setting purpose, and previewing texts.

Learning Log

Use the MARSI found in the Learning Log Appendix (LL8) to increase your knowledge about reading comprehension strategy assessment while you learn about your own strategy use.

ADD TO THE CLASS PROFILE—READING COMPREHENSION   Record three components for comprehension: Standardized, Instructional Grade Level, and Strategies Used.

1. In the *Standardized* (CompStand) column, record whether the student is Advanced, Proficient, Basic, Below Basic, or Far Below Basic on the standardized measure of comprehension.
2. In the *Instructional Grade Level* (Inst Lvl) column, record data from the Informal Reading Inventories.
3. In the *Strategies Used* (Strat) column, mark the strategies students are most and least likely to use independently.
   - "+" for strategies with a mean of 4.0 to 5.0
   - "√" for strategies with a mean of 2.0 to 3.9
   - "−" for strategies with a mean of 0 to 1.9

Figure 6.17 Shows Lao's reading comprehension entered on the Class Profile. Data from Lao's statewide assessment indicate that he is *Below Basic* in reading comprehension. Results from an Informal Reading Inventory conducted with Lao indicated that fifth- and sixth-grade text is at his *Instructional* level. This finding means that, even with support, Lao may be frustrated by his eighth-grade text. In addition, the QRI data show that Lao has trouble remembering the details of expository texts; he also has difficulty answering implicit comprehension questions—questions that require him to go beyond a literal understanding of the text.

Lao's results on the MARSI indicate strengths and areas for growth. The set of strategies that he uses most frequently are Global Reading Strategies. He sets purposes for reading, uses the text structure, and makes and confirms predictions. According to his survey, Lao is less likely to engage in strategies to support his reading (such as taking notes) or to solve problems that he encounters during reading. These findings open up some potential areas for strategy instruction.

Student	Language Proficiency			Vocabulary		Fluency			Comprehension					Motivation		
	L1	L2	Prof	Voc Stand	Cloze	Rate	Acc	Pros	Comp Stand	Inst Lvl	Strat G	Strat PS	Strat S	Self Con	Value Read	Interview/ Inventory
Lao	Hmong	Eng	Adv	Basic	Frust	Low	Frust	25%	BBasic	6th	+	✓	−	40%	80%	Enjoys working with partner

FIGURE 6.17   Lao's Reading Comprehension Data on the Class Profile

---

PAUSE and REFLECT 6.3

Consider the different types of comprehension assessments that you have experienced as a teacher and a learner. What can these assessments effectively measure? What do these assessments not measure?

Motivation

As explained in Chapter 5, motivation is a process by which a goal-directed activity is both initiated and sustained (Schunk, Pintrich, & Meece, 2008). One of the most widely used assessments for assessing motivation to read is the MRP or Motivation to Read Profile (Gambrell, Palmer, Codling, & Mazzoni, 1996). In 2007, this profile was adapted for use with adolescents (Pitcher, et al., 2007).

ADOLESCENT MOTIVATION TO READ PROFILE   The Adolescent Motivation to Read Profile consists of two parts: a reading survey and a conversational interview. The reading survey asks the student to answer 20 multiple-choice questions about their attitudes toward reading. These questions assess both Self-Concept as a Reader and the Value of Reading. The whole class completes this portion simultaneously. The conversational interview gives questions that a teacher or examiner asks individual students. These questions focus on the student's interests in three areas: narrative reading, informational reading, and general reading. The Teacher Tools Appendix includes the full assessment, with instructions.

Teacher Tool

The Adolescent Motivation to Read Profile (TT17) can be found in the Teacher Tools Appendix.

A scoring sheet (included in the Teacher Tools Appendix) assists the teacher in calculating scores for the motivation survey. Sub-cores for Self-Concept and Value of Reading can be calculated. For example, Lao's score on the Adolescent Motivation to Read Profile was 16/40 (40 percent) for Self-Concept and 32/40 (80 percent) for the Value of Reading. This data suggests that Lao does not think of himself as a strong reader; however, he thinks that reading is important.

The conversational interview provides a clearer image of the student's attitudes toward reading. In Lao's case, it revealed that he is interested in the military, and he enjoys hanging out with his friends and reading motorcycle magazines. An understanding of Lao's interests can lead to planning decisions that can increase motivation. For example, the teacher might make an effort to draw out his knowledge about the military in a discussion about the U.S. Civil War, a part of the eighth-grade social science curriculum. Pitcher et al. (2007) suggest that teachers use MRP results in planning developmentally appropriate curriculum and to help avoid a continual mismatch between reading assignments and student interests.

INFORMAL MOTIVATION INVENTORY   When there is not time to meet with students to talk about their interests, teachers give informal motivation inventories. An **Informal Motivation Inventory** is a survey of students' interests and attitudes toward reading. A whole class can simultaneously take the survey, giving the teacher a wealth of information to draw upon when building curricula. Informal Motivation Inventories are available on the Internet, in reading resource books, or as part of a textbook reading program. Many teachers design their own, with specific items that will give them important information about their students. Figure 6.18 shows an Informal Motivation Inventory.

The Informal Motivation Inventory tells more about what Lao finds both motivating and discouraging about reading. He enjoys working in a group, but does not like to read aloud parts of the text. He is bothered by his accent. Lao doesn't think he is a very good student because reading is hard for him.

Information from the Adolescent Motivation to Read Profile and the Informal Motivation Inventory help to complete the Class Profile.

Section 1: Questions. Please answer the following questions.

1. What do you like to do in your free time?
2. Who is your favorite person?
3. What is your favorite TV show or movie?
4. What is the best thing about school?
5. What is the worst thing about school?
6. How do you feel about reading?
7. What do you do when you get stuck while reading?
8. What do you usually do when you come to a word that you don't know?
9. If you could read anything, what would it be?

Section 2: Yes or No. For each item, circle yes or no.

I like reading when I read:

1.	Fiction	Yes	No
2.	Nonfiction	Yes	No
3.	Adventures	Yes	No
4.	Mysteries	Yes	No
5.	Newspapers	Yes	No
6.	Comics	Yes	No
7.	Magazines	Yes	No
8.	Textbooks	Yes	No
9.	Websites	Yes	No
10.	Email	Yes	No

I like reading about:

1.	Sports	Yes	No
2.	Celebrities	Yes	No
3.	Animals	Yes	No
4.	Science	Yes	No
5.	People	Yes	No
6.	History	Yes	No
7.	Technology	Yes	No
8.	Other_____	Yes	No

I believe that:

1.	reading is important	Yes	No
2.	I am a good reader	Yes	No
3.	being a good reader is important	Yes	No

I enjoy:

1.	Reading aloud	Yes	No
2.	Reading silently	Yes	No
3.	Reading by myself	Yes	No
4.	Reading in pairs	Yes	No
5.	Reading in groups	Yes	No
6.	Discussing what I read	Yes	No
7.	Helping others in class	Yes	No
8.	Reading Websites	Yes	No
9.	Other_____		

I need help with:

1.	Short words	Yes	No
2.	Long words	Yes	No
3.	Sounds of each letter	Yes	No
4.	Sounds of letters together	Yes	No
5.	Reading faster	Yes	No
6.	Reading aloud	Yes	No
7.	Remembering what I read	Yes	No
8.	Understanding what I read	Yes	No
9.	Learning from textbooks	Yes	No
10.	Other_____		

FIGURE 6.18 Informal Motivation Inventory. Adapted from *Bader Reading and Language Inventory,* 5th Edition

ADD TO THE CLASS PROFILE—MOTIVATION Record the three sources of motivation data: Self-Concept, Value of Reading, and important findings from the Interview/Survey (see Figure 6.19).

1. Record information about students' Self-Concepts and Value of Reading.
   a. Under *Self-Concept* (SC), calculate and record the percentage score (out of 40).
   b. Under *Value of Reading* (Val), calculate and record the percentage score (out of 40).
2. In the *Interview/Inventory* column, record information from the conversational interview of the Adolescent Motivation to Read Profile or the Informal Motivation Inventory.

After collecting data for all students, the Class Profile will be complete, like the one in Figure 6.20. For your use, the Teacher Tools Appendix includes a blank Class Profile.

Teacher Tool

For your use, a blank Class Profile (TT18) can be found in the Teacher Tools Appendix.

Student	Language Proficiency			Vocabulary		Fluency			Comprehension					Motivation		
	L1	L2	Prof	Voc Stand	Cloze	Rate	Acc	Pros	Comp Stand	Inst Lvl	Strat			Self Con	Value Read	Interview/ Inventory
											G	PS	S			
Lao	Hmong	Eng	Adv	Basic	Frust	Low	Frust	25%	BBasic	6th	+	✓	–	40%	80%	Enjoys working with partner

FIGURE 6.19   Lao's Motivation Data on the Class Profile

| Student | Language Proficiency | | | Vocabulary | | Fluency | | | Comprehension | | | | | Self Con | Value Read | Motivation |
	L1	L2	Prof	Voc Stand	Cloze	Rate	Acc	Pros	Comp Stand	Inst Lvl	G	PS	S			Interview/Inventory
Alec	Eng			Adv	Ind	High	Ind	92%	Adv	10th	+	✓	–	90%	90%	Wants to help others
Ava	Eng			Adv	Ind	High	Ind	100%	Adv	9th	+	✓	–	100%	90%	Wants to teach
Bella	Eng			Adv	Ind	High	Ind	90%	Adv	10th	+	✓	✓	90%	100%	Enjoys discussing text
Bianca	German	Eng	Adv	Prof	Inst	At	Inst	100%	Prof	8th	+	✓	–	90%	90%	Relies on help
Brandon	Eng			Prof	Inst	High	Frust	25%	Prof	7th	+	✓	✓	40%	90%	Dislikes reading aloud
Carson	Eng			Adv	Ind	High	Ind	92%	Adv	10th	+	+	+	80%	100%	Wants to help others
Casey	Eng			Adv	Inst	High	Frust	33%	Adv	8th	+	+	–	90%	80%	Enjoys discussing reading in groups
Ethan	Eng			Adv	Inst	High	Frust	25%	Adv	8th	+	+	✓	90%	80%	Enjoys discussing with partner
Garrett	Eng			Prof	Inst	At	Ind	50%	Prof	7th	+	✓	–	80%	80%	Enjoys discussing reading
Grant	Eng			Adv	Ind	High	Ind	84%	Adv	9th	+	+	✓	90%	90%	Wants to read at home
Jackie	Eng			Prof	Inst	High	Ind	41%	Prof	7th	+	✓	–	70%	80%	Enjoys discussing reading
Jana	Russian	Eng	Adv	Prof	Inst	High	Inst	41%	Prof	8th	+	✓	–	90%	90%	Relies on help
Johanna	German	Eng	Beg	Basic	Frust	Low	Frust	25%	FBB	4th	–	–	–	50%	20%	Doesn't want to read textbook
John	Eng			Prof	Inst	At	Ind	41%	Prof	7th	+	+	✓	50%	90%	Dislikes reading aloud
Jordan	Eng			Prof	Inst	At	Ind	50%	Prof	7th	+	+	–	80%	90%	Enjoys discussing with partner
Juan	Spanish	Eng	Adv	Prof	Ind	At	Inst	100%	Adv	9th	+	+	+	100%	100%	Enjoys reading aloud
Kia	Hmong	Eng	Int	Prof	Inst	Low	Frust	33%	Basic	7th	+	–	–	40%	80%	Trouble with text
Kristina	Eng			Basic	Frust	Low	Frust	33%	BB	6th	–	–	–	50%	30%	Dislikes reading, learning
Lao	Hmong	Eng	Adv	Basic	Frust	Low	Frust	25%	Basic	6th	+	✓	–	40%	80%	Enjoys working with partner
Lena	Eng			Adv	Ind	High	Ind	92%	Adv	9th	+	+	✓	90%	100%	Wants to read at home
Madison	Eng			Basic	Frust	Low	Frust	33%	BB	6th	–	–	–	40%	30%	Dislikes reading, learning
Maria	Spanish	Eng	Int	Prof	Inst	Low	Frust	33%	Basic	7th	+	–	–	40%	100%	Trouble with text, long words
Mia	Eng			Adv	Ind	High	Ind	92%	Adv	10th	+	+	+	90%	90%	Wants to help others
Raul	Spanish	Eng	Adv	Prof	Ind	At	Ind	92%	Adv	9th	✓	+	+	90%	90%	Enjoys discussing in groups
Tan	Hmong	Eng	Int	Basic	Frust	Low	Frust	33%	Basic	5th	✓	–	–	40%	30%	Dislikes reading aloud
Thao	Hmong	Eng	Int	Basic	Frust	Low	Frust	25%	BB	6th	–	–	–	30%	80%	Trouble w/text, dislikes reading aloud
Todd	Russian	Eng	Int.	Basic	Frust	Low	Frust	50%	FBB	4th	–	–	–	30%	70%	Dislikes reading aloud
Tou	Hmong	Eng	Beg	Basic	Frust	Low	Frust	50%	Basic	5th	–	–	–	40%	80%	Dislikes reading aloud
William	Eng			Prof	Inst	High	Frust	33%	Prof	8th	+	✓	✓	40%	90%	Dislikes reading aloud
Zach	Eng			Basic	Frust	Low	Frust	41%	BB	6th	–	–	–	50%	40%	Dislikes reading, learning

FIGURE 6.20 Completed Class Profile for an Eighth-grade Social Science Class

Chapter Summary

Assessment is a critical component of the LinC Cycle. While each teacher has a different role in regard to collecting and compiling data, all have access to assessment data that can help them address the adolescent literacy crisis. Effective content area teachers know the English language proficiency levels of students in their classes. They know their students' proficiency with vocabulary, fluency, and comprehension, and they understand what motivates their students to read. The tools provided in this chapter equip teachers to collect data efficiently, either by drawing data from standardized tests or by administering quick assessments.

The chapter began with Ms. Johnson, a new teacher who was surprised that her well-planned instructional strategy did not lead to the learning that she expected. By engaging in assessment, Ms. Johnson will be able to identify student needs and plan instruction that will lead to increased literacy development and content learning.

Resources

Gambrell, L. B., Palmer, B. M., Codling, R. M., & Mazzoni, S. A. (1996). Assessing motivation to read. *The Reading Teacher, 49*, 518–533.

Leslie, L., & Caldwell, J. (2011). *Qualitative reading inventory* (5th ed.). Boston: Pearson.

Mokhtari, K., & Reichard, C. A. (2002). Assessing students metacognitive awareness of reading strategies. *Educational Psychology, 94*(2), 249–259.

Pitcher, S., Albright, L., DeLaney, C., Walker, N., Seunarinesingh, K., Mogge, S., et al. (2007). Assessing adolescents' motivation to read. *Journal of Adolescent & Adult Literacy, 50*(5), 378–396.

References

Afflerbach, P., Pearson, P. D., & Paris, S. G. (2008). Clarifying differences between reading skills and reading strategies. *The Reading Teacher, 61*(5), 364–373.

Allington, R. L. (2002). What I've learned about effective reading instruction from a decade of studying exemplary classroom teachers. *Phi Delta Kappa Record*, 740–747.

California Department of Education (2000). California Standards Test: Released Test Questions, Grade 9 English. Retrieved June 29, 2008, from http://www.cde.ca.gov/ta/tg/sr/css05rtq.asp.

Dennis, D. (2008). Are assessment data really driving middle school instruction? What we can learn from one student's experience. *Journal of Adolescent & Adult Literacy, 51*(4), 578–587.

Dudley, A. M. (2005). Rethinking reading fluency for struggling adolescent readers. *Beyond Behavior: Journal of the Council for Children with Behavioral Disorders*, 16–22.

Flavell, J. H. (1976). Metacognitive aspects of problem solving. In L. B. Resnick (Ed.), *The nature of intelligence*. Hillsdale, NJ: Erlbaum.

Grigg, W., Donahue, P., & Dion, G. (2007). *The nation's report card: 12th grade reading and mathematics 2005*. Washington, DC: U.S. Department of Education, National Center for Education Statistics.

Hasbrouck, J., & Tindal, G. (2005). *Oral reading fluency: 90 years of measuremen* (Technical Report No. 33). Eugene, OR: Behavioral Research and Teaching, University of Oregon. Retrieved on July 14, 2008 at http://www.brtprojects.org/tech_reports.php

Ketterlin-Geller, L. R., McCoy, J. D., Twynman, T., & Tindal, G. (2006). Using a concept maze to assess student understanding of secondary-level content. *Assessment for Effective Intervention, 32*(2), 39–50.

Massachusetts Department of Education (2009). *Massachusetts comprehensive assessment system: Massachusetts grade 10 english language arts reading comprehension test*. Retrieved December, 2009 from http://www.doe.mass.edu/mcas/testitems. html?yr=09

National Center for Educational Statistics (2008). The NAEP glossary of terms. Retrieved July 18, 2008 from http://nces.ed.gov/nationsreportcard/about/interpretresults.asp.

Pikulski, J. J. (1990). Assessment: The role of tests in a literary assessment program. *The Reading Teacher, 43*(9), 686–688.

Schunk, D. H., Pintrich, P. R., & Meece, J. L. (2008). *Motivation in education: Theory, research and applications* (3rd ed.). Upper Saddle River, NJ: Pearson, Merrill, Prentice Hall.

South Carolina Department of Education (2009). English language development assessment: Grades 3-12 performance level descriptors. Retrieved September 30, 2009 from http://ed.sc.gov/agency/Accountability/Assessment/old/assessment/programs/elda/elda.html

Stiggins, R. (2008). *An introduction to student-involved assessment FOR learning, 5th ed.* Upper Saddle River, New Jersey: Pearson, Merrill, Prentice Hall.

CHAPTER 7

Reflect—Finding Patterns and Drawing Conclusions

It was late September, and Ms. Johnson had collected data on students' language proficiency, vocabulary, fluency, comprehension, and motivation. Getting the standardized test data was easy; the principal used the school's database to print out reports on the eighth-graders' results from the prior year. For the other data, she asked for help from all of the eighth-grade teachers and the district literacy coach to quickly gather what she needed.

By far, her favorite assessment was the Motivation to Read Profile. Ms. Johnson had always known that motivation impacted reading, but when she reflected on this data, she could see patterns across students in her classes. She looked at the data on the Class Profile for her fourth-period social science class, and what she saw surprised her. A majority of the class, all but five individuals, valued reading. Ms. Johnson knew that there was an "adolescent literacy crisis," so she expected these scores to be low. She let out a sigh of relief. But in the next column, she saw that many of the students did not have high self-concepts as readers. "I wonder why?" she thought. She looked across the Class Profile again and saw that about half of the class could not read at an eighth-grade level. This meant that reading the textbook independently was not an option. If, in the past, they had been assigned textbook reading at home, it is no wonder why they have low self-concepts as readers. Ms. Johnson knew that she would have to think carefully about this data so that she could choose the best instructional strategies to use with her class. "I wonder if I can help? Maybe if they can experience some success with reading the textbook, they will begin to see themselves as readers."

In the vignette, Ms. Johnson sees that the data can help her make instructional decisions. As she looks for patterns in the data, she engages in reflection about teaching and student learning. Reflection is more than just thinking about what one does. A reflective teacher gives careful thought to her experiences and how meaning is made from them. John Dewey, who wrote extensively about reflection in teaching, believed that **reflection** involves careful consideration of beliefs and practices, the evidence for those beliefs and practices, and the possible consequences (Dewey, 1933).

Reflective thought involves both content and process (Dewey, 1933; Hatton & Smith, 1995). With the LinC Cycle, the *content* of reflective thought is teacher knowledge. When integrating literacy in content area instruction, three types of teacher knowledge are especially important— knowledge about students, knowledge about curriculum, and knowledge about instructional methods (Colton & Sparks-Langer, 1993). The *process* of teacher reflection involves an interaction between a teacher's knowledge and new information in the environment. When engaged with the LinC Cycle, teachers use evidence and resources to inform their teaching practice.

Based on their knowledge, they plan, teach, and reteach. Reflection enables teachers to choose and use instructional strategies that lead to student learning.

Chapter 6 described how to create a Class Profile, a compilation of reading data for a class of students. This chapter demonstrates the process of reflection, in which a teacher carefully considers knowledge about students and the curriculum before planning and teaching.

PAUSE and REFLECT 7.1

Consider a time when you engaged in reflection about student learning. What was the content of your reflection? What reflective process did you use?

REFLECT ABOUT STUDENTS

When reflecting about student needs and strengths, Ms. Johnson considers both the class as a whole, and individual students.

The Class

The Class Profile in Figure 7.1 shows data for the students in Ms. Johnson's fourth-period U.S. history class. With this in hand, she is ready to reflect on the needs of the class.

The reflective process involves analyzing the Class Profile (Figure 7.1) to identify patterns, note exceptions, and draw conclusions. **Patterns** in the data exist when a particular assessment shows a common manner of performance shared by several students. One example of a pattern is visible in the *Motivation/Value of Reading* column. A majority of the class has a high value of reading. **Exceptions** are data that do not follow the pattern. For example, even though a majority of the class values reading, it is important to note that five students do not. Only after noting patterns and exceptions can a teacher draw conclusions about the data. **Conclusions** are statements that are based upon evidence.

Ms. Johnson engages in this reflective process for language proficiency, vocabulary, fluency, comprehension, and motivation. As she finds patterns and exceptions and draws conclusions, she records them on the Data Reflection Chart, shown in Figure 7.2.

Teacher Tool

A Data Reflection Chart (TT19) can be found in the Teacher Tools Appendix to assist you in reflecting upon the students you teach.

LANGUAGE PROFICIENCY   First, Ms. Johnson examines and notes patterns and exceptions for the language proficiency data.

Patterns

1. *Proficiency levels.* Ms. Johnson examines the *Language Proficiency* column on the Class Profile. Then, in the *Patterns* column on the Data Reflection Chart, she records the proficiency levels from the English Language Development Assessment. For example, the Class Profile in Figure 7.1 shows that a majority of students who are English learners are English proficient at the Intermediate (Int) or Advanced (Adv) levels. She makes a note of that fact in the *Patterns* column of Figure 7.3.
2. *Fluency rates.* Ms. Johnson looks at the fluency rates of English learners in the class. In this class, 8 of the 12 students who are English learners also need assistance in all areas of fluency.
3. *Vocabulary.* Vocabulary development is also an area of need for English learners in the class. Results of the standardized test suggest that 6 of the 12 English learners are not proficient in vocabulary.
4. *Comprehension.* The same 8 English learners who struggle with fluency also scored Basic or Below Basic for comprehension.
5. *Additional patterns.* Ms. Johnson notices that according to results on the MARSI (Metacognitive Awareness of Reading Strategy Inventory) the English learners tended to use Global Reading strategies (e.g., predictions) when reading. In addition, scores for an individual's vocabulary, fluency, and comprehension seem to be consistent.

| Student | Language Proficiency | | | Vocabulary | | Fluency | | | Comprehension | | | | | Self Con | Value Read | Motivation |
	L1	L2	Prof	Voc Stand	Cloze	Rate	Acc	Pros	Comp Stand	Inst Lvl	G	PS	S			Interview/Inventory
Alec	Eng			Adv	Ind	High	Ind	92%	Adv	10th	+	✓	–	90%	90%	Wants to help others
Ava	Eng			Adv	Ind	High	Ind	100%	Adv	9th	+	✓	–	100%	90%	Wants to teach
Bella	Eng			Adv	Ind	High	Ind	90%	Adv	10th	+	✓	✓	90%	100%	Enjoys discussing text
Bianca	German	Eng	Adv	Prof	Inst	At	Inst	100%	Prof	8th	+	✓	–	90%	90%	Relies on help
Brandon	Eng			Prof	Inst	High	Frust	25%	Prof	7th	+	✓	✓	40%	90%	Dislikes reading aloud
Carson	Eng			Adv	Ind	High	Ind	92%	Adv	10th	+	+	+	80%	100%	Wants to help others
Casey	Eng			Adv	Inst	High	Frust	33%	Adv	8th	+	+	–	90%	80%	Enjoys discussing reading in groups
Ethan	Eng			Adv	Inst	High	Frust	25%	Adv	8th	+	+	✓	90%	80%	Enjoys discussing with partner
Garrett	Eng			Prof	Inst	At	Ind	50%	Prof	7th	+	✓	–	80%	80%	Enjoys discussing reading
Grant	Eng			Adv	Ind	High	Ind	84%	Adv	9th	+	+	✓	90%	90%	Wants to read at home
Jackie	Eng			Prof	Inst	High	Ind	41%	Prof	7th	+	✓	–	70%	80%	Enjoys discussing reading
Jana	Russian	Eng	Adv	Prof	Inst	High	Inst	41%	Prof	8th	+	✓	–	90%	90%	Relies on help
Johanna	German	Eng	Beg	Basic	Frust	Low	Frust	25%	FBB	4th	–	–	–	50%	20%	Doesn't want to read textbook
John	Eng			Prof	Inst	At	Ind	41%	Prof	7th	+	+	✓	50%	90%	Dislikes reading aloud
Jordan	Eng			Prof	Inst	At	Ind	50%	Prof	7th	+	+	–	80%	90%	Enjoys discussing with partner

FIGURE 7.1 Completed Class Profile for An Eighth-grade Social Science Class

Student	Language Proficiency			Vocabulary		Fluency			Comprehension							Motivation
	L1	L2	Prof	Voc Stand	Cloze	Rate	Acc	Pros	Comp Stand	Inst Lvl	G	Strat PS	S	Self Con	Value Read	Interview/Inventory
Juan	Spanish	Eng	Adv	Prof	Ind	At	Inst	100%	Adv	9th	+	+	+	100%	100%	Enjoys reading aloud
Kia	Hmong	Eng	Int	Prof	Inst	Low	Frust	33%	Basic	7th	+	–	–	40%	80%	Trouble with text
Kristina	Eng			Basic	Frust	Low	Frust	33%	BB	6th	–	–	–	50%	30%	Dislikes reading, learning
Lao	Hmong	Eng	Adv	Basic	Frust	Low	Frust	25%	Basic	6th	+	✓	–	40%	80%	Enjoys working with partner
Lena	Eng			Adv	Ind	High	Ind	92%	Adv	9th	+	+	✓	90%	100%	Wants to read at home
Madison	Eng			Basic	Frust	Low	Frust	33%	BB	6th	–	–	–	40%	30%	Dislikes reading, learning
Maria	Spanish	Eng	Int	Prof	Inst	Low	Frust	33%	Basic	7th	+	–	–	40%	100%	Trouble with text, long words
Mia	Eng			Adv	Ind	High	Ind	92%	Adv	10th	+	+	+	90%	90%	Wants to help others
Raul	Spanish	Eng	Adv	Prof	Ind	At	Ind	92%	Adv	9th	✓	+	+	90%	90%	Enjoys discussing in groups
Tan	Hmong	Eng	Int	Basic	Frust	Low	Frust	33%	Basic	5th	✓	–	–	40%	30%	Dislikes reading aloud
Thao	Hmong	Eng	Int	Basic	Frust	Low	Frust	25%	BB	6th	–	–	–	30%	80%	Trouble w/text, dislikes reading aloud
Todd	Russian	Eng	Int.	Basic	Frust	Low	Frust	50%	FBB	4th	–	–	–	30%	70%	Dislikes reading aloud
Tou	Hmong	Eng	Beg	Basic	Frust	Low	Frust	50%	Basic	5th	–	–	–	40%	80%	Dislikes reading aloud
William	Eng	Eng		Prof	Inst	High	Frust	33%	Prof	8th	+	✓	✓	40%	90%	Dislikes reading aloud
Zach	Eng	Eng		Basic	Frust	Low	Frust	41%	BB	6th	–	–	–	50%	40%	Dislikes reading, learning

FIGURE 7.1 Continued

	Patterns	Exceptions	Conclusions
Language Proficiency			
Vocabulary			
Fluency			
Comprehension			
Motivation			

FIGURE 7.2   Data Reflection Chart to Guide Conclusions About Class Profile Data

Exceptions   In the *Exceptions* column, Ms. Johnson records any exceptions to the general data patterns. For example, unlike a majority of English learners in the class, Johanna and Tou each tested at a Beginning English proficiency level. And Jana, who scored at the Advanced level on the English Language Development Assessment, needs additional help with prosody.

Conclusions   Based on the data, Ms. Johnson concludes that her English learners need special emphasis on fluency, vocabulary, and reading comprehension. They would also benefit from learning additional reading strategies to help them solve comprehension problems as they read or to support their learning from the text (Problem-Solving and Support Strategies). She records her conclusions in the column on the Data Reflection Chart, as shown in Figure 7.3.

	Patterns	Exceptions	Conclusions
Language Proficiency	• 10 out of 12 English Learners in Advanced or Intermediate proficiency range • 8 out of 12 English Learners need help with all areas of fluency • 8 out of 12 Basic or below in comprehension • Half of English Learners are Proficient or above with vocabulary • Tendency to use Global Strategies or none at all (according to MARSI data) • Most scores show consistency between an individual's English proficiency level, fluency, vocabulary, and comprehension	• Johanna and Tou are both Beginning English Learners • Jana, an Advanced English Learner, is at or above grade level in all areas, but needs help with prosody	• Special focus on fluency, vocabulary, and comprehension, especially strategy use (MARSI Problem-Solving and Support Strategies)

FIGURE 7.3   Ms. Johnson's Reflections About the English Language Proficiency of Her Students

VOCABULARY   Ms. Johnson looks at the vocabulary data on the Class Profile and discovers patterns, identifies exceptions, and draws conclusions. She enters them on the Data Reflection Chart, as shown in Figure 7.4.

Patterns

1. *Standardized vocabulary scores.* Referring to the Class Profile, Ms. Johnson examines the *Voc Stand* (Standardized Vocabulary) column for patterns. She notices that her class is distributed across levels, with 9 Advanced, 12 Proficient, and 9 Basic. This means that over 2/3 of her class is at grade level or above in vocabulary knowledge.
2. *Cloze scores.* These scores give an indication of whether the vocabulary in the text is comprehensible to students. In this class, Ms. Johnson notes that for 21 of 30 students, the text's vocabulary is at an Instructional or Independent level. These students will require some instructional support to understand the terms used in the text. The 9 students who are frustrated by grade level vocabulary will get more explicit support throughout the reading process.
3. *Across vocabulary columns.* In the *Patterns* column of the Data Reflection Chart, Ms. Johnson records the students' performance on the Standardized Test (VStand) and the Cloze Procedure (Cloze). With this class, there is some consistency between the standardized test scores and the cloze scores. Generally, these two measures rise and fall together. For most students, a score of Basic, Below Basic, or Far Below Basic on the standardized test is associated with a score of Frustration on the Cloze Procedure. And, a score of Advanced on the standardized test is associated with a score of Independent on the Cloze Procedure.

Exceptions   In the *Exceptions* column, Ms. Johnson notes students who don't follow the general pattern. For example:

- Casey and Ethan scored Advanced on the standardized test of vocabulary, but they scored Instructional on the Cloze Procedure that was conducted with their social studies textbook. Both of these students need continued support with vocabulary, especially with words in content area textbooks.
- Raul and Juan scored Proficient on the standardized vocabulary test, but they scored Independent on the Cloze Procedure. Their understanding of vocabulary was higher when reading the textbook than when taking the standardized test. There could be many explanations for this finding. Ms. Johnson thinks that perhaps Raul and Juan do better with vocabulary when they read it in the context of a textbook, as in the Cloze Procedure.

Conclusions   Vocabulary in the textbook is at many of the students' instructional levels. This means that they will benefit from direct instruction in vocabulary before, during, and after reading. The 9 students who are frustrated by grade-level vocabulary will benefit especially from vocabulary instruction that occurs before they begin reading the text.

	Patterns	Exceptions	Conclusions
Vocabulary	• Good consistency between standardized test outcome and Cloze Procedure • For 21 of the 30 students, vocabulary in the text is at Instructional or Independent level	• Casey, Ethan—higher standardized scores than cloze scores • Raul, Juan—lower standardized scores than cloze scores	• The vocabulary in the text is at the Frustration level for 7 students—will need extra support for vocabulary

FIGURE 7.4   Ms. Johnson's Reflections About the Vocabulary Development of Her Students

PAUSE and REFLECT 7.2

Refer to the fluency data on the Class Profile in Figure 7.1. What patterns do you notice for reading rate, accuracy, and prosody? What conclusions can you draw from the data?

FLUENCY   Next, Ms. Johnson focuses on the fluency data on the Class Profile. She notices patterns, identifies exceptions, and draws conclusions about the data.

Patterns

1. *Rate.* As she looks at the Class Profile, Ms. Johnson notes that the fluency rate varies and is about evenly split between above, at, and below grade level.
2. *Accuracy.* She then looks at the *Acc* (Accuracy) column and notes that students' rates span between the Independent, Instructional, and Frustration levels.
3. *Prosody.* The *Prosody* column shows that 20 out of 30 students have low scores (50 percent or below) for prosody.
4. *Across fluency columns.* Ms. Johnson compares all three fluency columns and notices that there is consistency between students' rate and accuracy. For the most part, students who have a high rate are accurate in their reading (Instructional or Independent level). However, even some of the students who are quick, accurate readers struggle with their reading expression.
5. *Across all columns.* Ms. Johnson looks at the fluency scores in relation to vocabulary, comprehension, and motivation. She notes that students who are less fluent also scored Basic or Below Basic in comprehension. In addition, on the Motivation to Read Profile, these students reported that they dislike reading aloud.

Exceptions

- Casey and Ethan have quick reading rates, but they need work with accuracy and prosody.
- Brandon and William need work in fluency, but scored Proficient in reading comprehension. Their comprehension is outpacing their fluency. They need opportunities to develop their fluency so that their reading comprehension does not begin to falter as text becomes more complex to decode.

Conclusions   For fluency, 20 of the 30 students are low in prosody, which is defined as reading with appropriate intonation, expression, and phrasing. It is not surprising, then, that 7 students in the class dislike reading aloud. Ms. Johnson concludes that her students need instruction to develop their prosody while learning about the content area.

Some students (Casey and Ethan) need to slow down while reading, so they can focus on accuracy and prosody. Having a quick rate can sometimes be an obstacle to reading comprehension. Ms. Johnson enters her conclusions on the Data Reflection Chart. Figure 7.5 shows her reflections about fluency.

	Patterns	**Exceptions**	**Conclusions**
Fluency	• Majority of the class scored 50% or below in prosody • Students who score Basic or below in comprehension are also low in fluency	• Casey, Ethan—Both have a high rate, but low accuracy and prosody • Brandon, William—Low in fluency but Proficient in comprehension	• Need to work on prosody (reading with expression) • Instruction should stress accuracy rather than rate

FIGURE 7.5   Ms. Johnson's Reflections About the Fluency Development of Her Students

	Patterns	Exceptions	Conclusions
Comprehension	• 60% of class is Proficient or Advanced in comprehension • 40% reading below grade level • Most students used some strategies, but only 5 (all Advanced in comprehension) used all three categories of strategies • Majority of students scoring Basic or below in comprehension use no strategies	• Johanna, Todd—Far Below Basic, fourth-grade reading level • Mia, Carson, Bella, Alec—tenth-grade reading level	• Class needs help learning reading strategies, especially Support Strategies • Need to have supplemental reading materials from fourth to tenth-grade levels

FIGURE 7.6 Ms. Johnson's Reflections About the Comprehension Proficiencies of Her Students

COMPREHENSION After recording her reflections on the fluency data, Ms. Johnson examines the comprehension data on the Class Profile. She notes patterns and exceptions and then she draws conclusions about the data on the Data Reflection Chart, shown in Figure 7.6.

Patterns

1. *Standardized comprehension scores.* Ms. Johnson examines the *Comprehension* column of the Class Profile, focusing on the scores in the sub-column labeled *Comp Stand* (Standardized Comprehension Test). She notes that 19 students of the 30 (about 60 percent) in her class are Proficient or Advanced in comprehension. This 60 percent is reading at or above grade level, while the remaining 11 out of 30 tested below grade level in comprehension.
2. *Instructional level.* The scores in the *Inst Lvl* (Instructional Level) column indicate students' performance on a qualitative reading inventory. Ms. Johnson notes how many students are reading at or above the eighth-grade level for content area text. According to the reading inventory that was conducted with expository text, eighth-grade text is at the Instructional or Independent level for 14 out of 30 students.
3. *Strategies.* Ms. Johnson examines the data for students' use of strategies. The *Strat* (Strategies) column lists the type of strategies that students use: Global (G), Problem-Solving (PS), or Support (S). She notes that more students tend to use Global Reading Strategies (making predictions and previewing text) than the other two types of strategies.
4. *Across comprehension columns.* Ms. Johnson compares the strategy use for students at different levels of comprehension. For example, all of the 11 students who scored Advanced on the standardized comprehension test use strategies from two or three strategy categories. In contrast, students at the lower proficiency levels tend to use just one type of reading strategy, if any.
5. *Across all columns.* Comprehension scores tend to align with fluency and vocabulary scores. For the most part, students who are Proficient or above in comprehension are also strong in vocabulary and fluency. This result is not surprising—these three constructs are strongly and positively interrelated.

Exceptions

• Johanna and Todd are the only students who scored at the Far Below Basic level on the standardized comprehension test. In comparison with their classmates, Johanna and Todd will likely have more difficulty comprehending content area text.
• Four students—Alec, Bella, Carson, and Mia—read at the tenth-grade level. These eighth-grade students are more likely than their peers to be able to comprehend the class text.

Conclusions The class has a wide range of readers, from fourth- to tenth-grade level. This variety of reading levels means that many students will struggle with reading the eighth-grade history text. They will need extra instructional support, plus some supplementary reading material (like trade books) that focus on the content, but are written at appropriate grade levels. The more proficient readers might be interested in more challenging reading materials that supplement the content.

In addition, the majority of the class needs help learning reading strategies, especially Support Reading Strategies. Such strategies include note taking, paraphrasing, and self-questioning.

MOTIVATION   Lastly, Ms. Johnson turns her attention to the motivation data. She looks for patterns and exceptions, and she draws conclusions.

Patterns

1. *Self-Concept.* Ms. Johnson inspects the scores in the *Motivation* column labeled *Self Con* (Self-Concept). She notices that there is a range from 30 percent to 100 percent. Students in her class have varying opinions of themselves as readers.
2. *Value of Reading.* In the *Value Read* column (Value of Reading), Ms. Johnson notes that all but 5 students have a score of 80 percent or above. Most of the students in her class value reading.
3. *Motivation inventory.* By reading the *Interview/Inventory* column, Ms. Johnson sees that some of her students dislike reading aloud, and some find the text difficult. Many mention that they enjoy working with others, in a group or in pairs.
4. *Across motivation columns.* According to the Class Profile, there are more students who have a low Self-Concept than a low Value of Reading.
5. *Across all columns.* When looking across columns, Ms. Johnson notes that many of the students who have a low Value of Reading also struggle with comprehension, fluency, and vocabulary. In addition, there are five students (Zach, Tan, Madison, Johanna, and Kristina) who are low on all measures of motivation.

Exceptions

- Eight students have a low Self-Concept but a high Value of Reading. Because these students value reading, they will likely be receptive to strategies that help them strengthen their proficiencies with vocabulary, comprehension and fluency.

CONCLUSIONS   As a whole, the class values reading, but many lack the skills and strategies necessary for proficiency. Instruction will need to emphasize both building students' competence as readers and helping students form more positive self-concepts. Instructional strategies designed to initiate and sustain motivation will be especially important for the five students who have low motivation scores in all categories. Ms. Johnson decides she will need to look more closely at the motivation inventories of these students to see how she can best find a way to "hook" them into reading and learning.

Many of the students enjoy working together, which suggests that they would welcome instructional strategies involving group discussion. Furthermore, many students, especially those with low fluency, mentioned that they dislike reading aloud. Any oral reading in front of the class could be on a volunteer basis; assigned read aloud could happen with a partner. In addition, on their *Interview/Inventory*, four students mentioned that they enjoy teaching or helping others learn. These students might be good partners for those students who need extra help with fluency. Ms. Johnson enters her reflections on student motivation on the Data Reflection Chart. Figure 7.7 shows the complete chart with reflections for language proficiency, vocabulary, fluency, comprehension, and motivation.

Conclusion   Ms. Johnson reviews her completed Data Reflection Chart and concludes that she needs to design instruction that meets the following needs of her class.

- *Language proficiency.* For her English learners, design instruction that accounts for their English proficiency levels and focuses on fluency and comprehension strategies.
- *Vocabulary.* Build support for content vocabulary for all students, with a special focus on those students who struggle with terms in the text.

	Patterns	Exceptions	Conclusions
Language Proficiency	• 10 out of 12 English Learners in Advanced or Intermediate proficiency range • 8 out of 12 English Learners need help with all areas of fluency • 8 out of 12 Basic or below in comprehension • Half of English Learners are Proficient or above with vocabulary • Tendency to use Global Strategies or none at all (according to MARSI data) • Most scores show consistency between an individual's proficiency level, fluency, vocabulary, and comprehension	• Johanna and Tou are both beginning English Learners • Jana, an Advanced English Learner, is at or above grade level in all areas, but needs help with prosody	• Special focus on fluency, vocabulary, and comprehension, especially strategy use (MARSI Problem-Solving and Support Strategies)
Vocabulary	• Good consistency between standardized test outcome and Cloze Procedure • For 23 of 30 students, vocabulary in the text is at Instructional or Independent level	• Casey, Ethan—higher standardized scores than cloze scores • Raul, Juan—lower standardized scores than cloze scores	• The vocabulary in the text is at the Frustration level for 7 students—will need extra support for vocabulary
Fluency	• Majority of the class scored 50% or below in prosody • Students who are Basic or below in comprehension are also low in fluency	• Casey, Ethan—Both have a high rate, but low accuracy and prosody • Brandon, William—Low in fluency but Proficient in comprehension	• Need to work on prosody (reading with expression) • Instruction should stress accuracy rather than rate
Comprehension	• 60% of class is Proficient or Advanced in comprehension • 40% reading below grade level • Most students used some strategies, but only 5 (all Advanced in comprehension) used all three categories of strategies • Majority of students scoring Basic or below in comprehension use no strategies	• Johanna, Todd—Far below Basic, fourth-grade reading level • Mia, Carson, Bella, Alec—tenth-grade reading level	• Class needs help learning reading strategies, especially Support Strategies • Need to have supplemental reading materials from fourth to tenth-grade levels
Motivation	• Majority of class has high Value of Reading • Students who have low Self-Concept or Value of Reading also read below grade level • Five students are low on all measures of motivation • Several students dislike reading aloud (seem to be students with low fluency scores) • Many students enjoy working with peers	• 8 students have a low Self-Concept but a high Value of Reading	• Students need instruction that will boost competence and Self-Concept • Give opportunities for reading practice before asking to read aloud for others • Use methods that include cooperation and collaboration

FIGURE 7.7 Completed Data Reflection Chart

- *Fluency.* Design opportunities to practice fluency, especially prosody. Students will need a chance to practice before reading in front of a group. In addition, there should be an emphasis on accuracy rather than rate.
- *Comprehension.* Improve comprehension and increase students' strategy use, specifically Support and Problem-Solving Strategies.
- *Motivation.* Choose instructional strategies that will boost students' self-concepts as readers. Any strategy that helps students become more competent should be appropriate; however, methods that capitalize on students' social interactions might have the most benefit over time.

Learning Log

Use data from a sample Class Profile in the Learning Log Appendix to practice completing a Data Reflection Chart (LL9).

Ms. Johnson will use these conclusions to plan appropriate instruction to both build content knowledge and contribute to students' growth as readers and learners. Chapter 8 describes how she uses these conclusions to plan instruction for her eighth-graders.

Individual Students

While reflecting on the Class Profile gives valuable information for whole class instruction, it is often necessary to look more deeply at the strengths and needs of individual students. Ideally, thinking deeply about the needs of individual students would be part of the structure of middle and high schools. But, in reality, most teachers in intermediate and secondary environments do not have the time or resources to engage in this important activity for each of their students. There are, however, times when a teacher knows that careful thinking about one student's literacy needs can make a big difference. In these cases, teachers use an Individual Profile (Figure 7.8) to record assessment data and to draw conclusions.

Teacher Tool

An Individual Profile (TT20) can be found in the Teacher Tools Appendix to assist you in your reflection.

Most of the categories of data on the Individual Profile are similar to those on the Class Profile. English language proficiency, vocabulary, fluency, comprehension, and motivation all appear on both the Class Profile and the Individual Profile. The Individual Profile also includes a field for personal history; the teacher may know some facts about the student that impact language learning in the classroom.

COMPLETE THE INDIVIDUAL PROFILE This year, Ms. Johnson has been concerned about Lao, one of her students in her fourth-period class. She decides to reflect in more depth about Lao's strengths and needs. To assist her, she uses the Individual Profile shown in Figure 7.8.

To complete the Individual Profile, Ms. Johnson thinks about the data that is available about Lao as a reader. First, she records results from assessments for language proficiency, vocabulary, fluency, comprehension, and motivation.

Next, she records information about Lao's personal history. Each student brings a unique set of experiences to the classroom. Research shows both the power and the complexity of these variables—such as race and socioeconomic status—as they relate to learning (Oakes, Joseph, & Muir, 2004). Ms. Johnson has learned about Lao by examining his cumulative folder and by building a relationship with him. She knows that Lao's mother passed away two years ago. His father is a truck driver and works long, long days. When Lao gets home in the evening, he is under the care of his older sister. This information helps Ms. Johnson understand Lao and ways that his life outside of school impacts his success in school. She knows that for Lao to complete his homework, directions need to be clear, and he needs to have access to resources, like additional material at his reading level.

REFLECT ABOUT DATA FOR INDIVIDUAL STUDENTS The second step in completing the Individual Profile is to review the data, engage in reflection, and draw conclusions about instruction that will benefit the student. On the Individual Profile in Figure 7.8, Ms. Johnson records her conclusions about Lao's needs with content reading. She also notes his strengths.

Noting both strengths and areas for growth allows the teacher to draw balanced conclusions for future instruction. For example, the MARSI showed that Lao frequently uses strategies that prepare him to read (a strength). However, the vocabulary assessments suggest that he has difficulty with

---

STEP 1: COLLECT ASSESSMENT DATA

Name: *Lao*   **Grade:** *Eighth*   **Class:** *Social Science*

Language Proficiency

First Language: *Hmong*

Second Language: *English*   Proficiency: *Advanced*

Personal History

Lao was born in the United States. Hmong is spoken at home. Lives with dad and 3 sisters. Family situation makes it difficult to complete homework.

Vocabulary

- Standardized: *Basic*
- Cloze: 40% Level: ☐ Independent   ☐ Instructional   ■ Frustration

Fluency

- Rate: ☐ High   ☐ At Grade Level   ■ Low
- Accuracy: ☐ Independent   ☐ Instructional   ■ Frustration
- Prosody: 3 /12 or 25%

Comprehension

- Standardized:
  ☐ Advanced   ☐ Proficient   ■ Basic   ☐ Below Basic   ☐ Far Below Basic
- Qualitative Reading Inventory:
    Instructional Level: 6th
- Strategies:
    Global Mean: 4.0 Problem-Solving Mean: 3.6 Support Mean: 1.3

Motivation

- Self-Concept: 16/40 or 40 %
- Value of Reading: 32/40 or 80%
- Interview/Inventory: *Enjoys reading magazines/Web sites about motorcycles, military. Has computer at home, but connection is slow. Wants to build things. Can help fix anything. Enjoys group work. Doesn't like reading text. Dislikes reading aloud.*

STEP 2: REFLECT ON ASSESSMENT DATA

Conclusions:

- Vocabulary: Below grade level. Has trouble using context to figure out word meaning. He would benefit from vocabulary instruction before he reads the text.
- Fluency: Low fluency in all areas. Lao needs practice, but not in front of the class!
- Comprehension: Reads below grade level. Has trouble remembering details and answering implicit questions about text. Uses Global Reading Strategies, some Problem-Solving strategies. Can continue to build on these and add Support Strategies—instruction that focuses on what to do during reading to help remember details.
- Motivation: Low Self-Concept, high Value of Reading. He needs reading that has a purpose, at a level that he can read without a struggle. Has several interests and talents that might motivate him to learn about social science. Might be interested in learning about inventions and about US military history. Enjoys group work.

FIGURE 7.8   Lao's Individual Profile

vocabulary while reading his text (area for growth). So, Lao might benefit from focusing on new vocabulary *before* he reads.

The assessment data reveals other patterns that can help Ms. Johnson make instructional decisions. The motivation inventories indicate that Lao enjoys discussing reading with friends. The reading comprehension assessments show that Lao needs support while reading. These two pieces of evidence suggest that Lao would benefit from reading instruction that takes place in cooperative groups.

Learning Log

Use the Individual Profile in the Learning Log Appendix to practice drawing conclusions about a student (LL10).

It is not necessary to complete the Individual Profile for every student. However, some teachers with self-contained classrooms and/or extra resources may choose to do so. In addition, the Individual Profile can be used to help teachers decide whether to seek additional interventions for students. Schools that are engaged in Response to Intervention (Fuchs & Fuchs, 2001) or other tiered intervention and support models will find it useful to have a one-page summary, like the Individual Profile, that gives an overview of the student's content reading proficiency.

Ms. Johnson has focused much of her reflection upon her students, both the class as a whole and as individuals. Next she reflects about the eighth-grade history curriculum.

REFLECT ABOUT THE CURRICULUM

Ms. Johnson is well versed in the content of history, especially U.S. history, the focus of her eighth-grade course. In addition, she has recently learned more about literacy learning, both in general and inside the social sciences. With her prior knowledge as a base, she considers instructional standards and the eighth-grade history text.

Standards

CONTENT STANDARDS The **content standards** define the knowledge, concepts, and skills that each student should master at each grade level, Kindergarten through grade 12. They are the basis for state-sponsored standardized tests. Throughout the United States, content standards exist for a variety of subjects, from agriculture to world languages. Each state is responsible for approving its own content standards. However, most are based upon sets of national standards developed by organizations of teachers and experts in the field. For example, the National Council for Teachers of English (NCTE) created English standards that states use as a foundation for developing their own. And, as of the writing of this book, 46 states have agreed to work toward a common set of national standards for English and mathematics.

Because states approve and publish their own standards, each state has a unique way of organizing them. Often, standards are grouped by grade level, subdivided by topic, and numbered for easy reference. The language in standards identifies an expectation, and teachers translate these expectations into goals and learning objectives.

PAUSE and REFLECT 7.3

Consider one set of content standards in your state. What is the structure of these standards? Choose one grade level. What are students expected to know and be able to do by the end of that grade?

In Ms. Johnson's state, the eighth-grade U.S. history standards focus on "United States History and Geography—Growth and Conflict." Eighth-graders review events prior to the formation of the United States, then they concentrate on major events that occurred between the Constitution and World War I. Ms. Johnson is beginning a unit on the Civil War, focusing on its causes and consequences. Her next set of lessons will examine the differences between the Northern and Southern United States in the 1860s.

ENGLISH/LANGUAGE ARTS STANDARDS   Next, Ms. Johnson considers the English/language arts standards. Even though her content area is social science, she reviewed the English/language arts standards at the beginning of the year. She thinks about the four domains in the California standards (reading, writing, written and oral language conventions, and speaking and listening).

Reading   Reading standards include expectations for fluency, vocabulary, and comprehension. The standards include expectations that students will learn to read both narrative and expository text. For this set of lessons, Ms. Johnson focuses on the standards that refer to expository text. In particular, eighth graders focus on content vocabulary, specifically the meaning of specialized vocabulary in the content areas. They practice reading informational text and learn to use text structure, organization, and purpose to connect the essential ideas of text (California Department of Education, 2002). These standards are essential to students' proficiency with text in social science and all content domains.

Writing   These standards include attention to both writing strategies and writing applications. For example, eighth graders learn to write clear and focused essays that include a solid introduction, supporting evidence, and a conclusion. In social science, expressing one's ideas clearly, in writing, is essential.

Written and Oral Language Conventions   These standards include attention to English language conventions: spelling, grammar, punctuation, and mechanics. For example, eighth graders learn to use varied sentence types to show personal style as a writer and speaker. Ms. Johnson knows that her students practice with language conventions so they can communicate their opinions clearly.

Listening and Speaking   These standards include comprehending presentations, organizing and delivering oral presentations, and evaluating oral and media communications. Eighth graders learn how to orally support a thesis and include different perspectives from a variety of sources. She sees that these standards, like the other English/language arts standards, overlap with her goals of helping students become more adept at historical thinking.

Ms. Johnson decides to focus on reading, but her choice of strategies will also support student growth in writing, English language conventions, and listening/speaking.

PAUSE and REFLECT 7.4

Consider the English/language arts standards in your state. What is the structure of these standards? Choose one grade level. What are students expected to know and be able to do by the end of that grade?

ENGLISH LANGUAGE DEVELOPMENT STANDARDS   Ms. Johnson also considers the English language development (ELD) standards. Some states incorporate the ELD standards into the English/language arts standards. Others use the standards developed by an educational organization entitled Teachers of English to Speakers of Other Languages (TESOL). In California the English language development standards give a progression based on language acquisition—Beginning, Intermediate, and Advanced Proficiency. These standards are described as an "on-ramp" to the English/language arts standards (Carr & Lagunoff, 2002). With increasing levels of proficiency, students can ultimately access the rigorous English/language arts standards.

Resource

TESOL standards are available at www.tesol.org

For example, Ms. Johnson knows that during the year she will need to teach students to evaluate the structural patterns of text. She uses the English language development standards to help her identify appropriate learning goals for students at different levels of English development. She:

1. identifies the English/language arts standards.
2. reflects about what the standard is asking students to know and be able to do.
3. looks for English language development standards that help eighth-grade English learners approach the language arts standard.

Ms. Johnson understands that the English/language arts standard is asking students to evaluate the text's structure and whether the ideas flow logically. The English language development standards suggest the following goals for English learners:

- Beginning English Learners: Orally identify cause/effect and fact/opinion statements in text.
- Intermediate English Learners: Understand and orally identify the basic components of informational text.
- Advanced English Learners: Analyze a variety of rhetorical styles found in informational text (California Department of Education, 2002).

Notice that as the standards move from Beginning, to Intermediate, to Advanced proficiencies, they become more linguistically demanding. When she plans her next set of lessons, she will need to keep in mind the English proficiency levels of her students, particularly if she uses writing to assess their learning from the text.

PAUSE and REFLECT 7.5

Consider the English language development standards in your state. What is the structure of these standards? What are students with different English proficiency levels expected to know and be able to do?

By examining the history/social science, English/language arts, and English language development standards, Ms. Johnson understands what students should know and be able to do by the end of eighth grade. Now that Ms. Johnson has a solid understanding of students' needs and has considered the standards, her next step is to reflect about the text.

The Text

Effective teachers carefully review each book or reading before including it in a lesson. In most districts, teachers use state-adopted texts. Some districts encourage teachers to supplement the core content book with other texts. Whether the book is officially adopted or not, the text type, features, and readability can impact student learning.

TEXT TYPE   To effectively support student learning from a text, it is essential for the teacher to understand the different types of text and how they impact learning. Research shows that when students understand differences in text types, both their writing and reading comprehension improve (Armbruster & Anderson, 1989).

In most middle and high school classrooms, students read text that falls into two broad categories—**narrative** or **expository**. Narrative texts relay a story and generally have the following elements: plot, setting, characters, and theme. Expository text, on the other hand, is intended to teach about a concept. Expository text is more complex, has difficult vocabulary, unfamiliar sentence structure, and various text structures. Students will most often see expository text in their textbooks and narrative text in a novel or story. Each lends itself to different structures and needs to be approached differently by the reader. In addition, there may be a motivational difference for students when reading different types of text.

Most students are exposed to narrative text from a young age and continue to experience narratives in picture books, oral stories, movies, and television. While many young students enjoy reading nonfiction, much of the reading in the early grades is narrative in form. Early in elementary school, usually around grade four, the proportion of narrative to expository text changes. A good reader of narrative text is not always proficient with expository text. Students need to be guided through the transition so that they know what to expect with expository text.

The adopted textbook for Ms. Johnson's social science class is entitled *U.S. History*. While it does contain some narrative historical accounts, most of the text is expository. Based upon data from the Motivation to Read Profile, Ms. Johnson knows that many of her students dislike textbooks and struggle to make meaning from them. However, she also recognizes that learning to read informational text is essential for success inside and outside of school. She turns her focus to the features of the textbook, hoping to find elements that will guide her students as they read.

Teacher Tool

For use in your planning, a blank Text Profile (TT21) can be found in the Teacher Tools Appendix.

TEXT FEATURES   Ms. Johnson examines the textbook and notes its features—the characteristics that can assist student learning. As she evaluates each text feature, she makes notes on the Text Profile in Figure 7.9.

Table of Contents   In this U.S. history text, the table of contents shows a clear progression of topics and shows page numbers to help students find the location of units, chapters, and sections.

Headings   Ms. Johnson also notes the headings, or announcements of the main topic of the upcoming text. Font size of headings is usually larger and bolder than that of the text. In this text, there are different levels of heading, signaled by changes in color. Main headings are red, and subheadings are blue. She will need to draw students' attention to the headings because she knows that many of her students skip them when reading.

Vocabulary   The important terms in this section appear in bold font, and the definition is highlighted in the text. Ms. Johnson likes that these textbook authors wrote definitions in the context of the paragraph or sentence, so that students will have extra support while reading. Students can also find each term and its definition in a glossary at the back of the text.

Figures/Charts/Graphs   Ms. Johnson notes visuals that give students more information about the content in the text. Figures are diagrams or pictures representing text information,

Text Title: *U.S. History*	
Text Features	**Notes**
Table of Contents	*Units, chapters, and page numbers*
Headings	*Section headings are red, topic headings are blue, subheadings are red*
Vocabulary	*Important vocabulary bolded, and definition highlighted within the paragraph*
Figures/Charts/ Graphs	*Figures, charts, and graphs to support text*
Illustrations/Photos	*Lifelike illustrations and photos*
Time Lines/Maps	*Colorful maps, noting events, and locations*
Captions	*Captions posted under charts, paintings, illustrations, time lines, and maps*
Glossary/Index	*Glossary in English and Spanish (blue edges); Index (gold edges)*
Appendix	*Includes atlas, gazetteer, presidents, state facts, supreme court decisions, historical documents*
Font Type/Size	*Times New Roman, 14pt.*
White Space	*Single spaced with adequate white space between sections*
Readability	*Ninth grade*

FIGURE 7.9   Completed Text Profile for an Eighth-grade U.S. History Textbook

charts summarize information, and graphs summarize numerical data. These components help students understand the content area concepts. Charts are especially helpful because they give information as well as comparisons and processes between concepts (Robb, Klemp, & Schwartz, 2002).

Illustrations/Photographs   Ms. Johnson observes that in the social studies text, there are both illustrations and photographs to aid comprehension. Illustrations and photographs give a visual representation of the concepts in the text. These visuals can be especially helpful when students have no background knowledge about a topic and need a picture to help them understand. In fact, reviewing just the pictures can give a good indication about what content will be presented (Robb, et al., 2002).

Time Lines/Maps   The text also includes time lines and maps to give her students information about events and places. Time lines summarize dated text information and provide a visual organization of that information. Maps offer readers an understanding of location, distance, and direction about specific places. Ms. Johnson's students can use these maps, with illustrations and photographs, to reinforce their understanding of the concepts in the book.

Captions   Publishers provide captions with figures, charts, graphs, illustrations, photographs, time lines, and maps. Captions tell readers about the visual display. In this history text, all visuals include clear captions.

Glossary and Index   Ms. Johnson's history text also includes a glossary and an index, both in the back of the book. Students can use the glossary to help them define vocabulary terms and use the index to locate a person, place, or idea within the textbook.

Appendix   The appendix is also located at the back of the book and provides the students with additional information to support the text. For example, in this history text the appendix includes additional maps. If Ms. Johnson makes her students aware of this appendix, it can become another useful, informative resource.

Font Type/Size   The font type and size varies from text to text and influences reading fluency. Serif fonts, like Times New Roman, have details on the ends of some of the letters. These details aid struggling readers by making the words easier to read (Hartley, 1994). Also fonts that are larger (14 point) and more widely spaced enhance reading speed and accuracy (Hartley, 1984). Decreasing the font size often leads to an increase in reading errors. In the history text, Ms. Johnson decides that the font is easily readable.

White Space   The amount of white space (or leading) between lines of text also impacts reading. Readers can better follow the line of text if there is more space between lines (Bloodsworth, 1993). Ms. Johnson notes that there is enough white space to make the text reader-friendly.

After considering the text features, she concludes that several will assist her students. Because many of her students read below grade level, the maps and charts will be particularly helpful. The bold vocabulary terms and glossary will assist all of her students, especially English learners, as they build vocabulary.

Even with all of these features, Ms. Johnson wonders whether this text will cause frustration for her students. She decides to determine its readability.

READABILITY OF TEXT   The text's **readability**, or difficulty, plays an important role in student comprehension. Even the most proficient readers will be frustrated by a text that is too difficult—due to its vocabulary, sentence structure, or format. For example, Bella reads tenth-grade text at an instructional level. The eighth-grade text should not be too problematic for her. However, if this eighth-grader were to face a twelfth-grade text, she could become frustrated—a state that would hamper both her learning and motivation. Most often, content teachers use a textbook that is written for a particular grade level. However, sometimes the actual reading level is different from the grade level. In addition, teachers who choose to use supplementary reading materials may wonder whether they are too difficult for their students. Fortunately, there are two ways to readily estimate text difficulty: the Fry Readability Formula, and the Flesch-Kincaid Scale.

Fry Readability Formula   In the 1970s, Edward Fry, a reading specialist, developed a readability formula that has been used for decades (Fry, 1977). According to the Fry Readability Formula, the text's readability can be predicted by the word length and sentence length.

To calculate the readability of the text:

1. Randomly select a text section from the book and count out 100 words.
2. Count the number of syllables in those 100 words.
3. Count the number of sentences in those 100 words.
4. Repeat steps 1, 2, and 3 using three different passages from the book.
5. Calculate the average number of syllables and average number of sentences.
6. Using the Fry Graph (Figure 7.10), plot the readability (syllables on x axis, sentences on y axis).

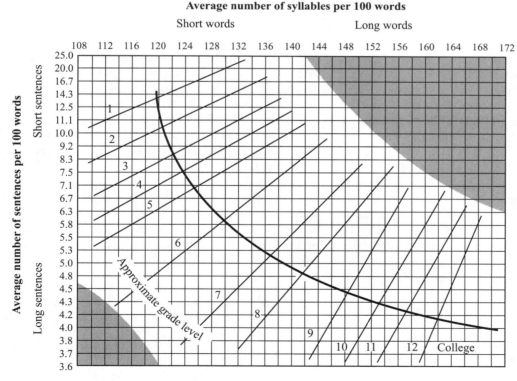

FIGURE 7.10   Fry Graph for Estimating Text Readability

Resource

To calculate the readability of a word-processed text or a Web site, see www.readability.info/. For a selection of several readability tools, visit www.interventioncentral.org.

Learning Log

Use your content area textbook in conjunction with the Text Profile (LL11) from the Learning Log Appendix to practice analyzing your content area textbook.

Flesch-Kincaid Scale   It is possible to check the readability of electronic text by using tools built into a word processing program. If using Microsoft Word (2004), readability information is based on the Flesch-Kincaid scale, which calculates readability in a way similar to the Fry formula.

1. Set the preferences on the computer.
  a. On the menu bar, choose "preferences," then select "spelling and grammar."
  b. Check the box "check spelling with grammar."
  c. Select "show readability statistics."
2. Calculate readability.
  a. Go back to the document and highlight some or all of the text.
  b. On the menu bar, choose "grammar."
  c. After Word checks the document for grammar and spelling, a table appears that will show the readability level.

Ms. Johnson uses the online readability formula and finds that her eighth-grade text is actually written at a ninth-grade level. She enters it on the Text Profile (Figure 7.9). This finding surprises her. It means that even students who are reading at grade level will need extra support when reading. Ms. Johnson looks back at the *Inst Lvl* column on the Class Profile and sees that 21 of her 30 students read below a ninth-grade level She can expect about 2/3 of the class to struggle when reading the textbook. Ms. Johnson knows that the readability number does not account for every factor—such as having supportive text features. However, she will have to consider this discrepancy between student reading levels and the text's readability when planning her lessons.

Chapter Summary

Reflection is an essential step in effectively teaching literacy in the context of content area instruction. The content of reflection includes the teacher's knowledge and experience, especially as it relates to the students and the curriculum. The process of reflection allows teachers to think about the standards and the text in light of their students' needs.

For student assessment data to inform instruction, teachers reflect on the data to find patterns, exceptions to those patterns, and draw conclusions. This process can be used with data for a whole class or for individual students. In either case, reflecting on the data allows the teacher to become ready to teach in a way that will positively impact student learning.

The curriculum becomes part of the reflective process when teachers consider the standards and the text. To bridge literacy and content instruction, teachers understand the content standards, English/language arts standards, and the English language development standards. They also acknowledge the significant characteristics of their class texts, including text types, text features, and readability levels.

In the opening vignette, Ms. Johnson wonders whether she will be able to help her students enhance their self-concepts as readers. If she reflects on what she knows about her students and the curriculum, she will be able to make informed decisions about which instructional strategies to choose. She will make a difference.

RESOURCES

California Department of Education (2000). *History-social science content standards for California public schools, kindergarten through grade twelve.*

California Department of Education (2002). *English-Language development standards for California public schools, kindergarten through grade twelve.*

Carr, J., & Lagunoff, R. (2002). *A map of standards for English language learners.* San Francisco: WestEd.

Fry, E. (1977). *Elementary reading instruction.* New York: McGraw-Hill.

REFERENCES

Armbruster, B. B., & Anderson, T. H. (1989). Teaching text structure to improve reading and writing. *The Reading Teacher, 43*(2), 130–137.

Bloodsworth, J. G. (1993). *Legibility of print.* East Lansing, MI: National Center for Research on Teacher Learning.

Colton, A. B., & Sparks-Langer, G. M. (1993). A conceptual framework to guide the development of teacher reflection and decision making. *Journal of Teacher Education, 44*(1), 45–54.

Dewey, J. (1933). *How we think (Rev.ed): A restatement of the relation of reflective thinking to the educative process.* Boston, MA: D.C. Heath & Co.

Fuchs, D., & Fuchs, L. S. (2001). Responsiveness to Intervention: A blueprint for practitioners, policymakers, and parents. *Teaching Exceptional Children, 38*(1), 57–61.

Hartley, J. (1994). *Designing instructional text* (2nd ed.). London, UK: Kogan Page.

Hatton, N., & Smith, D. (1995). Reflection in teacher education: Towards definition and implementation. *Teaching and Teacher Education, 11*(1), 33–49.

Hughes, L. E., & Wilkins, A. J. (2000). Typography in children's reading schemes may be suboptimal: Evidence from measures of reading rate. *Journal of Research in Reading, 23*(3), 314–324.

Oakes, J., Joseph, R., & Muir, K. (2004). Access and achievement in mathematics and science: Inequalities that endure and change. In J. A. Banks & C. M. Banks (Eds.), *Handbook of Research on Multicultural Education* (2 ed., pp. 69–90). San Francisco: Jossey-Bass.

Robb, L., Klemp, R., & Schwartz, W. (2002). *Reader's handbook: A student guide for reading and learning.* Wilmington, MA: Great Source.

CHAPTER 8

Plan—Making Informed Decisions

At 3:30, Ms. Johnson rushed into the classroom, her arms filled with folders, papers, and books. The other teachers on the eighth-grade team sat around a table, in the empty classroom, chatting about the day.

"Sorry I'm late."

The others looked at her knowingly. "Don't worry—we all remember our first year of teaching. You're holding up pretty well."

She took a seat in a student-sized chair. "I don't feel like it. Actually, I'm overwhelmed. I've been focusing on my fourth-period U.S. history class, trying to learn as much as possible about them. And now I know that they are all over the map with reading. There are some that read at a fourth-grade level and some that read at a tenth-grade level." Ms. Ramirez, a math teacher responded. "I know that group. They all come to me for math."

"And most of them have me for science," Mr. Blake added.

Ms. Johnson continued, "Some read fluently, some don't; many of them believe they are horrible readers. I want to help them all become better at reading and understanding the social science text. And I'm not sure what to do."

Mrs. Lincoln, the English teacher responded, "We should talk about it. None of us is a reading 'expert,' but maybe together we can come up with some plans to support reading across all of our classes."

Planning has always been central to the process of teaching. But this group of eighth-grade teachers, who are committed to student learning, is undertaking a more important planning task. Even though each has a different subject focus, they have decided to work together to develop student literacy. Admittedly, they are not trained reading specialists, but they all know some instructional strategies that, when applied thoughtfully, will help their students. They know that gains made in literacy will help their students succeed in all of their classes and will prepare them for high school and beyond.

In Chapter 7, Ms. Johnson reflected about student needs and the curriculum. In this chapter, she uses those reflections to help her decide which instructional strategies will best meet the needs of her students. To help record her plans, Ms. Johnson uses a LinC Teaching Plan (Figure 8.1) that incorporates her knowledge of the student, the text, the content, and instructional strategies. The LinC Teaching Plan helps teachers prepare to engage their students in instruction that builds knowledge of subject matter and strengthens student vocabulary, fluency, comprehension, and motivation.

Teacher Tool

The Teacher Tools Appendix includes a blackline master of the LinC Teaching Plan (TT22) to assist you in your planning.

PAUSE and REFLECT 8.1

Recall a lesson that you planned. What process did you use to develop your instructional plan?

Class		Topic	
LEARNING OUTCOMES			
	Objectives		**Assessments**
Content Area			
English/ Language Arts			
English Language Development			
TEXT			
Pages			
Type/Structure			
Features			
VOCABULARY			
Level 1 Essential (Before Reading)			
Level 2 Related (Before Reading)			
Level 3 Critical (During/After)			
Level 4 Not-Essential			
INSTRUCTIONAL STRATEGIES			
Lesson 1			
Vocabulary			
Fluency			
Comprehension			
Motivation			
Lesson 2			
Vocabulary			
Fluency			
Comprehension			
Motivation			
Lesson 3			
Vocabulary			
Fluency			
Comprehension			
Motivation			

FIGURE 8.1   LinC Teaching Plan

To build the LinC Teaching Plan, teachers engage in five steps. They establish learning outcomes, know the text, choose vocabulary for instruction, review student needs, and select instructional strategies. Each of these reflective planning activities is essential in building a LinC Teaching Plan that meets the needs of students.

ESTABLISH LEARNING OUTCOMES

Central to curriculum development is the notion of establishing learning outcomes. In thinking about what students will learn, Ms. Johnson needs to determine the objectives and methods of assessment. **Objectives** identify the new knowledge, skills, or attitudes that students can demonstrate as a result of instruction. The assessments measure student progress toward each of those objectives. Ms. Johnson uses her knowledge about U.S. history and literacy to establish learning outcomes for the content area and for English /language arts. In addition, she uses the English language development standards to guide her thinking.

Content Area

OBJECTIVES   Ms. Johnson is beginning a unit on the U.S. Civil War. She is a teacher in California, so she identifies the California social science standard: Students analyze the multiple causes, key events, and complex consequences of the civil war (California Department of Education, 2000). One essential concept in meeting this standard is to understand the differences between the Northern and Southern states at the beginning of the Civil War. She decides upon an objective. As a result of instruction, students will be able to:

- compare the advantages and disadvantages of the Northern and Southern states as they entered the U.S. Civil War.

ASSESSMENT   She plans to assess their understandings by having students write a paragraph comparing the advantages of the North and the South. The content should include details about the railroad, economy, military, and geography.

English/Language Arts

OBJECTIVES   Ms. Johnson is not the English teacher, and yet she notices ways in which her instruction can support students' reading, writing, listening, and speaking. She decides that her lesson will support vocabulary development, recording ideas from text, and summary writing. As a result of the instruction, students will be able to:

- use vocabulary terms from the text in speaking and writing.
- use a graphic organizer to record ideas in the text.
- write a summary based on the text (with an introduction, supporting evidence, and a conclusion).

ASSESSMENT   There are several ways that Ms. Johnson will be able to assess student learning. When she reads the summary, she will look for the student's use of content vocabulary. To assess whether students successfully used a graphic organizer, she will collect and examine graphic organizers to see if they include details from the text. When she reads the summary, she will look for writing components, including an introduction, supporting details, and a conclusion.

English Language Development

Ms. Johnson knows that several of her students, especially those who are beginning and intermediate English learners, will need extra support during the lessons. She expects that many of her English learners will struggle with writing a summary. If she uses a Written Summary to test

Learning Outcomes		
	Objectives	**Assessments**
Content Area	1. *Compare the advantages and disadvantages of the Northern and Southern states as they entered the U.S. Civil War.*	1. *Summary paragraph: Does it include details about the population, railroad, economy, military, and geography?*
English/ Language Arts	1. *Use vocabulary terms from the text in speaking and writing.* 2. *Use a graphic organizer to record ideas in the text.* 3. *Write a summary based on the text.*	1. *Summary paragraph: Does it include content vocabulary?* 2. *Graphic organizer: Does the student record ideas from the text?* 3. *Does summary include introduction, supporting details, and a conclusion?*
English Language Development	Beginning: orally compare/contrast the North and South Intermediate: write short statements comparing the North and South Advanced: write several sentences comparing the North and South	

FIGURE 8.2   Learning Outcomes Entered on the LinC Teaching Plan

students' understanding of the concepts, some of her students will not be able to express their knowledge. For guidance, she consults the English language development standards. After reviewing the standards, she identifies learning outcomes for students of various English proficiency levels.

- Beginning English learners will be able to orally compare/contrast the North and South.
- Intermediate English learners will be able to write short statements comparing the North and South.
- Advanced English learners will be able to write several well-developed sentences comparing the North and South.

Ms. Johnson has established learning outcomes. She enters them on the LinC Teaching Plan, as shown in Figure 8.2. Now that she has established learning outcomes, her next step is to get to know the text.

PAUSE and REFLECT 8.2

In your content area, how do you assess student learning? How might a student's level of English proficiency impact his or her success with demonstrating learning?

KNOW THE TEXT

In Chapter 7, Ms. Johnson reflected about the textbook, and she recorded her thoughts on the Text Profile. These notes were general thoughts about the textbook, and now she focuses on a specific text section. As she prepares to teach, she reads the section of the textbook that will be the focus of the upcoming lessons. This section of text, shown in Figure 8.3, compares the Northern and Southern United States at the start of the Civil War. She reads the text, mindful of the text's structure and features.

Structure

As she reads this text segment, she identifies the text structure as compare/contrast. In this case, the structure of the text is consistent with, and supportive of, her instructional objectives. She wants students to be able to compare the North and the South, and the text will help them toward that goal.

Because she knows the structure of the text, she can appropriately match a graphic organizer to the text and use this visual representation to improve comprehension (Armbruster & Anderson, 1989). Figure 8.4 lists different text structures and corresponding graphic organizers (introduced in Chapter 4) that teachers can use for increasing comprehension. With this compare/contrast text segment, Ms. Johnson will want to use one of three types of graphic organizers: a Venn Diagram, a Compare/Contrast Matrix, or an Inference Graphic Organizer.

Pennsylvania, New Jersey, and the states north of them rallied to the president's call. The crucial slave states of the Upper South—North Carolina, Tennessee, Virginia, and Arkansas—seceded. They provided soldiers and supplies to the South. Mary Boykin Chesnut, whose husband became a Confederate congressman, wrote in her diary during this time:

"I did not know that one could live in such days of excitement…Everybody tells you half of something, and then rushes off…to hear the last news."

Wedged between the North and the South were the key **border states** of Delaware, Kentucky, Maryland, and Missouri—slave states that did not join the Confederacy. Kentucky and Missouri controlled parts of important rivers. Maryland separated the Union capital, Washington, D.C., from the North.

People in the border states were deeply divided on the war. The president's own wife,

Mary Todd Lincoln, had four brothers from Kentucky who fought for the Confederacy. Lincoln sent federal troops into the border states to help keep them in the Union. He also sent soldiers into western Virginia, where Union loyalties were strong. West Virginia set up its own state government in 1863.

Northern Resources

Numbers tell an important story about the Civil War. Consider the North's advantages. It could draw soldiers and workers from a population of 22 million, compared with the South's 5.5 million. One of its greatest advantages was its network of roads, canals, and railroads. Some 22,000 miles of railroad track could move soldiers and supplies throughout the North. The South had only about 9,000 miles of track.

In the North, the Civil War stimulated economic growth. To supply the military, the production of coal, iron, wheat, and wool increased. Also, the export of corn, wheat, beef,

FIGURE 8.3   Section of an Eighth-Grade U.S. History Textbook.   *Illustrations from HOLT SOCIAL STUDIES: UNITED STATES HISTORY Copyright © by William Francis Deverell. Reprinted by Holt, Rinehart and Winston, reproduced by permission of publisher Holt, Rinehart and Winston Publishing Company*

and pork to Europe doubled. In the South, the export of resources decreased because of the Union blockade.

Finally, the Union had money. It had a more developed economy, banking system, and currency. The South had to start printing its own Confederate dollars. Some states printed their own money, too. This led to financial chaos.

Taking advantage of the Union's strengths, General **Winfield Scott** developed a two-part strategy: (1) destroy the South's economy with a naval blockade of southern ports; (2) gain control of the Mississippi River to divide the South. Other leaders urged an attack on Richmond, Virginia, the Confederate capital.

Southern Resources

The Confederacy had advantages as well. With its strong military tradition, the South put many brilliant officers into battle. Southern farms provided food for its armies. The South's best advantage, however, was strategic. It needed only to defend itself until the North grew tired of fighting.

The North had to invade and control the South. To accomplish this, the Union army had to travel huge distances. For example, the distance from northern Virginia to central Georgia is about the length of Scotland and England combined. Because of distances such as this, the North had to maintain long supply lines.

In addition, wilderness covered much of the South. Armies found this land difficult to cross. Also, in Virginia, many of the rivers ran from east to west. Because of this, they formed a natural defense against an army that attacked from the north to the south. As a result, Northern generals were often forced to attack Confederate troops from the side rather than from the front. Furthermore, because Southerners fought mostly on their home soil, they were often familiar with the area.

The South hoped to wear down the North and to capture Washington, D.C. Confederate president Jefferson Davis also tried to win foreign allies through **cotton diplomacy**. This was the idea that Great Britain would support the Confederacy because it needed the South's raw cotton to supply its booming textile industry. Cotton diplomacy did not work as the South had hoped. Britain had large supplies of cotton, and it got more from India and Egypt.

READING CHECK **Comparing** What advantages did the North and South have leading up to the war?

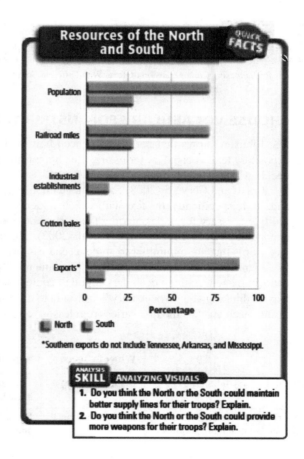

Resources of the North and South

QUICK FACTS

*Southern exports do not include Tennessee, Arkansas, and Mississippi.

SKILL ANALYZING VISUALS
1. Do you think the North or the South could maintain better supply lines for their troops? Explain.
2. Do you think the North or the South could provide more weapons for their troops? Explain.

FIGURE 8.3   continued

Significant Features

On the LinC Teaching Plan, Ms. Johnson notes some of the most significant features of this text section. Both the U.S. map and the chart showing resources of the North and South will help students comprehend the text. Students might also use these visuals as support when writing their essay. Ms. Johnson also looks at the headings; she will remember to point out the red and blue headings when the text changes topics.

Text Example	Structure	Purpose	Appropriate Graphic Organizers
History of Jazz	Sequential	Describe the events in order	MAIN IDEA/DETAIL INFERENCE
World Religions	Descriptive	Give details about a person, place, thing, or idea (nouns)	MAIN IDEA/DETAIL COMPARE/CONTRAST MATRIX INFERENCE
Atomic Bombings at Hiroshima and Nagasaki	Cause/Effect	Explain why something happens	OUTCOME INFERENCE
Substance Abuse	Persuasive	Convince reader to believe a point of view	EVIDENCE GUIDE INFERENCE
Styles of Artists: Impressionism (Monet) and Fauvism (Matisse)	Compare/Contrast	Show similarities and differences	COMPARE/CONTRAST MATRIX VENN DIAGRAM INFERENCE
Global Warming	Problem/Solution	Explain a problem and its solutions	EVIDENCE GUIDE INFERENCE

FIGURE 8.4   Graphic Organizers for Increasing Comprehension of Texts With Different Structures

CHOOSE VOCABULARY FOR INSTRUCTION

Ms. Johnson knows that her students need help with learning key vocabulary. However, with expository text, vocabulary terms are often numerous and represent deep concepts. How does she decide which words to include in instruction?

Bravo and Cervetti (2008) recommend choosing words to study based upon the curriculum and, more specifically, the text with which students will be engaged. The best choices are high-utility, necessary for understanding the document, and have strong conceptual connections with one another (Beck, McKeown, & Kucan, 2002). The goal in selecting words is to target vocabulary words that are unfamiliar to students and essential to understanding the text.

Flannigan and Greenwood (2007) recommend a four level system, designed for organizing, choosing, and teaching vocabulary found in content area text. Figure 8.5 shows this system. This way of thinking about vocabulary is useful in that it is dynamic—different vocabulary terms will fit into each level as the text varies from lesson to lesson.

LEVELS	Description	When to Teach	Type of Instruction
Level 1	Words essential to understanding the reading.	Before Reading	Time intensive; use strategies to build full word knowledge.
Level 2	"Foot in the door" words. Related to the content and needed to understand the reading.	Before Reading	If new label and new concept, need short definition and example. If new label and old concept, need synonym or simple definition.
Level 3	Words critical to understanding the content, but not critical to the reading. • clearly defined in reading • high-utility; students will see in other settings • demonstrate the patterns of language	During and After Reading	Use strategies to teach in a meaningful context and/or access independent use of strategies.
Level 4	Words that don't serve the lesson objectives.	Don't Teach	

FIGURE 8.5   Four Levels of Content Vocabulary. *Chart compiled from information in Flanigan and Greenwood (2007)*

- *Level 1.* Words at Level 1 are essential to understanding the reading. These terms require advanced teaching in order to ensure that all students understand the concept and the term.
- *Level 2.* Level 2 words are called "foot in the door" words because they provide the reader access to information in the reading. The best time to teach these words is before content instruction begins. Instruction of Level 2 words is often more quickly paced than instruction with Level 1 words.
- *Level 3.* Level 3 words are critical to understanding the content, but not critical to the reading. These words are perfect for reviewing and teaching during and after reading.
- *Level 4.* Level 4 words are those that should not be taught during the lesson. If a word falls into this category, it doesn't mean that it should *never* be taught, it just means that it does not fit with the current learning objectives.

When teaching using the four-level system, it is important to understand what the students already know. Teachers can teach Level 1 words as new labels for concepts that students already know. For example, most students will have an understanding of the concept of "hot," making it easier to learn vocabulary words that are related, such as "scalding." Level 2 words may be labels for concepts that students don't know. For example, the word "equilibrium" might be both a new word and a new concept for a middle or high school student. Thus, much of the vocabulary instruction in the content areas includes Level 1 and Level 2 vocabulary terms.

Many content area textbook publishers have already highlighted or italicized vocabulary that they feel is relevant to the text passage or content area being studied. Teachers are not obligated to choose the same vocabulary terms the publisher has chosen; they can use their own professional judgment and then select engaging strategies to build vocabulary.

In the text section that Ms. Johnson plans to use (Figure 8.3), very few words are bolded. Ms. Johnson knows that her students will find other words difficult. She identifies words that her students might not know, especially when used in the context of the reading.

- *Level 1:* advantages, disadvantages, union, confederate
- *Level 2:* decreased, natural defense, economic, currency, stimulated, blockade, allies, supply lines
- *Level 3:* cotton diplomacy

Learning Log

Use a section of your content area textbook to practice deciding which words to teach (LL12).

She writes these words on the LinC Teaching Plan, as shown in Figure 8.6. Now that Ms. Johnson has established learning outcomes, knows the text, and has selected vocabulary, she is ready to review student needs and select specific instructional strategies.

TEXT	
Pages	*512-513*
Type/Structure	*expository, compare/contrast*
Features	*map, chart, headings*
VOCABULARY	
Level 1 Essential (Before Reading)	*advantages, disadvantages, union, confederate*
Level 2 Related (Before Reading)	*decreased, natural defense, economic, currency, stimulated, blockade, allies, supply lines*
Level 3 Critical (During/After)	*cotton diplomacy*
Level 4 Not-Essential	

FIGURE 8.6   Text and Vocabulary Entered on the LinC Teaching Plan

REVIEW STUDENT NEEDS

Just before she chooses strategies, Ms. Johnson takes a few minutes to review what she knows about her students. When Ms. Johnson reflected about her Class Profile, she came to the following conclusions about what her students needed:

- *Language Proficiency.* For her English learners, design instruction that accounts for their English proficiency levels and focuses on fluency, vocabulary, and comprehension strategies.
- *Vocabulary.* Build support for content vocabulary for all students, with a special focus on those students who struggle with terms in the text.
- *Fluency.* Design opportunities to practice fluency, especially prosody (reading with expression). Students will need a chance to practice reading before reading in front of a group. In addition, there should be an emphasis on accuracy rather than rate.
- *Comprehension.* Improve comprehension and increase students' strategy use, specifically Support and Problem-Solving Strategies.
- *Motivation.* Choose instructional strategies that will boost students' self-concepts as readers. Any strategy that helps students become more competent should be appropriate; however, methods that capitalize on students' social interactions might have the most benefit over time.

With these thoughts in mind, Ms. Johnson begins to select instructional strategies and enter them on the LinC Teaching Plan.

PAUSE and REFLECT 8.2

Think about an instructional strategy that you have used. How did you choose that strategy? In what ways did it impact student learning?

SELECT INSTRUCTIONAL STRATEGIES

Selecting instructional strategies is the most critical part of the LinC Cycle. It is an intentional act. Teachers assess and reflect so they can decide which instructional strategies to use. As Ms. Johnson teaches about the North and the South, she will be using strategies that support vocabulary, fluency, reading comprehension, and motivation.

Ms. Johnson is now ready to choose appropriate instructional strategies to meet students' needs. She uses Figure 8.7, the Strategy Summary Chart, to make these instructional decisions. The Strategy Summary Chart includes each literacy component (vocabulary, fluency, comprehension, motivation), the goals of instruction, and strategies that meet that goal. For example, one of the literacy components is fluency. For fluency, there are three goals: model fluency, guide fluency, and provide practice for fluency. The *Strategies for Instruction* column lists instructional strategies that meet each goal. If, for example, a teacher wishes to guide fluency, he might choose one of two strategies—Guided Fluency Development Instruction or Adapted Retrospective Miscue Analysis.

Vocabulary

Teacher Tool

A Strategy Summary Chart is available in the Teacher Tools Appendix (TT23) to assist you in your planning.

Most of the class needs instruction in content area vocabulary. She has chosen to teach terms that fall mostly into Levels 1 and 2. Words that fit into these levels should be taught before reading and reinforced during reading. Ms. Johnson decides that her students will benefit if she teaches these words in a meaningful context. She refers to Figure 8.7 and sees that the <u>Vocabulary Rating Guide*</u> is one strategy that will meet this goal of vocabulary instruction. First, she will introduce level 1 and level 2 terms before reading. Then, during instruction, she will reinforce these terms. After instruction, students can see whether their understanding of the terms changes.

---

*Chapters 2 through 5 give complete procedures for all underlined strategies.

Literacy Component	Goals of Instruction	Strategies for Instruction
Vocabulary	Build Full Concept Knowledge	• Concept of Definition Map • Semantic Feature Analysis • Pre-Teaching Vocabulary
	Teach Words in a Meaningful Context	• Vocabulary Rating Guide • List-Group-Label • Vocabulary Visits
	Encourage Independent Use of Strategies	• Word Analysis • Contextual Redefinition • Dictionary Use • Personal Dictionary
Fluency	Model Fluency	• Teacher Read Aloud • Generated Read Aloud
	Guide Fluency	• Guided Fluency Instruction • Adapted Retrospective Miscue Analysis
	Provide Practice for Fluency	• Repeated Reading • Wide, Independent Reading
Comprehension	Activate and Build Background Knowledge	• K-W-L Strategy Chart • Text Box/Bag Activity • Survey Strategy and Guide
	Use Graphic Organizers	• Main Idea/Detail Graphic Organizer • Outcome Graphic Organizer • Evidence Guide Graphic Organizer • Compare/Contrast Matrix • Inference Graphic Organizer
	Summarize	• Written Summaries • Oral Summaries • Visual Summaries • Cornell Notes
	Ask and Answer Questions	• SQ3R (Survey, Question, Read, Recite, Review) • QAR (Question-Answer Relationship)
	Monitor Comprehension	• Interactive Think Aloud • Comprehension Monitoring Strategy Guide
	Use Multiple Reading Strategies	• Reciprocal Teaching • PLAN (Predict, Locate, Add, Note)
Motivation	Foster Student Control and Choice	• Socratic Seminars • WebQuests
	Encourage Collaboration	• Learning Clubs • PALS (Peer Assisted Learning Strategies)
	Ensure Mastery of Content and Literacy Skills	• Scaffolded Reading Experiences • CORI (Concept-Oriented Reading Instruction

FIGURE 8.7   Strategy Summary Chart: A List of Instructional Strategies from Chapters Two through Five

Fluency

In addition, many students benefit from instruction to improve fluency, and prosody in particular. Therefore, <u>Guided Fluency Development Instruction</u> (GFDI) is an appropriate choice. In GFDI, Ms. Johnson will be able to guide students through the text. In addition, <u>Repeated Reading</u> will provide students with independent fluency practice. For Repeated Reading, she will have students work in pairs, an especially good choice for students who need fluency practice, but who are not ready to read in front of a group.

Comprehension

Because some English learners and English-only students cannot yet read the text independently, explicit instruction in and support of comprehension strategies will be essential. Support with comprehension is also important because of the difficulty of the text—its readability level is ninth grade. Ms. Johnson will use the <u>Survey Strategy and Guide</u> to preview the text features in the section.

One of Ms. Johnson's conclusions about her students is that most will benefit from instruction in Problem-Solving Strategies. She refers to Figure 8.8 to see which instructional methods most effectively build Problem-Solving Strategies. Figure 8.8 shows the three categories of reading strategies that the MARSI addresses. For each one, it lists instructional strategies from Chapter 4 that best support each type of reading strategy. For Problem-Solving Strategies, Figure 8.8 suggests three instructional strategies: Interactive Think Aloud, Comprehension Monitoring Strategy Guide, and Reciprocal Teaching. Ms. Johnson decides to use the <u>Interactive Think Aloud</u>. She will think aloud as she reads aloud, modeling problem solving reading strategies for students with the content area text. To prepare for this strategy, she reads the text and makes notes of phrases and sentences that might cause her students to struggle with comprehension. Over time, students will be ready to use Problem-Solving Strategies independently.

Global Reading Strategies
- K-W-L Strategy Chart
- Text Box/Bag Activity
- Survey Strategy and Guide
- Cornell Notes
- Survey, Question, Read, Recite, Review (SQ3R)

Problem-Solving Strategies
- Interactive Think Aloud
- Comprehension Monitoring Guide
- Reciprocal Teaching

Support Reading Strategies
- Main Idea/ Detail Graphic Organizer
- Outcome Graphic Organizer
- Evidence Guide Graphic Organizer
- Compare/Contrast Matrix
- Inference Graphic Organizer
- Written Summaries
- Oral Summaries
- Visual Summaries
- Cornell Notes
- Survey, Question, Read, Recite, Review (SQ3R)
- Reciprocal Teaching
- Predict, Locate, Add, Note (PLAN)

FIGURE 8.8 Comprehension Instruction That Builds Three Categories of Reading Strategies: Global, Problem-Solving, and Support

Most of the students in this class do not use Support Reading Strategies independently. Therefore, they will require explicit instruction to learn how to use strategies to support their reading. Graphic organizers and summary strategies work best at the beginning of the year, because students can focus on one type of strategy at a time with this difficult text. Therefore, Ms. Johnson decides to use a <u>Compare/Contrast Matrix</u> because it matches the objective and the structure of the text. As students complete this graphic organizer, they will be recording some of the similarities and differences between the North and South. At the same time, they will be learning to use a strategy that supports their reading. Using graphic organizers during reading will add to students' abilities to note important details in content text.

In addition, students will complete <u>Written Summaries</u> after reading to be sure they under-stand the content. These summaries will give students additional practice with the grade level writing standards. While most of her class is engaged in writing summaries, she will meet indi-vidually with her Beginning and Intermediate English learners. She will ask each, with words and images, to explain the advantages of the North and South. In this way, she will differentiate instruction for her English learners. **Differentiated instruction** is an approach to teaching that includes active planning for student individual differences. By planning ahead for students' indi-vidual needs, Ms. Johnson hopes to build a successful learning experience for her students.

Resource

For more about differentiated instruction, see *Differentiation in Practice: A Practical Guide for Differentiated Curriculum Grades 9–12.*

Motivation

The instructional sequence will also seek to initiate and sustain student motivation. In this class, many students have a low Self-Concept and are eager to feel successful with the text. Ms. Johnson remembers that in order to develop student motivation, instruction should ensure mastery of con-tent and literacy skills. To decide which strategy will work best, she consults Figure 8.9. This fig-ure lists every instructional strategy from Chapters 2 through 5 and indicates whether that strategy promotes choice, collaboration, or mastery.

Ms. Johnson determines that a <u>Scaffolded Reading Experience</u> will work best with these eighth-grade students because the readability of the text (ninth grade) is above most students' reading levels. For the sequence of lessons to be a Scaffolded Reading Experience, instructional strategies need to support students before, during, and after reading. Ms. Johnson will use the Vocabulary Rating Guide and the Survey Strategy before reading. In addition, she will spark their interest in the Civil War with a reading from a novel. During reading, she plans to engage students in Guided Fluency Development Instruction and an Interactive Think Aloud. Completing the Compare/Contrast Matrix will further support their comprehension. After reading, the students will return to their Vocabulary Rating Guide and reflect upon their vocabulary growth. Ms. Johnson's plan is to help students improve their competence as readers and, as a result, improve their self-concepts.

Conclusion

After a process of assessment, reflection, and planning, Ms. Johnson concludes that she will use the following instructional strategies:

- Vocabulary Rating Guide
- Guided Fluency Development Instruction (GFDI)
- Repeated Reading
- Survey Strategy
- Interactive Think Aloud
- Compare/Contrast Matrix
- Written Summaries
- Scaffolded Reading Experience

After deciding which strategies to use, Ms. Johnson writes them on the LinC Teaching Plan. Figure 8.10 shows the complete LinC Teaching Plan that Ms. Johnson prepared for her eighth-grade social science class.

Strategy		Motivational Principles		
Name	Chapter	Choice	Collaboration	Mastery
Concept of Definition Map	2		X	X
Semantic Feature Analysis	2			X
Pre-Teaching Vocabulary	2			X
Vocabulary Rating Guide	2		X	X
List-Group-Label	2	X		X
Vocabulary Visits	2	X	X	X
Word Analysis	2		X	X
Contextual Redefinition	2	X		X
Dictionary Use	2			X
Personal Dictionary	2	X		X
Teacher Read Aloud	3			X
Generated Read Aloud	3	X		X
Guided Fluency Development Instruction	3		X	X
Adapted Retrospective Miscue Analysis	3			X
Repeated Reading	3	X	X	X
Wide, Independent Reading	3	X		X
K-W-L Strategy Chart	4	X	X	X
Text Box/Bag Activity	4		X	X
Survey Strategy and Guide	4	X	X	X
Main Idea/Detail Graphic Organizer	4			X
Outcome Graphic Organizer	4			X
Evidence Guide Graphic Organizer	4	X		X
Compare/Contrast Matrix	4			X
Inference Graphic Organizer	4			X
Written Summaries	4	X		X
Oral Summaries	4	X		X
Visual Summaries	4	X		X
Cornell Notes	4	X		X
SQ3R	4			X
QAR	4			X
Interactive Think Aloud	4	X	X	X
Comprehension Monitoring Guide	4	X	X	X
Reciprocal Teaching	4	X	X	X
PLAN (Predict, Locate, Add, Note)	4	X	X	X
Socratic Seminars	5	X	X	X
WebQuests	5	X	X	X
Learning Clubs	5	X	X	X
Peer-Assisted Learning Strategies (PALS)	5		X	X
Scaffolded Reading Experience	5		X	X
Concept-Oriented Reading Instruction (CORI)	5	X	X	X

FIGURE 8.9 Strategies to Promote Choice, Collaboration, and Mastery

Class	Eighth-Grade Social Science		Topic	Civil War

LEARNING OUTCOMES			
	Objectives		**Assessments**
Content Area	1. Compare the advantages of the Northern and Southern states as they entered the U.S. Civil War.		1. Summary paragraph: Does it include details about the population, railroad, economy, military, and geography?
English/ Language Arts	1. Use vocabulary terms from the text in speaking and writing. 2. Use a graphic organizer to record ideas from the text. 3. Write a summary based on the text.		1. Summary paragraph: Does it include content vocabulary? 2. Graphic organizer: Does the student record ideas from the text? 3. Does summary include introduction, supporting details, and a conclusion?
English Language Development	*Beginning: orally compare/contrast the North and South* *Intermediate: write short statements comparing the North and South* *Advanced: write several sentences comparing the North and South*		

TEXT	
Pages	*512-513*
Type/Structure	*expository, compare/contrast*
Features	*map, chart, headings*

VOCABULARY	
Level 1 Essential (Before Reading)	*advantages, disadvantages, union, confederate*
Level 2 Related (Before Reading)	*decreased, natural defense, economic, currency, stimulated, blockade, allies, supply lines*
Level 3 Critical (During/After)	*cotton diplomacy*
Level 4 Not-Essential	

INSTRUCTIONAL STRATEGIES	
Lesson 1	
Vocabulary	*Vocabulary Rating Guide*
Fluency	
Comprehension	*Survey Strategy*
Motivation	*Scaffolded Reading Experience*
Lesson 2	
Vocabulary	
Fluency	*Guided Fluency Development Instruction, Repeated Reading*
Comprehension	*Interactive Think Aloud, Compare/Contrast Graphic Organizer*
Motivation	*Scaffolded Reading Experience*
Lesson 3	
Vocabulary	*Vocabulary Rating Guide*
Fluency	
Comprehension	*Written Summary (Compare/Contrast)*
Motivation	*Scaffolded Reading Experience*

FIGURE 8.10 Ms. Johnson's LinC Teaching Plan

Learning Log

Complete a LinC Teaching Plan for a lesson sequence in your content area (LL13).

Note that it is not necessary to include strategies for every literacy component every day; it is more important to make informed choices about which strategies to use. In addition, the chronological order of the instructional strategies each day can be flexible. It might make more sense to use a comprehension instructional strategy first, followed by one that addresses fluency.

Note, too, that many vocabulary, fluency, and comprehension strategies also enhance motivation. When recording strategies on the "motivation" line in the LinC Teaching Plan, record methods that are specifically chosen to initiate and sustain motivation, like those described in Chapter 5.

Chapter Summary

In order to choose appropriate instructional strategies, teachers go through a planning process. They clearly understand three sets of grade-level standards—for English/language arts, English language development, and the content area. They optimize learning from a text by understanding the features, type, structure, readability, and vocabulary of the text. And, finally, they choose strategies to strengthen each student's content knowledge and literacy development.

After recording instructional strategies on a LinC Teaching Plan, instruction can begin.

To prepare to teach, Ms. Johnson selected instructional strategies carefully. Assessment and reflection informed her instructional plans. She now looks forward to beginning this sequence of lessons, designed specifically to support content learning and literacy development.

Resources

California Department of Education (2000). *History-social science content standards for California public schools, kindergarten through grade twelve.*

Flanigan, K., & Greenwood, S. C. (2007). Effective content vocabulary instruction in the middle: Matching students, purposes, words and strategies. *Journal of Adolescent & Adult Literacy, 51*(3), 226–238.

Tomlinson, C.A. (2005). *Differentiation in practice: A resource guide for differentiating curriculum, Grades 9-12.* Alexandria, VA: ASCD.

References

Armbruster, B. B., & Anderson, T. H. (1989). Teaching text structure to improve reading and writing. *The Reading Teacher, 43*(2), 130–137.

Beck, I. L., McKeown, M. G., & Kucan, L. (2002). *Bringing words to life: Robust vocabulary instruction.* New York: Guilford.

Bravo, M. A., & Cervetti, G. N. (2008). Teaching vocabulary through text and experience in content areas. In A. E. Farstrup & S. J. Samuels (Eds.), *What research has to say about vocabulary instruction* (130-149). Newark, DE: International Reading Association.

Deverell, W. F., & White, D.G. (2009). *United States history.* Boston, MA: Holt McDougal.

CHAPTER 9

Teach and Reteach—Using the LinC Cycle

Ms. Johnson had invested time in assessment, reflection, and planning. She had begun teaching, and during the first two lessons, the instructional strategies had been successful. She was happy to see that students were engaged with the text, but what had they learned? It was time for the final lesson on the North and South, and Ms. Johnson asked students to take out their Vocabulary Rating Guides.

"Remember on Monday when you rated the words?" she asked, rhetorically. "Now it's time to rate them again. Let's see which ones you feel comfortable with now. In the column marked 'after instruction,' you're going to rate your level of understanding with a 1, 2, 3, or 4. Remember the ratings go from 1, meaning you don't recognize the word and haven't heard it before, to a 4, which means you fully understand the meaning of the word."

She began reading the words one by one, and she watched as students thought about how well they understood the vocabulary. Her eye traveled over to Lao, who sat at table four, nodding his head almost imperceptibly as he marked his page.

After she had read the words, Ms. Johnson was ready for students to show how much they'd learned. "So, let's see who had a change in their understanding of the first word 'disadvantage.' Thumbs up means your rating went up, flat hand for stayed the same, thumbs down means rating went down."

She looked around and saw that everyone had either a thumb up or a flat hand. "Okay," she continued, "raise your hand if your final rating is a 4."

Lao looked up, smiled, and raised his hand slowly. Ms. Johnson asked for a volunteer to share his or her definition and they went on to the next word.

For almost every word, Lao had his thumb up. On the word "blockade," Lao volunteered to use the word in a sentence. "The ships made a blockade in Charleston Harbor."

Ms. Johnson kept her calm exterior, but inside, she was ready to bubble over. Lao and his class had been able to access the vocabulary in the reading. This was a far cry from last week, when they read the text on their own and weren't able to remember or talk about what they had read. She couldn't wait to share the news with her eighth-grade team.

Chapters 5, 6, and 7 described how teachers assess, reflect, and plan for instruction. This chapter explains the next stage of the LinC Cycle—teach and reteach. In a culmination of her planning, Ms. Johnson uses her LinC Teaching Plan to guide students through the text. But the process is not over—she also assesses student progress and measures their learning. Her goal is to plan future instruction that continually meets her students' needs.

TEACH: THE LINC TEACHING PLAN IN ACTION

Ms. Johnson refers to her LinC Teaching Plan (Figure 9.1) and begins her three-day lesson for her fourth-period, eighth-grade social science class. To give the series of lessons context, it is important to know that her class has already explored some of the events leading up to the Civil War. They know the geography of the United States in the 1860s and have a U.S. map of that time period available for reference in the classroom.

Day 1

SCAFFOLDED READING EXPERIENCE   To get students interested in the reading, Ms. Johnson reads aloud from the novel *Two Brothers: One North, One South* (Jones, 2008). She and the students discuss how the Civil War tore families apart. She asks students to imagine what it would be like to be fighting against family and friends. They take a moment to respond to that question in their notebooks. In addition, in order to prepare them for success with the content of the text, she uses the Survey Strategy and Vocabulary Rating Guide. Each of these strategies supports students' reading before they even begin to read the text.

SURVEY STRATEGY   Ms. Johnson asks students to open their texts, and she guides them in using the Survey Strategy to identify features of the section that will give rise to further understanding (headings/subheadings, vocabulary terms, map, chart, and captions). She then asks the students to work with their neighbors to identify the structure of the text on pages 512 and 513. The class helps her identify that this is written in a compare/contrast structure. They note important signal words, such as "advantages" and "disadvantages." **Signal words** are terms that help the reader identify the text structure.

VOCABULARY RATING GUIDE   Ms. Johnson distributes a Vocabulary Rating Guide (Figure 9.2). She reads the directions. Then she reads each term, uses it in a sentence, and asks the students to rate each term with a number 1, 2, 3, or 4. She asks them to work with their partners to define and find synonyms for these terms. She models the process with the first two vocabulary terms. Then, as they work with their partners, she monitors their progress as they complete the Vocabulary Rating Guide. Some use the dictionary and thesauri from the class library. Two pairs use the classroom computers to look up the terms and choose the appropriate definitions. After the class has completed the rating guide, they discuss the terms, their definitions, and the initial ratings of the terms.

> **PAUSE and REFLECT 9.1**
>
> Choose one of the instructional strategies that Ms. Johnson used on Day 1. In what ways does this strategy support student literacy?

Day 2

GUIDED FLUENCY DEVELOPMENT INSTRUCTION   Ms. Johnson guides students in reading the section entitled "Northern Resources." She models fluent reading and word analysis strategies. For example, she reads the sentence "To supply the military, the production of coal, iron, wheat, and wood increased." As she reads, she makes sure that she reads at an appropriate pace, and she pauses when she sees a comma. After she reads the sentence, she asks students if they know the word "increased." She continues, sometimes reading alone, and sometimes having students read chorally with her.

INTERACTIVE THINK ALOUD   During the Guided Fluency Development Instruction, Ms. Johnson is also focused on comprehension. For example, Ms. Johnson reads the sentence "In the North, the Civil War stimulated economic growth." She pauses to say aloud, "'Economic,'

Class	Eighth-Grade Social Science		Topic	Civil War

LEARNING OUTCOMES ———

	Objectives	Assessments
Content Area	1. *Compare the advantages of the Northern and Southern states as they entered the U.S. Civil War.*	1. *Summary paragraph: Does it include details about the population, railroad, economy, military, and geography?*
English/ Language Arts	1. *Use vocabulary terms from the text in speaking and writing.* 2. *Use a graphic organizer to record ideas from the text.* 3. *Write a summary based on the text.*	1. *Summary paragraph: Does it include content vocabulary?* 2. *Graphic organizer: Does the student record ideas from the text?* 3. *Does summary include introduction, supporting details, and a conclusion?*
English Language Development	*Beginning: orally compare/contrast the North and South* *Intermediate: write short statements comparing the North and South* *Advanced: write several sentences comparing the North and South*	

TEXT

Pages	*512-513*
Type/Structure	*expository, compare/contrast*
Features	*map, chart, headings*

VOCABULARY

Level 1 Essential (Before Reading)	*advantages, disadvantages, union, confederate*
Level 2 Related (Before Reading)	*decreased, natural defense, economic, currency, stimulated, blockade, allies, supply lines*
Level 3 Critical (During/After)	*cotton diplomacy*
Level 4 Not-Essential	

INSTRUCTIONAL STRATEGIES

Lesson 1	
Vocabulary	*Vocabulary Rating Guide*
Fluency	
Comprehension	*Survey Strategy*
Motivation	*Scaffolded Reading Experience*
Lesson 2	
Vocabulary	
Fluency	*Guided Fluency Development Instruction, Repeated Reading*
Comprehension	*Interactive Think Aloud, Compare/Contrast Graphic Organizer*
Motivation	*Scaffolded Reading Experience*
Lesson 3	
Vocabulary	*Vocabulary Rating Guide*
Fluency	
Comprehension	*Written Summary (Compare/Contrast)*
Motivation	*Scaffolded Reading Experience*

FIGURE 9.1 Ms. Johnson's LinC Teaching Plan

Vocabulary Rating Guide

Text title: Northern Resources, Southern Resources

1. I don't recognize this word, and I have never heard it before.
2. I recognize the word, but I don't know what it means.
3. I have a basic understanding of the word.
4. I understand the word and can use it flexibly, in most contexts. I could teach it to others.

Vocabulary Word	Before Instruction				After Instruction				Definition	Synonym
	1	2	3	4	1	2	3	4		
1. advantage										
2. disadvantage										
3. union										
4. confederacy										
5. decrease										
6. natural defense										
7. economic										
8. currency										
9. stimulated										
10. blockade										
11. allies										
12. supply lines										
13. cotton diplomacy										

FIGURE 9.2 Vocabulary Rating Guide Handout for Students

'stimulated' . . . those are two of our vocabulary words." They discuss the meaning of that sentence, and why wars, throughout history, have sparked an increased production of goods.

REPEATED READING   After reading the first section together as a class, Ms. Johnson asks students to orally reread it with their partners and to complete the Compare/Contrast Matrix. During this Repeated Reading, students take turns practicing fluent reading.

COMPARE/CONTRAST MATRIX   Ms. Johnson draws a Compare/Contrast Matrix on the whiteboard (Figure 9.3) and has students copy it into their notebooks. She explains that they will be using this graphic organizer to compare the advantages and disadvantages of the North and South. On the left side, she writes the words "North" and "South." They look back at the reading and, together, identify the titles of each column. She asks, "How should we compare them? What terms should we use?" Across the top, she writes the terms for comparison. She and the students discuss why each of those categories is important in determining who has an advantage in war. She models how to complete the first column of the graphic organizer. Then, students complete the organizer during their Repeated Reading practice with their partner. As she gives directions, she mentions that students can use short phrases and visual symbols in the graphic organizer.

When the class has finished entering the advantages of the North, they continue reading the next section ("Southern Resources"). As they did with the first section, they progress through the instructional strategies: Guided Fluency Development Instruction, Interactive Think Aloud, Repeated Reading, and Compare/Contrast Matrix.

SCAFFOLDED READING EXPERIENCE   Throughout Day 2, Ms. Johnson supports student motivation with a Scaffolded Reading Experience. Each of the four strategies is designed to support students' comprehension of the text during reading. As students engage with each of these instructional strategies, they focus on the meaning of the text, and Ms. Johnson guides them toward gaining mastery with fluency, vocabulary, and comprehension.

PAUSE and REFLECT 9.2

Choose one of the instructional strategies that Ms. Johnson used on Day 2. In what ways does this strategy support student literacy?

	Population (size of army)	Railroad (getting supplies)	Economy (goods and money)	Military (training, strength of officers)	Geography (difficulty of fighting)
North					
South					

FIGURE 9.3   Compare/Contrast Matrix

Day 3

VOCABULARY RATING GUIDE   On the third class day, after students have finished their Compare/Contrast Matrix, Ms. Johnson has her class revisit their Vocabulary Rating Guides. She reads each term, and students rate their understanding. As a class, they discuss how their understanding of these terms changed over the last few lessons.

WRITTEN SUMMARY   Ms. Johnson tells the class that each person will be completing a Written Summary—a short essay on the advantages of the North and the South. First, she asks each student to turn to his or her partner and explain what they remember about the advantages of the North and the South. Next, she shows them how their Compare/Contrast Matrices can help them as they write. Using an overhead projector, she shows a sample graphic organizer. They then discuss the best format for the essay. They agree that they would like to write an introduction, one paragraph on the North, one paragraph on the South, and a conclusion. They talk about possible information to include in the introduction. Next, she models how to take the information from the graphic organizer and write it as a sentence. For example, the first box (North and Population) reads 22 million. She turns this information into a sentence: "The population of the North was 22 million." She gives students time to begin writing. While they are writing, she calls up her beginning English learners and asks them to explain orally the advantages of the North and the South. By providing an alternative to the writing assignment, she is differentiating instruction and assessment (Tomlinson, 1999) and honoring the differences in English proficiency among her students.

SCAFFOLDED READING EXPERIENCE   Like Days 1 and 2, Day 3 is embedded with motivational scaffolds. Both instructional strategies are designed to ensure that students understand what they have read and are able to express it in writing. The support of literacy development does not end when the reading is finished. Instead, it continues as Ms. Johnson helps students extend and apply what they have learned.

She closes the lesson by having students read and share their essays with a partner. She then reads another section of the novel *Two Brothers: One North, One South* (Jones, 2008). She ties the novel to what they have learned about the advantages of the North and the South in the Civil War.

Throughout this lesson sequence, Ms. Johnson embeds literacy in context and focuses on content reading. She provides explicit instruction in vocabulary, fluency, and comprehension, while initiating and sustaining their motivation to learn. She scaffolds student learning by modeling tasks before asking students to engage in them independently. Now she turns her attention to evaluating student learning.

PAUSE and REFLECT 9.3

Choose one of the instructional strategies that Ms. Johnson used on Day 3. In what ways does this strategy support student literacy?

ASSESS STUDENT LEARNING

To assess student learning, Ms. Johnson reviews her lesson objectives and evaluates learning outcomes. After carefully examining student work, she reaches conclusions about her next steps for instruction.

Review Lesson Objectives

Ms. Johnson reviews her lesson's learning objectives.

- Social science objective(s). Students will be able to:
  - compare the advantages of the Northern and Southern states as they entered the U.S. Civil War.

- Language arts objective(s). Students will be able to:
  - use the vocabulary terms from the text in speaking and writing.
  - use a graphic organizer to record ideas from the text.
  - write a summary based on the text.
- English/language development objective(s).
  - Beginning English learners will be able to orally compare/contrast the North and South.
  - Intermediate English learners will be able to write short statements comparing the North and South.
  - Advanced English learners will be able to write several well-developed sentences comparing the North and South.

In her teaching, Ms. Johnson supported literacy proficiencies other than those listed in the objectives. For example, she supported fluency, and the students practiced it. However, it is important to keep her learning outcomes simple and measurable for each lesson. In other lessons, she will have an opportunity to focus on other objectives.

Evaluate Learning Outcomes

For the class, Ms. Johnson evaluates student learning about the social science content, vocabulary understanding, graphic organizer use, and summary writing.

SOCIAL SCIENCE CONTENT   The evidence for learning about the content is the Written Summary. By examining the class set of essays, Ms. Johnson notes that students have a good understanding of the content. All students were able to describe advantages of the North and advantages of the South.

Recall that Ms. Johnson met individually with each of her Beginning English learners during the independent writing time. During that time she was able to assess whether each had learned the content. Her Beginning English learners, for example, were able to briefly describe, through words and drawn symbols, the advantages of the North and the South. When she read the work from her other Intermediate and Advanced English learners, it was clear that they had grasped the content.

As a class, the group seemed to have trouble understanding why the economy of the North and South could impact the war. There was broad understanding that money is needed to fight a war. However, the idea that foreign trade supports economies was new to many students. Ms. Johnson realized that she will need to reteach the difference in the economies between the North and South.

VOCABULARY   Were students able to learn the vocabulary? Based on a review of their Vocabulary Rating Guides, students reported that they had a better understanding of the vocabulary at the end of the lesson. The majority of students felt that they had full word knowledge of several terms ("advantages," "disadvantages," "union," "confederate," "natural," "defense"). At the end of the lesson, no one rated any word with a score of 1 ("I don't recognize this word, and I have never heard it before"). But the true test of vocabulary understanding is whether students were then able to use it correctly in speaking and writing. In the essay, many of the students used the terms. For example, in Figure 9.4, Lena's essay includes the terms: "advantages," "economy," "natural defense," "Union," "Confederate," "supply lines," and "blockade." She used all correctly. But Ms. Johnson notes that the majority of students used just 6 or 7 terms (of 12) in their essays. In the future, she will need to help students become even more comfortable with these new terms so that they will use them when writing.

GRAPHIC ORGANIZER   Recall that one of Ms. Johnson's objectives was to teach students to take notes on a graphic organizer. This tool would help their need to develop strategies that support their reading. All but two students had detailed Compare/Contrast Matrices. For the sake of comparison, Figure 9.5 shows an example of a detailed graphic organizer, and an example of a less detailed graphic organizer. In Figure 9.5, Madison's graphic organizer is short on details. In the "Economy" column, for example, she does not list the goods or exports. On

Lena

Advantages of the North and South

At the start of the Civil War, both the North and the South had advantages. If we think about their population, railroad, <u>economy</u>, military, and geography, we can see many of the <u>advantages</u>.

The North had advantages because of its population, railroad, and <u>economy</u>. The North had a higher population. This meant that there were more people to recruit for the <u>Union</u> Army. The North also had many more miles of railroad tracks so that they had a <u>supply line</u> to their troops. They had 22,000 miles compared to 9,000 miles of railroad track in the South. The North also had a better <u>economy</u>. They produced coal, iron, wheat, and wool. They made money by exporting these things to Europe. The South, on the other hand, had trouble exporting goods because the Union navy made a <u>blockade</u> of ships to stop trade.

The South's military and geography brought some <u>advantages</u>. They had many brilliant military officers who wanted to defend the <u>Confederacy's</u> way of life. Their farms produced food for soldiers. And, most of the fighting occurred in the South, so they were able to fight on their "home turf." And that wasn't easy for the North, because the South was an area filled with wilderness, a <u>natural defense.</u>

When the Civil War began, both sides used their <u>advantages</u> to try to win. But in the end, one side would come out ahead.

FIGURE 9.4 Lena's Essay "Advantages of the North and South"

A. Madison's Compare/Contrast Matrix

	Population (size of army)	Railroad (getting supplies)	Economy (goods and money)	Military (training, strength of officers)	Geography (difficulty of fighting)
North	22 million	22,000 miles	Had money		
South	2 million	9,000 miles	No exports		A lot of wilderness

B. Lena's Compare/Contrast Matrix

	Population (size of army)	Railroad (getting supplies)	Economy (goods and money)	Military (training, strength of officers)	Geography (difficulty of fighting)
North	22 million	22,000 miles	Produced coal, iron, wheat, wool. Exported corn, wheat, beef, and pork to Europe. Banking system and currency.		Varied terrain, but mostly fought battles in the South.
South	2 million	9,000 miles	Exports dropped because of the Union blockade. Farms produced food for soldiers. Had to print new Confederate money.	Brilliant officers	Natural defense: Wilderness covered much of the South. Most fighting occurred on the South's home soil.

FIGURE 9.5 Two Compare/Contrast Matrices on the North and the South

the other hand, in Lena's graphic organizer (Figure 9.5), she lists products of the North and mentions the naval blockade of the South. This student work shows that Madison, and a student with a similar type of graphic organizer (Garrett), will need further instruction on how to take notes on a graphic organizer.

COMPARE/CONTRAST WRITTEN SUMMARY   There was a difference in how well-developed students' essays were. Take, for example, Madison's essay. A quick glance shows that it lacks detail. Why? Ms. Johnson looks at Madison's essay and graphic organizer, side-by-side, for a clue. (Figure 9.6). Madison's graphic organizer is not detailed. So, it is not surprising that her essay is also short on details. And there appears to be another problem. Even when a detail is entered on Madison's graphic organizer, it doesn't always make it to the essay. So, it appears that Madison has some trouble creating sentences from the notes on her graphic organizer.

Ms. Johnson matches students' graphic organizers with their essays, and she notes that students with less developed essays had one of these two issues:

- they did not have enough detail on their graphic organizers,
- or they had trouble transferring the information to their essays.

She knows that future instruction will need to help students with both of these issues. Ms. Johnson recalls that she did do some modeling of how to transfer information from the graphic organizer to a well-written essay. However, she now sees that it will require more instructional attention. In future lessons, she will model, once again, how to use notes to build a paragraph or essay. In addition, she decides to meet with Madison and Garrett to talk with them about their writing to see if this is a problem that they have had in the past.

At the other end of the spectrum were students who had very detailed graphic organizers and well-developed essays. Figure 9.7 shows Alec's graphic organizer and essay. On his graphic organizer, Alec included details that went beyond the reading. Ms. Johnson remembered that at one point during the lesson, Alec had asked whether he could look up something on the computer. She saw what he added to the graphic organizer. Under the "Military" column,

Madison's Compare/Contrast Matrix

	Population (size of army)	Railroad (getting supplies)	Economy (goods and money)	Military (training, strength of officers)	Geography (difficulty of fighting)
North	22 million	22,000 miles	Had money		
South	2 million	9,000 miles	No exports		A lot of wilderness

Madison's Compare/Contrast Essay

Madison

<u>Advantages</u> of the North and South

The North and South both had <u>advantages</u>. The North had more people than the South. It had a bigger army. The North also had a railroad to get supplies to soldiers. And they had more money. The South had farms to feed their soldiers. Also it was hard for the North to fight there because of the wilderness. They couldn't get ships out because of the <u>blockade</u>.

FIGURE 9.6   Madison's Graphic Organizer and Essay

Alec's Compare/Contrast Matrix

	Population (size of army)	Railroad (getting supplies)	Economy (goods and money)	Military (training, strength of officers)	Geography (difficulty of fighting)
North	22 million	22,000 miles Supply line to the soldiers.	Produced coal, iron, wheat, wool. Exported corn, wheat, beef, and pork to Europe. Banking system, and currency	Ulysses S. Grant Major Robert Anderson (Fort Sumter) Lieutentant General Thomas "Stonewall" Jackson	Varied terrain. Most battles fought in the South.
South	2 million	9,000 miles	Cotton, but blockade made that difficult. Farms produced food for soldiers. Printed currency	Brilliant officers Robert E. Lee William T. Sherman	Natural defense: Wilderness, fields, swamps. Most battles on South's homeland.

Alec's Compare/Contrast Essay

Alec

<u>**Advantages**</u> **of the North and South**

The North and the South each had advantages when they started the Civil War. The North's <u>advantages</u> were its population, railroad, and <u>economy</u>. The South's advantage was its military and the natural defense provided by its geography.

The North had several <u>advantages</u>. The North had a bigger population, miles of railroad tracks, and a strong <u>economy</u>. With a population of 22 million, they had plenty of people to serve in the military. A 22,000-mile railroad system helped serve as a <u>supply line</u> to their troops. The South had just 9,000 miles of track to transfer food and weapons. Furthermore, the North's <u>economy</u> was more stable. They produced goods like coal, iron, wheat, and wool that they could use themselves and export to Europe. Exports earned them extra money. Because of the naval <u>blockade</u>, the South could not export goods to Europe. The South produced an abundance of cotton, but because of the naval <u>blockade</u> they were unable to export it.

The South's military and geography brought some <u>advantages</u>. They had many brilliant military officers who wanted to defend the <u>Confederacy</u>'s way of life. One, Robert E. Lee, had distinguished himself during the Mexican-American War. Lincoln invited him to lead the Union army, but he chose to fight for the <u>Confederacy</u>. Another <u>advantage</u> of the South was the geography. Most of the South was barren and wild, which made a good <u>natural defense</u> for the <u>Confederate</u> Army. This would prove to be an <u>advantage</u> because much of the fighting occurred in the South, because the South was an area filled with wilderness, a <u>natural defense.</u>

When the Civil War began, both sides used their <u>advantages</u> to try to win. But in the end, one side would come out ahead.

FIGURE 9.7   Alec's Graphic Organizer and Essay

Alec wrote the names of Union and Confederacy officers. Then, when he wrote his essay, he included some information about Robert E. Lee.

Ms. Johnson realized that all students would have benefited from an opportunity to use an outside source to complete their charts. She makes a mental note for her next lesson.

CONCLUSION   By examining student work, she comes to some conclusions about future lessons. She knows she will need to:

1. Explain how economies are impacted by national events, such as war.
2. Make an extra effort to highlight important vocabulary words during reading, and show students how to use these terms in their writing.

3. Model how to take notes on a graphic organizer. This will be especially important for Garrett and Madison, who had trouble recording details on their Compare/Contrast Matrix.

4. Model how to take information from a graphic organizer and write well-constructed sentences.

These goals will become part of future lessons.

PAUSE and REFLECT 9.4

Consider Ms. Johnson's conclusions. How might she address these learning goals in future lessons?

DESIGN FUTURE INSTRUCTION

Reteaching is more than simply reiterating what has already been taught using the same instructional methods. It involves using evidence of student learning to decide directions for future teaching. When Ms. Johnson examined student work and thought about student learning, she concluded that future lessons would need to reinforce certain aspects of content knowledge and literacy proficiency. Her upcoming lessons will focus on major events in the Civil War. She thinks about how upcoming instruction will continue to support student learning.

Social Science Content

Ms. Johnson plans to teach students more about how the economies of the North and South impacted the war and its outcome. To do this, she will gather information that compares the financial status of the North and South in the 1860s. If students can see real examples of supply and demand for goods, they will likely gain a better understanding of wartime economies. In addition, Ms. Johnson will bring in information about current military expenses. It might be interesting for students to compare the expense of current wars with the expense of the Civil War.

Vocabulary

As the class learns about the Civil War, the vocabulary terms from these lessons will continue to appear. Each time she notices a vocabulary term, she will draw attention to it. One of her colleagues, Mr. Blake, makes an effort to use the class's vocabulary words when he speaks to his students. When he uses a vocabulary word, he says it with strong emphasis so that students realize he is saying a vocabulary word. She decides to try this method. Also, when she coaches individuals on their writing, she will be aware of places where they might be able to use the new vocabulary words. Supporting the words during speaking and writing will likely help students become more comfortable with using the words.

Graphic Organizers

During the next portion of instruction, Ms. Johnson will be having students complete an Outcome Graphic Organizer to document events in the Civil War. She will spend some time with the whole class focused on how to take notes; then she will work with a small group as the rest of the class works independently or in pairs. Students who need more guidance will receive it, while students who don't (like Alec) will be able to fill in their graphic organizers without interruption.

Writing

During this lesson, Ms. Johnson realized that students need more help in transforming their notes into detailed sentences. In her next lesson, when she uses the Outcome Graphic Organizer, she will have another opportunity to help students transfer their notes into carefully constructed paragraphs. She will seek opportunities to have quick writing conferences with individual students so that she can model how to write engaging sentences that include essential information.

Conclusion

In thinking about reteaching, Ms. Johnson shows her commitment to student learning. Student work from lessons tells her more than how well students learned the content—it tells her about students' abilities to understand and express ideas. Before she began this lesson sequence, Ms. Johnson decided to support students' vocabulary, fluency, comprehension, and motivation. Each of the strategies that she chose was purposeful in addressing student needs and grade level standards. And now she sees that students are on their way to becoming more proficient in essential literacy skills and strategies.

Chapter Summary

When using the LinC Cycle, a thoughtful process of assessment, reflection, and planning culminates in teaching a lesson. Teachers use the LinC Teaching Plan to help guide them during instruction. But, after teaching, the LinC Cycle does not end. The teacher assesses student learning and plans future instruction. The continuous cycle of assessment, reflection, planning, teaching, and reteaching guides teachers to match their commitment to adolescent literacy with the tools to make it happen.

By engaging with the LinC Cycle, Ms. Johnson is now able to intentionally plan instruction that leads to growth in both content learning and literacy development. As the school year progresses, she will continue to use data as information to guide her instructional choices. And, when her students begin 9th grade, they will be more prepared to face the challenges of high school content learning.

Resource

Jones, D.H. (2008). *Two brothers, one north, one south.* Tarzana, CA: Staghorn.

Reference

Tomlinson, C. A. (1999). *The differentiated classroom: Responding to the needs of all learners.* Upper Saddle River, NJ: Pearson/Merrill/Prentice Hall.

Teacher Tools

TEACHER TOOL 1   Concept of Definition Map

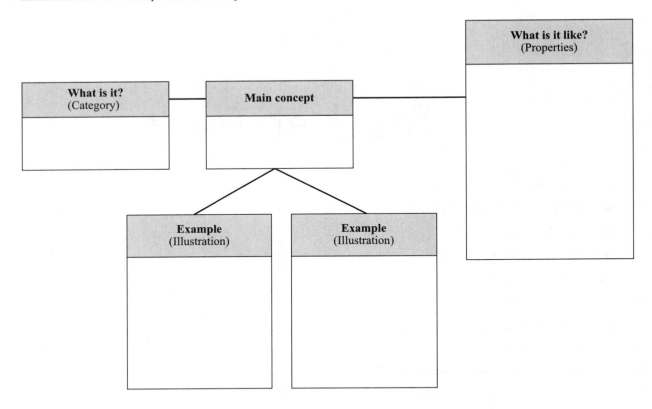

TEACHER TOOL 2   Visual Association Chart

Vocabulary Term	What is it?	What does it look like?

TEACHER TOOL 3 Vocabulary Note Card

Definition	Properties

Term

Examples	Non-Examples

TEACHER TOOL 4   Pre-Teaching Vocabulary Chart

Term	Synonym	Definition/Example	Image

Vocabulary Rating Guide

Text title: _____

1. I don't recognize this word, and I have never heard it before.
2. I recognize the word, but I don't know what it means.
3. I have a basic understanding of the word.
4. I understand the word and can use it flexibly, in most contexts. I could teach it to others.

Vocabulary Word	Before Instruction				After Instruction				Definition	Synonym
	1	2	3	4	1	2	3	4		

TEACHER TOOL 6   Contextual Redefinition Chart

Term	Word-level Clues	Context Clues	Predicted Meaning	Actual Meaning

TEACHER TOOL 7   Personal Dictionary

Date	Source	Page	Term	Definition

K (things I *know*)	W (things I *want* to know)	L (things I *learned*)

TEACHER TOOL 9 Main Idea/Detail Graphic Organizer

Paragraph	Main Idea	Details

TEACHER TOOL 10 Outcome Graphic Organizer

Paragraph #s	Details	Outcome

TEACHER TOOL 11   Evidence Guide Graphic Organizer

Theories	Supporting Evidence	Evidence Against

TEACHER TOOL 13   Inference Graphic Organizer

Sub-Heading	Details From the Text	What You Know	Inference (SI)

TEACHER TOOL 14   Observation/Inference Chart

OBSERVATION	INFERENCE

TEACHER TOOL 15   Reciprocal Teaching Organizer

Predict

I think . . .

Question

Factual

Who?
What?
When?
Where?

Interpretive

Why?
How?

The main point is . . .

I thought . . .

When I read, I realized . . .

Summarize

Clarify

TEACHER TOOL 16 MARSI: Metacognitive Awareness of Reading Strategies Inventory

---

Metacognitive Awareness of Reading Strategies Inventory Directions

Listed on the next page are statements about what people do when they read academic or school-related materials, such as textbooks or library books.

Five numbers follow each statement (1, 2, 3, 4, 5), and each number means the following:

- **1** means "I **never or almost never** do this."
- **2** means "I do this **only occasionally**."
- **3** means "I **sometimes** do this" (50% of the time).
- **4** means "I **usually** do this."
- **5** means "I **always or almost always** do this."

After reading each statement, circle the number (1, 2, 3, 4, or 5) that applies to you using the scale provided. Please note that there are no right or wrong answers to the statements in this inventory.

Scoring Rubric

Directions:

1. Write your response to each statement (i.e., 1, 2, 3, 4, or 5) in each of the blanks.
2. Add up the scores under each column. Place the result on the line under each column.
3. Divide the subscale score by the number of statements in each column to get the average for each subscale.
4. Calculate the average for the whole inventory by adding up the subscale scores and dividing by 30.
5. Compare your results to those shown below.
6. Discuss your results with your teacher or tutor.

Global Reading Strategies		Problem-Solving Strategies		Support Reading Strategies		Overall Reading Strategies
1.	19.	8.	27.	2.	20.	GLOB
3.	22.	11.	30.	5.	24.	PROB
4.	23.	13.		6.	28.	SUP
7.	25.	16.		9.		
10.	26.	18.		12.		
14.	29.	21.		15.		
17.						
GLOB Score		PROB score		SUP score		Overall score
GLOB Mean		PROB mean		SUP mean		Overall mean

Interpreting your scores: The overall average indicates how often you use reading strategies when reading academic materials. The average for each subscale of the inventory shows which group of strategies (i.e., global, problem-solving, and support strategies) you use most when reading. With this information, you can tell if you score very high or very low in any of these strategy groups. Note, however, that the best possible use of these strategies depends on your reading ability in English, the type of material read, and your purpose for reading it. A low score on any of the subscales or parts of the inventory indicates that there may be some strategies in these parts that you might want to learn about and consider using when reading.

TEACHER TOOL 16   Continued

Name: _____   Date: _____

Metacognitive Awareness of Reading Strategies Inventory

1.	I have a purpose in mind when I read.	1	2	3	4	5
2.	I take notes while reading to help me understand what I read.	1	2	3	4	5
3.	I think about what I know to help me understand what I read.	1	2	3	4	5
4.	I preview the text to see what it's about before reading it.	1	2	3	4	5
5.	When the text becomes difficult, I read aloud to help me understand what I read.	1	2	3	4	5
6.	I summarize what I read to reflect on important information in the text.	1	2	3	4	5
7.	I think about whether the content of the text fits my reading purpose.	1	2	3	4	5
8.	I read slowly but carefully to be sure I understand what I'm reading.	1	2	3	4	5
9.	I discuss what I read with others to check my understanding.	1	2	3	4	5
10.	I skim the text first by noting characteristics like length and organization.	1	2	3	4	5
11.	I try to get back on track when I lose concentration.	1	2	3	4	5
12.	I underline or circle information in the text to help me remember it.	1	2	3	4	5
13.	I adjust my reading speed according to what I'm reading.	1	2	3	4	5
14.	I decide what to read closely and what to ignore.	1	2	3	4	5
15.	I use reference materials, such as dictionaries, to help me understand what I read.	1	2	3	4	5
16.	When the text becomes difficult, I pay closer attention to what I'm reading.	1	2	3	4	5
17.	I use tables, figures, and pictures in the text to increase my understanding.	1	2	3	4	5
18.	I stop from time to time and think about what I'm reading.	1	2	3	4	5
19.	I use context clues to help me better understand what I'm reading.	1	2	3	4	5
20.	I paraphrase (restate ideas in my own words) to better understand what I'm reading.	1	2	3	4	5
21.	I try to picture or visualize information to help remember what I read.	1	2	3	4	5
22.	I use typographical aids like boldface and italics to identify key information.	1	2	3	4	5
23.	I critically analyze and evaluate the information presented in the text.	1	2	3	4	5
24.	I go back and forth in the text to find relationships among ideas in it.	1	2	3	4	5
25.	I check my understanding when I come across conflicting information.	1	2	3	4	5
26.	I try to guess what the material is about when I read.	1	2	3	4	5
27.	When the text becomes difficult, I reread to increase my understanding.	1	2	3	4	5
28.	I ask myself questions I like to have answered in the text.	1	2	3	4	5
29.	I check to see if my guesses about the text are right or wrong.	1	2	3	4	5
30.	I try to guess the meaning of unknown words or phrases.	1	2	3	4	5

TEACHER TOOL 17   Adolescent Motivation to Read Profile

Adolescent Motivation to Read Profile: Reading Survey Directions.

Teacher Directions

Distribute copies of the Adolescent Motivation to Read Survey. Ask students to write their names on the space provided.

Say: *I am going to read some sentences to you. I want to know how you feel about your reading. There are no right or wrong answers. I really want to know how you honestly feel about reading. I will read each sentence twice. Do not mark your answer until I tell you to. The first time I read the sentence I want you to think about the best answer for you. The second time I read the sentence I want you to fill in the space beside your best answer. Mark only one answer. If you have any questions during the survey, raise your hand. Are there any questions before we begin? Remember: Do not mark your answer until I tell you to. Okay, let's begin.*

Read the first sample item:
Say:
Sample 1: I am in (pause) sixth grade, (pause) seventh grade, (pause) eighth grade, (pause) ninth grade, (pause) tenth grade, (pause) eleventh grade, (pause) twelfth grade.

Read the first sample again.
Say:
This time as I read the sentence, mark the answer that is right for you. I am in (pause) sixth grade, (pause) seventh grade, (pause) eighth grade, (pause) ninth grade, (pause) tenth grade, (pause) eleventh grade, (pause) twelfth grade.

Read the second sample item.
Say:
Sample 2: I am a (pause) female, (pause) male.
Say: *Now, get ready to mark your answer.*
I am a (pause) female, (pause) male.

Read the remaining items in the same way (e.g., number _____, sentence stem followed by a pause, each option followed by a pause, and then give specific directions for students to mark their answers while you repeat the entire item).

Scoring Directions

The survey has 20 items based on a 4-point scale. The highest total score possible is 80 points. On some items the response options are ordered least positive to most positive (see item 2 below) with the least positive response option having a value of 1 point and the most positive option having a point value of 4. On other items, however, the response options are reversed (see item 1 below). In those cases it will be necessary to recode the response options. Items where recoding is required are starred on the scoring sheet.

Example: Here is how Maria completed items 1 and 2 on the reading survey.

1. My friends think I am _____.
   ❏ a very good reader
   ■ a good reader
   ❏ an OK reader
   ❏ a poor reader
2. Reading a book is something I like to do.
   ❏ Never
   ❏ Not very often
   ❏ Sometimes
   ■ Often

To score item 1 it is first necessary to recode the response options so that
a poor reader equals 1 point,
an OK reader equals 2 points,
a good reader equals 3 points, and
a very good reader equals 4 points.

Because Maria answered that she is a good reader, the point value for that item, 3, is entered on the first line of the Self-Concept column on the scoring sheet. See next page.

The response options for item 2 are ordered least positive (1 point) to most positive (4 points), so scoring item 2 is easy. Simply enter the point value associated with Maria's response. Because Maria selected the fourth option, a 4 is entered for item 2 under the Value of Reading column on the scoring sheet. See next page.

TEACHER TOOL 17 Continued

Motivation to Read Profile: Reading Survey Scoring Sheet

Student name: _____

Grade: _____ Teacher: _____

Administration date: _____

Recoding scale
1=4
2=3
3=2
4=1

Self-Concept as a Reader			Value of Reading	
*recode	1.			2.
	3.		*recode	4.
*recode	5.			6.
*recode	7.		*recode	8.
	9.		*recode	10.
	11.			12.
	13.			14.
*recode	15.			16.
	17.		*recode	18.
	19.		*recode	20.
SC raw score	/40		V raw score	/40
Full survey raw score (Self-Concept & Value):				/80
Percentages			Self-Concept	
			Value	
			Full survey	
Comments:				

To calculate the Self-Concept raw score and the Value raw score, add all student responses in the respective column.

The full survey raw score is obtained by combining the column raw scores. To convert the raw scores to percentage scores, divide student raw scores by the total possible score (40 for each subscale, 80 for the full survey).

Pitcher, S., Albright, L., DeLaney, C., Walker, N., Seunarinesingh, K., Mogge, S., Headley, K., Ridgeway, V., Peck, S., Hunt, R., Dunston P. (2007). Assessing adolescents' motivation to read. *Journal of Adolescent & Adult Literacy, 50* (5), 378–396. Copyright 2007 by the International Reading Association (www.reading.org). Reprinted with permission.

TEACHER TOOL 17   Continued

Adolescent Motivation to Read Profile: Reading Survey

Name: _____   Date: _____

Sample 1: I am in _____.
❏ Sixth grade
❏ Seventh grade
❏ Eighth grade
❏ Ninth grade
❏ Tenth grade
❏ Eleventh grade
❏ Twelfth grade

Sample 2: I am a _____.
❏ Female
❏ Male

Sample 3: My race/ethnicity is
_____.
❏ African-American
❏ Asian/Asian American
❏ Caucasian
❏ Hispanic
❏ Native American
❏ Multiracial/Multiethnic
❏ Other: Please specify _____

1. My friends think I am
_____.
❏ a very good reader
❏ a good reader
❏ an OK reader
❏ a poor reader

2. Reading a book is something I like
to do.
❏ Never
❏ Not very often
❏ Sometimes
❏ Often

3. I read _____.
❏ not as well as my friends
❏ about the same as my friends
❏ a little better than my friends
❏ a lot better than my friends

4. My best friends think reading is
_____.
❏ really fun
❏ fun
❏ OK to do
❏ no fun at all

5. When I come to a word I don't know,
I can _____.
❏ almost always figure it out
❏ sometimes figure it out
❏ almost never figure it out
❏ never figure it out

6. I tell my friends about good books
I read.
❏ I never do this
❏ I almost never do this
❏ I do this some of the time
❏ I do this a lot

7. When I am reading by myself,
I understand _____.
❏ almost everything I read
❏ some of what I read
❏ almost none of what I read
❏ none of what I read

8. People who read a lot are
_____.
❏ very interesting
❏ interesting
❏ not very interesting
❏ boring

9. I am _____.
❏ a poor reader
❏ an OK reader
❏ a good reader
❏ a very good reader

10. I think libraries are _____.
❏ a great place to spend time
❏ an interesting place to spend time
❏ an OK place to spend time
❏ a boring place to spend time

11. I worry about what other kids think
about my reading _____.
❏ every day
❏ almost every day
❏ once in a while
❏ never

12. Knowing how to read well is
_____.
❏ not very important
❏ sort of important
❏ important
❏ very important

13. When my teacher asks me a question
about what I have read, I
_____.
❏ can never think of an answer
❏ have trouble thinking of an answer
❏ sometimes think of an answer
❏ always think of an answer

14. I think reading is _____.
❏ a boring way to spend time
❏ an OK way to spend time
❏ an interesting way to spend time
❏ a great way to spend time

15. Reading is _____.
❏ very easy for me
❏ kind of easy for me
❏ kind of hard for me
❏ very hard for me

16. As an adult, I will spend
_____.
❏ none of my time reading
❏ very little time reading
❏ some of my time reading
❏ a lot of my time reading

17. When I am in a group talking
about what we are reading,
I _____.
❏ almost never talk about my ideas
❏ sometimes talk about my ideas
❏ almost always talk about my ideas
❏ always talk about my ideas

18. I would like for my teachers to read
out loud in my classes
_____.
❏ every day
❏ almost every day
❏ once in a while
❏ never

19. When I read out loud I am a
_____.
❏ poor reader
❏ OK reader
❏ good reader
❏ very good reader

20. When someone gives me a book for
a present, I feel _____.
❏ very happy
❏ sort of happy
❏ sort of unhappy
❏ unhappy

Adolescent Motivation to Read Profile: Conversational Interview

Teacher Directions:

1. Duplicate the conversational interview (see below and next page) so that you have a form for each child.
2. Choose in advance the section(s) or specific questions you want to ask from the conversational interview.
3. Reviewing the information on students' reading surveys may provide information about additional questions that could be added to the interview.
4. Familiarize yourself with the basic questions provided in the interview prior to the interview session in order to establish a more conversational setting.
5. Select a quiet corner of the room and a calm period of the day for the interview.
6. Allow ample time for conducting the conversational interview.
7. Follow up on interesting comments and responses to gain a fuller understanding of students' reading experiences.
8. Record students' responses in as much detail as possible. If time and resources permit, you may want to audiotape answers to A1 and B1 to be transcribed after the interview for more in-depth analysis.
9. Enjoy this special time with each student!

Conversational Interview

A. Emphasis: Narrative text

Suggested prompt (designed to engage student in a natural conversation):

I have been reading a good book. I was talking with_____about it last night. I enjoy talking about what I am reading with my friends and family. Today, I would like to hear about what you have been reading and if you can share it.

1. Tell me about the most interesting story or book you have read recently. Take a few minutes to think about it (wait time). Now, tell me about the book.
   Probe: What else can you tell me? Is there anything else?
2. How did you know or find out about this book?
   (Some possible responses: assigned, chosen, in school, out of school)
3. Why was this story interesting to you?

B. Emphasis: Informational text

Suggested prompt (designed to engage student in a natural conversation):

Often we read to find out or learn about something that interests us. For example, a student I recently worked with enjoyed reading about his favorite sports teams on the Internet. I am going to ask you some questions about what you like to read to learn about.

1. Think about something important that you learned recently, not from your teacher and not from television, but from something you have read. What did you read about? (Wait time.) Tell me about what you learned.
   Probe: What else could you tell me? Is there anything else?
2. How did you know or find out about reading material on this?
   (Some possible responses: assigned, chosen, in school, out of school)
3. Why was reading this important to you?

TEACHER TOOL 17 Continued

C. Emphasis: General reading

1. Did you read anything at home yesterday? What?
2. Do you have anything at school (in your desk, locker, or book bag) today that you are reading?
   Tell me about them.
3. Tell me about your favorite author.
4. What do you think you have to learn to be a better reader?
5. Do you know about any books right now that you'd like to read?
   Tell me about them.
6. How did you find out about these books?
7. What are some things that get you really excited about reading?
   Tell me about. . . .
8. Who gets you really interested and excited about reading?
   Tell me more about what they do.
9. Do you have a computer in your home?
   If they answer yes, ask the following questions:
   How much time do you spend on the computer a day?
   What do you usually do?
   What do you like to read when you are on the Internet?
   If they answer no, ask the following questions:
   If you did have a computer in your home, what would you like to do with it?
   Is there anything on the Internet that you would like to be able to read?

D. Emphasis: School reading in comparison to home reading

1. In what class do you most like to read?
   Why?

2. In what class do you feel the reading is the most difficult?
   Why?

3. Have any of your teachers done something with reading that you really enjoyed?
   Could you explain some of what was done?

4. Do you share and discuss books, magazines, or other reading materials with your friends outside of school?
   What?
   How often?
   Where?

5. Do you write letters or email to friends or family?
   How often?

6. Do you share any of the following reading materials with members of your family:
   newspapers, magazines, religious materials, games?
   With whom?
   How often?

7. Do you belong to any clubs or organizations for which you read and write?
   Could you explain what kind of reading it is?

TEACHER TOOL 18   Class Profile

Student	Language Proficiency			Vocabulary		Fluency			Comprehension						Motivation		
	L1	L2	Prof	Voc Stand	Cloze	Rate	Acc	Pros	Comp Stand	Inst Lvl	Strat			Self Con	Value Read	Interview/ Inventory
											G	PS	S			

TEACHER TOOL 19   Data Reflection Chart

	Patterns	Exceptions	Conclusions
Language Proficiency			
Vocabulary			
Fluency			
Comprehension			
Motivation			

TEACHER TOOL 20   Individual Profile

STEP 1: COLLECT ASSESSMENT DATA

Name:	Grade:	Class:

Language Proficiency

First Language:
Second Language: Proficiency:

Personal History

Vocabulary

- Standardized:
- Cloze:
     Percent_____ Level: ❑ Independent   ❑ Instructional   ❑ Frustration

Fluency

- Rate: ❑ High   ❑ At Grade Level   ❑ Low
- Accuracy: ❑ Independent   ❑ Instructional   ❑ Frustration
- Prosody: _____/12 or _____%

Comprehension

- Standardized:
     ❑ Advanced   ❑ Proficient   ❑ Basic   ❑ Below Basic   ❑ Far Below Basic
- Qualitative Reading Inventory:
     Instructional Level: _____
- Strategies:
     Global Mean: _____ Problem-Solving Mean: _____ Support Mean: _____

Motivation

- Self-Concept: _____/40 or _____%
- Value of Reading: _____/40 or _____%
- Interview/Inventory:

STEP 2: REFLECT ON ASSESSMENT DATA

What do you know about the student? Strengths? Areas for growth?
What instruction would support this student?

Conclusions:

TEACHER TOOL 21   Text Profile

Text Title:	
Text Features	**Notes**
Table of Contents	
Headings	
Vocabulary	
Figures/Charts/ Graphs	
Illustrations/Photos	
Time Lines/Maps	
Captions	
Glossary/Index	
Appendix	
Font Type/Size	
White Space	
Readability	

TEACHER TOOL 22 The LinC Teaching Plan

LinC Teaching Plan

Class		Topic
LEARNING OUTCOMES		
	Objectives	**Assessments**
Content Area		
English/ Language Arts		
English Language Development		
TEXT		
Pages		
Type/Structure		
Features		
VOCABULARY		
Level 1 Essential (Before Reading)		
Level 2 Related (Before Reading)		
Level 3 Critical (During/After)		
Level 4 Not-Essential		
INSTRUCTIONAL STRATEGIES		
Lesson 1		
Vocabulary		
Fluency		
Comprehension		
Motivation		
Lesson 2		
Vocabulary		
Fluency		
Comprehension		
Motivation		
Lesson 3		
Vocabulary		
Fluency		
Comprehension		
Motivation		

TEACHER TOOL 23   Strategy Summary Chart

Literacy Component	Goals of Instruction	Strategies for Instruction
Vocabulary	Build Full Concept Knowledge	• Concept of Definition Map • Semantic Feature Analysis • Pre-Teaching Vocabulary
	Teach Words in a Meaningful Context	• Vocabulary Rating Guide • List-Group-Label • Vocabulary Visits
	Encourage Independent Use of Strategies	• Word Analysis • Contextual Redefinition • Dictionary Use • Personal Dictionary
Fluency	Model Fluency	• Teacher Read Aloud • Generated Read Aloud
	Guide Fluency	• Guided Fluency Development Instruction • Adapted Retrospective Miscue Analysis
	Provide Practice for Fluency	• Repeated Reading • Wide, Independent Reading
Comprehension	Activate and Build Background Knowledge	• K-W-L Strategy Chart • Text Box/Bag Activity • Survey Strategy and Guide
	Use Graphic Organizers	• Main Idea/Detail Graphic Organizer • Outcome Graphic Organizer • Evidence Guide Graphic Organizer • Compare/Contrast Matrix • Inference Graphic Organizer
	Summarize	• Written Summaries • Oral Summaries • Visual Summaries • Cornell Notes
	Ask and Answer Questions	• SQ3R (Survey, Question, Read, Recite, Review) • QAR (Question-Answer Relationship)
	Monitor Comprehension	• Interactive Think Aloud • Comprehension Monitoring Strategy Guide
	Use Multiple Reading Strategies	• Reciprocal Teaching • PLAN (Predict, Locate, Add, Note)
Motivation	Foster Student Control and Choice	• Socratic Seminars • WebQuests
	Encourage Collaboration	• Learning Clubs • PALS (Peer Assisted Learning Strategies)
	Ensure Mastery of Content and Literacy Skills	• Scaffolded Reading Experiences • CORI (Concept-Oriented Reading Instruction

Learning Logs

Vocabulary Rating Guide
Text title: LinC – Chapter 2

Directions: Before reading Chapter 2, read each vocabulary term and rate your understanding. During reading, record the definition and suggest a synonym. Definitions can be found in the context of the sentence or in the glossary. After reading Chapter 2, rate your understanding of each concept again.

1. I don't recognize this word, and I have never heard it before.
2. I recognize the word, but I don't know what it means.
3. I have a basic understanding of the word.
4. I understand the word and can use it flexibly, in most contexts. I could teach it to others.

Vocabulary Word	Before Instruction				After Instruction				Definition	Synonym
	1	2	3	4	1	2	3	4		
Matthew Effect										
academic vocabulary										
content-specific academic vocabulary										
content-general academic vocabulary										
label										
concept										
semantic mapping										
semantic features										
context										
realia										
word consciousness										
morphological analysis										
context clues										

LEARNING LOG 2 K-W-L Strategy Chart

K (things I *know*)	W (things I *want* to learn)	L (things I *learned*)
Before Reading *Record words, phrases, or terms that you are familiar with about reading comprehension.*	*Before Reading* *Record questions you have about reading comprehension.*	*After Reading* *Record concepts learned while reading this chapter.*

LEARNING LOG 3   Main Idea/Detail Graphic Organizer

Section *Note how the subheadings representing each type of graphic organizer have been recorded below.*	**Main Idea** *Determine the main idea of each section and record it below.*	**Details** *Record significant details from each section, in note format, during reading.*
Outcome		
Evidence Guide		
Compare/Contrast Matrix		
Inference		

LEARNING LOG 4   Summary Paragraph Template

Directions: After reading the text, write a summary paragraph about "Summarize."

   1. *Write the topic sentence. Include the title of the section, authors, and main idea.*

   For example—

   In Chapter 4 of LinC, written by Miller and Veatch, we read about the "Use of Graphic Organizers" to support student reading comprehension.

Topic Sentence:

   2. *Write sentences detailing the text. Write at least two significant things about the text.*

   This text would appropriately need to be summarized with four details—one for each subsection (written summary, oral summary, visual summary, and Cornell Notes).

Detail Sentences:

   3. *Write a supported inference, sharing your reflections about this section of the text.*

   Consider how you will implement this strategy into your teaching. Begin with the thought "I think that . . ."

Supported Inference Sentence:

   4. *Write a conclusion sentence, restating the main idea. Try to begin with a transition word.*

Conclusion Sentence:

LEARNING LOG 5 QAR Strategy

Directions:

1. *Read "Ask and Answer Questions."*
2. *Label the following questions using the QAR categories (Refer to Figure 4.22 for more information.)*
   a. *Right There*
   b. *Think and Search*
   c. *Author and You/Inference*
   d. *On Your Own*
3. *Answer these questions to help you deepen your understanding of this section.*

1. _____ Would you have been more successful as a middle or high school student if you had explicitly learned how to ask and answer questions about the text?

2. _____ Both SQ3R and QAR can be used to help students increase their understanding of the text. How are these strategies different?

3. _____ Why do you think students can be more successful with reading the text and answering the text questions if they learn how to identify different types of questions using the QAR strategy?

4. _____ What is a benefit of students learning to answer different types of questions about text?

LEARNING LOG 6 Comprehension Monitoring Strategy Guide

Directions: Circle whether you agree or disagree with each statement. If you disagree, write why.

Agree/Disagree **1.** Teachers should teach using multiple strategy instruction with all content area lessons.

_____

_____

_____

Agree/Disagree **2.** Reciprocal teaching involves the steps of predicting, clarifying, questioning, and summarizing.

_____

_____

_____

Agree/Disagree **3.** PLAN is most effectively used with science instruction.

_____

_____

_____

Agree/Disagree **4.** Using PLAN is similar to using a Concept of Definition Map (Chapter 2).

_____

_____

_____

LEARNING LOG 7   Fluency Assessment

Directions: Calculate the student's rate and accuracy.

- *// follows the last word read in one minute*
- ***Bolded*** *words indicate miscues*

The Confederacy had advantages as well. With its strong	9
military tradition, the South put many brilliant officers	17
into battle. Southern farms provided food for its armies.	26
The South's best advantage, however, was **strategic**. It	34
needed only to defend itself until the North grew tired of	45
fighting. The North had to invade and control the South.	55
To **accomplish** this, the Union army had to travel huge	65
distances. For example, the distance from northern Virginia	72
to central Georgia is about the length of Scotland and	82
England **combined**. Because of distances such as this, the	91
North had to maintain long supply lines. In addition,	100
wilderness covered much of the South. Armies found this	109
land difficult to cross. Also, in Virginia, many **of** the	119
rivers ran from east to west. Because of this, they formed	130
a natural **defense** against an army that attacked from the	140
north to the south. As a result, Northern generals were **//**	150
often forced to attack Confederate troops from the side	159
rather than from the front. Furthermore, because	166
Southerners fought mostly on their home soil, they were	174
often familiar with the area. The South hoped to wear down	185
the North and to capture Washington, D.C. Confederate	194
president Jefferson Davis also tried to win foreign allies	203
through cotton diplomacy.	206

Text from Deverell, W. F., & White, D. G. (2009). *United States History*. Boston, MA: Holt McDougal.

LEARNING LOG 8   MARSI: Metacognitive Awareness of Reading Strategies Inventory.

Metacognitive Awareness of Reading Strategies Inventory

Directions: Listed below are statements about what people do when they read academic or school-related materials, such as textbooks or library books.

Five numbers follow each statement (1, 2, 3, 4, 5), and each number means the following:

- **1** means "I **never or almost never** do this."
- **2** means "I do this **only occasionally**."
- **3** means "I **sometimes** do this" (50% of the time).
- **4** means "I **usually** do this."
- **5** means "I **always or almost always** do this."

After reading each statement, circle the number (1, 2, 3, 4, or 5) that applies to you using the scale provided. Please note that there are no right or wrong answers to the statements in this inventory.

LEARNING LOG 8 (Continued)

Metacognitive Awareness of Reading Strategies Inventory

1.	I have a purpose in mind when I read.	1	2	3	4	5
2.	I take notes while reading to help me understand what I read.	1	2	3	4	5
3.	I think about what I know to help me understand what I read.	1	2	3	4	5
4.	I preview the text to see what it's about before reading it.	1	2	3	4	5
5.	When the text becomes difficult, I read aloud to help me understand what I read.	1	2	3	4	5
6.	I summarize what I read to reflect on important information in the text.	1	2	3	4	5
7.	I think about whether the content of the text fits my reading purpose.	1	2	3	4	5
8.	I read slowly but carefully to be sure I understand what I'm reading.	1	2	3	4	5
9.	I discuss what I read with others to check my understanding.	1	2	3	4	5
10.	I skim the text first by noting characteristics like length and organization.	1	2	3	4	5
11.	I try to get back on track when I lose concentration.	1	2	3	4	5
12.	I underline or circle information in the text to help me remember it.	1	2	3	4	5
13.	I adjust my reading speed according to what I'm reading.	1	2	3	4	5
14.	I decide what to read closely and what to ignore.	1	2	3	4	5
15.	I use reference materials such as dictionaries to help me understand what I read.	1	2	3	4	5
16.	When the text becomes difficult, I pay closer attention to what I'm reading.	1	2	3	4	5
17.	I use tables, figures, and pictures in the text to increase my understanding.	1	2	3	4	5
18.	I stop from time to time and think about what I'm reading.	1	2	3	4	5
19.	I use context clues to help me better understand what I'm reading.	1	2	3	4	5
20.	I paraphrase (restate ideas in my own words) to better understand what I'm reading.	1	2	3	4	5
21.	I try to picture or visualize information to help remember what I read.	1	2	3	4	5
22.	I use typographical aids like boldface and italics to identify key information.	1	2	3	4	5
23.	I critically analyze and evaluate the information presented in the text.	1	2	3	4	5
24.	I go back and forth in the text to find relationships among ideas in it.	1	2	3	4	5
25.	I check my understanding when I come across conflicting information.	1	2	3	4	5
26.	I try to guess what the material is about when I read.	1	2	3	4	5
27.	When the text becomes difficult, I reread to increase my understanding.	1	2	3	4	5
28.	I ask myself questions I like to have answered in the text.	1	2	3	4	5
29.	I check to see if my guesses about the text are right or wrong.	1	2	3	4	5
30.	I try to guess the meaning of unknown words or phrases.	1	2	3	4	5

LEARNING LOG 8 Continued

Scoring Directions

1. *Write your response to each statement (i.e., 1, 2, 3, 4, or 5) in each of the blanks.*
2. *Add up the scores under each column. Place the result on the line under each column.*
3. *Divide the subscale score by the number of statements in each column to get the average for each subscale.*
4. *Calculate the average for the whole inventory by adding up the subscale scores and dividing by 30.*
5. *Compare your results to those shown below.*
6. *Discuss your results with your teacher or tutor.*

Global Reading Strategies		Problem-Solving Strategies		Support Reading Strategies		Overall Reading Strategies
1.	19.	8.	27.	2.	20.	GLOB
3.	22.	11.	30.	5.	24.	PROB
4.	23.	13.		6.	28.	SUP
7.	25.	16.		9.		
10.	26.	18.		12.		
14.	29.	21.		15.		
17.						
GLOB Score		PROB score		SUP score		Overall score
GLOB Mean		PROB mean		SUP mean		Overall mean

Interpreting your scores: The overall average indicates how often you use reading strategies when reading academic materials. The average for each subscale of the inventory shows which group of strategies (i.e., global, problem solving, and support strategies) you use most when reading. With this information, you can tell if you score very high or very low in any of these strategy groups. Note, however, that the best possible use of these strategies depends on your reading ability in English, the type of material read, and your purpose for reading it. A low score on any of the subscales or parts of the inventory indicates that there may be some strategies in these parts that you might want to learn about and consider using when reading.

Categories of Reading Strategies

Global Reading Strategies
Examples include setting purpose for reading, activating prior knowledge, checking whether text content fits purpose, predicting what text is about, confirming predictions, previewing text for content, skimming to note text characteristics, making decisions in relation to what to read closely, using context clues, using text structure, and using other textual features to enhance reading comprehension. (Items 1, 3, 4, 7, 10, 14, 17, 19, 22, 23, 25, 26, 29)

Problem -Solving Strategies
Examples include reading slowly and carefully, adjusting reading rate, paying close attention to reading, pausing to reflect on reading, rereading, visualizing information read, reading text out loud, and guessing meaning of unknown words. (Items 8, 11, 13, 16, 18, 21, 27, 30)

Support Reading Strategies
Examples include taking notes while reading, paraphrasing text information, revisiting previously read information, asking self questions, using reference materials as aids, underlining text information, discussing reading with others, and writing summaries of reading. (Items 2, 5, 6, 9, 12, 15, 20, 24, 28)

LEARNING LOG 9 Data Reflection

Directions: Examine the data on the ninth-grade class profile. Think about patterns and exceptions in the data, and complete the Data Reflection.

Student	Language Proficiency			Vocabulary		Fluency			Comprehension					Motivation		
	L1	L2	Prof	Voc Stand	Cloze	Rate	Acc	Pros	Comp Stand	Inst Lvl	G	PS	S	Self Con	Value Read	Interview/Inventory
Aaron	English			Basic	Frust	Low	Frust	25%	FBB	4th	+	✓	–	20%	70%	Trouble reading at home.
Angela	Spanish	English	Adv	Prof	Ind	At	Inst	92%	Prof	9th	+	✓	–	80%	90%	Likes to work in pairs.
Brent	English			Prof	Inst	At	Inst	75%	Prof	9th	+	✓	✓	80%	90%	Dislikes reading aloud.
Brian	English			Basic	Frust	Low	Frust	50%	Basic	6th	+	✓	–	50%	80%	Likes working in groups.
Caleb	English			Adv	Ind	At	Ind	100%	Adv	10th	+	✓	✓	90%	90%	Dislikes reading aloud.
Chris	English			Prof	Inst	At	Ind	75%	Adv	10th	+	+	+	80%	90%	Trouble with homework.
Derek	English			Prof	Inst	At	Inst	75%	Prof	9th	+	+	–	90%	100%	Enjoys helping others.
Ellie	English			Prof	Inst	At	Inst	50%	Prof	8th	+	+	✓	70%	90%	Trouble with text.
Hailey	English			Adv	Inst	High	Inst	92%	Adv	12th	+	✓	–	100%	100%	Likes reading aloud.
Hayden	English			Basic	Frust	Low	Frust	25%	BB	4th	+	+	✓	20%	80%	Doesn't like reading.
Jennifer	English			Prof	Inst	At	Ind	92%	Prof	9th	+	✓	–	80%	80%	Enjoys helping others.
Julia	English			Prof	Inst	At	Inst	50%	BB	5th	+	✓	–	40%	80%	Dislikes school reading.
Kara	English			Adv	Ind	High	Int	100%	Adv	10th	–	–	–	90%	100%	Likes working in groups.
Connor	English			Basic	Frust	Low	Frust	25%	FBB	3rd	+	+	✓	30%	80%	Trouble with text.
Kia	Hmong	English	Int	Prof	Inst	Low	Frust	33%	FBB	3rd	+	+	–	30%	70%	Dislikes reading aloud.
Kristen	English			Adv	Ind	Low	Ind	100%	Adv	10th	+	+	+	90%	100%	Trouble with text.
Long	Hmong	English	Int	Prof	Instr	At	Ind	92%	Prof	8th	+	–	–	60%	90%	Dislikes reading aloud.
Moira	English			Adv	Inst	At	Inst	83%	Prof	9th	–	–	–	80%	90%	Wants more study skills.
Nina	English			Basic	Frust	Low	Frust	25%	Basic	6th	+	✓	–	50%	80%	Wants more study skills
Pablo	Spanish	English	Int	Basic	Frust	Low	Frust	25%	Basic	7th	+	+	✓	70%	90%	Trouble with text.
Patricia	English			Adv	Inst	High	Inst	83%	Prof	9th	–	–	–	70%	90%	Trouble with text.
Todd	English			Prof	Inst	At	Ind	100%	Adv	10th	+	–	–	100%	100%	Likes group work.
Sebastian	Spanish	English	Adv	Adv	Ind	High	Inst	100%	Adv	12th	+	+	+	90%	100%	Likes group work.
Wyatt	English			Adv	Inst	At	Inst	92%	Prof	9th	✓	+	+	90%	90%	Likes working in pairs.

Data Reflection Chart

	Patterns	Exceptions
Language Proficiency		
Vocabulary		
Fluency		
Comprehension		
Motivation		

LEARNING LOG 10   Individual Profile

STEP 1: COLLECT ASSESSMENT DATA

Name:	Grade:	Class:

Language Proficiency

First Language:
Second Language: Proficiency:

Personal History

Vocabulary

- Standardized:
- Cloze:
   Percent_____ Level: ❑ Independent ❑ Instructional ❑ Frustration

Fluency

- Rate: ❑ High ❑ At Grade Level ❑ Low
- Accuracy: ❑ Independent ❑ Instructional ❑ Frustration
- Prosody: _____/12 or _____%

Comprehension

- Standardized:
   ❑ Advanced ❑ Proficient ❑ Basic ❑ Below Basic ❑ Far Below Basic
- Qualitative Reading Inventory:
   Instructional Level: _____
- Strategies:
   Global Mean: _____ Problem-Solving Mean: _____ Support Mean: _____

Motivation

- Self-Concept: _____/40 or _____%
- Value of Reading: _____/40 or _____%
- Interview/Inventory:

STEP 2: REFLECT ON ASSESSMENT DATA

What do you know about the student? Strengths? Areas for growth?
What instruction would support this student?

Conclusions:

LEARNING LOG 11   Text Profile

Directions: Choose a content area textbook. Complete the text profile.

Text Title:	
Text Features	**Notes**
Table of Contents	
Headings	
Vocabulary	
Figures/Charts/Graphs	
Illustrations/Photos	
Time Lines/Maps	
Captions	
Glossary/Index	
Appendix	
Font Type/Size	
White Space	
Readability	

LEARNING LOG 12 Four Levels of Content Vocabulary

Directions: Choose a section of a content area text. Decide which vocabulary words are important to teach, and categorize them into level 1, 2, 3, or 4. Then enter the words in the "Vocabulary" column on the chart.

LEVELS	Description	When to Teach	Type of Instruction	Vocabulary
Level 1	Words essential to understanding reading.	Before Reading	Time intensive; use strategies to build full word knowledge.	
Level 2	"Foot in the door" words. Related to content, and needed to understand reading.	Before Reading	If new label/new concept need short definition, example. If new label and old concept, need synonym or simple definition.	
Level 3	Words critical to understanding of content, but not critical to reading. • clearly defined in reading, • high-utility; students will see in other settings • demonstrating the patterns of language	During and After Reading	Use strategies to Teach in a meaningful context and/or access independent use of strategies.	Take up whole page people will unite here
Level 4	Words that don't serve lesson objectives	Don't Teach		

Chart compiled from information in Flanigan and Greenwood (2007).

LEARNING LOG 13   LinC Teaching Plan

Directions: Complete the LinC Teaching Plan for a lesson sequence in a content area.

Class		Topic	
LEARNING OUTCOMES			
	Objectives	**Assessments**	
Content Area			
English/ Language Arts			
English Language Development			
TEXT			
Pages			
Type/Structure			
Features			
VOCABULARY			
Level 1 Essential (Before Reading)			
Level 2 Related (Before Reading)			
Level 3 Critical (During/After)			
Level 4 Not-Essential			
INSTRUCTIONAL STRATEGIES			
Lesson 1			
Vocabulary			
Fluency			
Comprehension			
Motivation			
Lesson 2			
Vocabulary			
Fluency			
Comprehension			
Motivation			
Lesson 3			
Vocabulary			
Fluency			
Comprehension			
Motivation			

GLOSSARY

Academic vocabulary words specific to learning in the content areas, describe content-specific knowledge and complex processes, and create cohesion in discourse.

Accuracy reading or decoding text without making errors (omissions, additions, or miscues).

Advanced term used to describe performance on standardized assessments that demonstrates superior mastery of knowledge and skills that are fundamental for proficient grade-level work.

Assessment to gather evidence of student learning for the purpose of informing instruction.

Basic term used to describe performance on standardized assessments that demonstrates partial mastery of knowledge and skills that are fundamental for proficient grade-level work.

Basic literacy skills, such as decoding, that give readers access to print and help them break the code of a text.

Book Talk an oral sharing of a book.

Choral Reading text read in unison.

Cloze Procedure vocabulary assessment measuring whether students can understand words in context; words are omitted from a text passage and the student must choose the correct word to fill in the blank.

Cloze reading students read significant words or phrases that have been omitted as the teacher reads the rest of the text aloud.

Collaborative Retrospective Miscue Analysis students take on the role of the teacher in recording and interpreting miscue analysis results.

Concept an abstract thought.

Concept Maze vocabulary assessment measuring whether students can understand key concept words from the content.

Conclusions statements based upon evidence.

Content-general academic vocabulary a word that occurs across domains and can change meaning depending upon the context.

Content-specific academic vocabulary a word associated with a particular discipline.

Content standards standards that define the knowledge, concepts, and skills that each student should master at each grade level, Kindergarten through grade 12

Context the environment in which a concept is taught and understood.

Context clues using clues within the context of the text to determine the meaning of unknown words.

Curriculum Based Measure (CBM) a measurement system created with items that represent the grade-level curriculum.

Deep fluency explicit awareness of one's own text processing, intrinsic motivation to practice, and autonomy.

Diagnostic an assessment that uncovers strengths and areas for growth.

Differentiated instruction an approach to teaching that includes active planning for individual student differences.

Direct experiences enriching experiences, such as visiting a natural history museum or handling historical artifacts.

Disciplinary literacy specialized literacy that occurs in a discipline.

Draw Aloud drawing a visual representation that summarizes the reading while orally discussing its features.

Echo Reading students repeat the text in unison after the teacher has read it aloud.

English learner a nonnative English speaker.

Exceptions data that do not follow the pattern.

Explicit strategy instruction teacher shows students how and when to use a reading strategy as a tool to help their comprehension.

Expository content area text

Expression using a correct tone of voice based upon grammatical symbols within the text

Fluency reading a text accurately, at an appropriate rate, with appropriate expression.

Fluent English proficient a nonnative English speaker whose proficiency with English is comparable to a native English speaker.

Formative an assessment that supports learning by allowing the teacher to evaluate what a student has learned so that instruction can be modified for subsequent lessons.

Frustration level even with assistance, the text is too difficult for the student.

Global Reading Strategy a cognitive tool that readers can use to aid comprehension when reading any text, such as having a purpose in mind while reading.

Gradual Release of Responsibility Model teachers model strategies and give opportunities for guided practice before students independently apply the strategy.

Graphic organizers visual organizers that help students organize ideas from text.

Guided practice a student repeats the modeled procedure with teacher support.

Home Language Survey a survey that parents/guardians must complete when they enroll their child in a U.S. public school to identify limited English language proficiency.

Independent level the student can read the text without assistance.

Independent practice A student repeats the modeled procedure without direct teacher intervention.

Indirect experiences experiences that teachers create to build on prior knowledge.

Informal Motivation Inventory a survey of students' interests and attitudes toward reading

Informal Reading Inventory an individually administered battery of assessments designed to determine a student's reading instructional needs.

Initiation-Response-Evaluation (IRE) a response strategy where the teacher asks a question, the student answers, and the teacher evaluates the response.

Instructional level student can read the text with some assistance.

Instructional strategies teaching methods chosen to reach a particular learning outcome.

Intermediate literacy learning to comprehend texts of different types, and learning literacy strategies that cross domains.

Intonation the rising or falling of pitch of the voice

Jigsaw student becomes an expert about one aspect of the text and exchanges their knowledge with other students.

Label words that represent objects or ideas.

Literacy the ability to identify, understand, interpret, create, communicate, compute, and use printed and written materials across varying contexts.

Mastery goals goals that focus on guiding students toward finding meaning in the text.

Mastery orientation student is focused on making meaning from text; the purpose of reading is to increase conceptual understanding.

Matthew Effect "The rich (rich with vocabulary) get richer and the poor (limited vocabulary) get poorer" (Stanovich, 1986).

Metacognition one's own knowledge about one's thinking.

Modeled practice a process by which a teacher demonstrates a procedure.

Morphological analysis using word parts to determine the meaning of unknown words.

Motivation a process by which a goal-directed activity is both initiated and sustained.

Multiple strategy instruction an instructional practice when several reading strategies are taught simultaneously.

Narrative text that most often relays a story and generally has the following elements: plot, setting, characters, and theme.

Newspapers in Education companies donate funds to supply classrooms with sets of newspapers for student lessons and independent reading.

Note making summarizing the text in the form of notes.

Note taking recording notes given during a lecture.

Objectives the new knowledge, skills, or attitudes that students can demonstrate as a result of instruction.

Open-ended questions questions without obvious answers.

Paired Reading students are paired together by the teacher according to literacy skill levels to practice reading.

Partner Repeated Reading students read to each other and no corrective feedback is given.

Patterns particular assessment findings that occur across several students in a class.

Performance orientation a student is engaged in reading to complete a task or "make the grade."

Personal interest an enduring characteristic of an individual. (eg. Brandon really wants to be a fighter pilot when he grows up just like his grandfather. He has a personal interest in reading as much as he can about this topic.)

Phrasing using grammatical structures (commas and periods) to denote pauses and breaks in thought while reading.

Planning a process whereby teachers systematically decide what students should learn and the methods that will be used for instruction and assessment.

Problem-Solving Strategy a cognitive tool, such as rereading, that readers use to correct comprehension.

Professional Learning Community teachers take collective responsibility for the education of all students at their school.

Proficient term used to describe performance on standardized assessments that demonstrates solid mastery of knowledge and skills that are fundamental for proficient grade-level work.

Prosody vocal stress in speech (intonation, expression, phrasing).

Rate the speed at which one reads.

Read Around students select their favorite section from the text to showcase their fluency as they read it aloud.

Readability a text's difficulty, usually communicated with a particular grade level number.

Reader's Theatre students repeatedly practice the reading of a passage to perform later as part of a play or skit.

Reading a complex process in which the reader constructs meaning from text.

Reading comprehension the process of using one's own prior knowledge and the writer's cues from the text to infer the author's intended meaning.

Reading skills automatic actions that result in decoding and comprehension.

Reading strategies deliberate actions that readers make in an effort to construct meaning from text.

Realia actual objects used to teach vocabulary.

Reflection to give careful consideration to beliefs and practices, the evidence for those beliefs and practices, and the possible consequences.

Reluctant reader a reader who is capable of reading, but, when faced with a particular task, chooses not to.

Response to Intervention a tiered intervention and support model.

Reteaching implementing instruction in a different way that will lead to positive learning outcomes.

Revised Radio Reading students practice reading a passage orally in the style of a radio announcer.

Say it Like the Character teachers use a piece of narrative text full of dialogue to teach how reading with different voices enhances meaning.

Scaffold to teach with the intention of gradually releasing responsibility to the student.

Scan eyes move rapidly over the text to locate specific information.

Schema theory a theory to describe how readers use prior knowledge in reading.

Self-Concept a student's perception of his or her own reading competence.

Self-efficacy a student's confidence in their own reading abilities.

Self-monitoring the ability to monitor one's own comprehension.

Semantic features differences that can be noted among the meanings of words, concepts, events, or processes.

Semantic mapping a strategy using lines and geometric shapes to show the relationship between concepts and sub-concepts.

Signal words terms that help the reader identify the text structure.

Situational interest the contextual features that make some task or activity interesting.

Skim read the first sentence of each paragraph to understand the main idea.

Standardized test an assessment that is administered and scored in a consistent, predetermined manner.

Strategic fluency the balancing of speed control, meaning extraction, and level of confidence with text.

Summative an assessment that tests learning as a result of a unit of study.

Support Reading Strategy a cognitive tool, such as note taking, that assists the reader as he or she reads the text.

Surface fluency the use of phonological decoding, site word recognition, use of content and grammatical structure.

Teaching A complex process by which the teacher, a reflective decision maker, implements instruction aimed at positively impacting change in students.

Think Aloud orally sharing the stages of one's thought process for others to hear.

Topic Talk a talk given by a teacher to share information about an upcoming concept.

Value of Reading placing importance on the act of reading.

Venn Diagram a graphic organizer using two overlapping circles to compare and contrast two concepts.

Vocabulary difficulty of language in text.

Wait time time to allow students to think about the answers.

Whole Class RMA Strategy Lessons teacher uses an overhead or a projector to display a copy of a student's miscue analysis, which leads to a discussion about how to recognize the different types of miscues.

Word consciousness an awareness of words and their features.

Word sort a vocabulary strategy whereby words are sorted into categories based upon word structure.

Write Aloud orally sharing one's thought process while engaged in writing a summary of the reading.